AFRICAN RAINBOW

Also by Mirella Ricciardi
Vanishing Africa
African Saga

Also by Lorenzo Ricciardi
The Voyage of the Mir-El-Lah

AFRICAN RAINBOW

ACROSS AFRICA BY BOAT

Lorenzo & Mirella Ricciardi

WILLIAM MORROW AND COMPANY, INC.
NEW YORK

Mirella Ricciardi used Fuji film 100 SA and Olympus OM2 cameras
with 70–250 and 35–70 zoom lenses and a 21 mm wide-angle lens

First published by Ebury Press
an imprint of Century Hutchinson Ltd
Brookmount House, 62–65 Chandos Place
London WC2N 4NW

First impression 1989

Quotations from *Livingstone's Lake* by Oliver Ransford
by kind permission of John Murray (Publishers) Ltd,
and from *The River Congo* by Peter Forbath
by kind permission of Secker & Warburg Ltd.
The photograph on p. 239 by Don McCullin is reproduced by his kind permission.

Library of Congress Catalog Card Number: 89-061765
ISBN: 0-688-08959-3

Printed in Italy
First U.S. Edition
1   2   3   4   5   6   7   8   9   10

CONTENTS

This book is dedicated to the African people and to all those who, on any front, fight the battles for conservation.

An unending pleasure is derived from the exploration of new unvisited and unexplored regions. Each eminence is eagerly climbed in the hope of viewing new prospects, each forest traversed with a strong idea prevailing that at the other end some grand feature of nature may be revealed. The morrow's journey is longed for in the hope that something new may be discovered. For the traveller who is a true lover of 'wild Nature', where can she be found in such variety as in Africa, where is she so mysterious, fantastic and savage, where are her charms so strong, her moods so strange . . . .

H. M. STANLEY

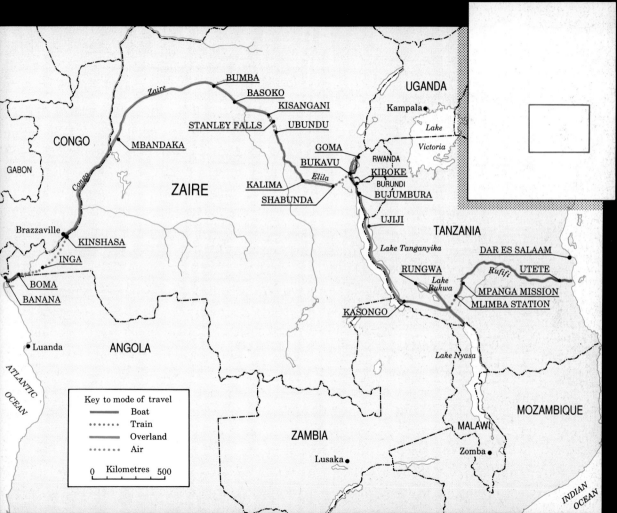

Key to mode of travel

- ——— Boat
- ········· Train
- ——— Overland
- ········· Air

0   Kilometres   500

PREFACE

MIRELLA: 'THE RICCIARDIS ARE VICTIMS OF WHAT BAUDELAIRE called the "great malady" – horror of one's home,' the late English author Bruce Chatwin once said of us. This is only half true in as much as I am also a Cancerian, and Cancerians are homemakers, but there is an Italian proverb which says, 'God makes them and then he couples them.' This is indeed true of us, for Lorenzo, like myself, is an inveterate traveller and, because we both suffer from the 'great malady', it has been the cause of many a crisis, since we always tend to want to be where we are not; it has, however, also led to a highly interesting and varied life.

Some good angel must have once whispered to my guiding mother to put a camera into my hands, so that I could use it where she used her crayons and clay. My mother was an artist and passed on to me a fragment of her talent. Though I never learned to draw, I inherited her eye for beauty and the camera became my tool. In this way my mother saved my life. If there were only one thing I could now pass on to my children, it would be, 'Find yourselves an activity you enjoy, stick to it and be good at it, for there is nothing more rewarding and healing than an absorbing distraction, especially if you can also earn your living from it.'

From the Niger to the Nile, from the Arabian Peninsula to the East African coast and now across Africa by boat on a 5,000-mile journey on the rivers and lakes of the Equator, my vision quests have rewarded me more than most other things in life and have given purpose to my travels.

I can still vividly remember how, on one of my African trips some years ago, I discovered Djenne in Mali. After hours crammed into an overpacked *taxi-brousse*, in the heat and dust of midday, the Great Mosque appeared ahead of us, the colour of burnished sand rising proudly from the flat desert. It was market day and around it, in billowing waves of colour, the people moved about their business, draped in flowing robes and crowned with large, shady hats sequinned with the glint of pure gold from the great earrings on the women's ears.

A few years later, on a rough road along the Nile between Bore and Juba in the Sudan, I sighted a Dinka cattle encampment spread out on the river bank, enveloped in a transparent haze of evening smoke. The river was quite still, reflecting the scene in a double image. For a long, silent moment I looked at it, almost afraid it would fade before my eyes; I reached for my camera. The vision is still with me. A rainstorm was rolling across the desert pushing a strong wind that whipped up the sand, swirling the smoke and momentarily obliterating everything. The tall, naked Dinka glided about the compound tying down the cowhide roofs of their huts with leather thongs, then huddled together beneath them. There was something ageless and ritualistic in their movements. I could smell the advancing rain – that rain sacred to the African, especially to the nomad, for from it springs their life.

I was born in Africa – in Kenya, where in 1930 my mother and father ended a year-long foot safari through the then Belgian Congo. My mother was French and came from an illustrious family in Paris who owned *Le Matin*, the leading daily newspaper of France at the time. Her father, Philippe Bunau-Varilla, was, at the age of twenty-seven, made engineer-in-chief of the Panama Canal project by Ferdinand de Lesseps, whose vision became Philippe's obsession. The success of the Panama venture brought huge financial rewards. My mother's family position conditioned her outlook on life: proud of the wealth and achievements of her father and uncle (joint owners of *Le Matin*), she was nevertheless contemptuous of a world in which a woman's mind was conditioned to accept selfish masculine indulgence. After two failed marriages, she moved to an artist's studio in Montparnasse, where she lived on her own, absorbed in her art and studying with the great French sculptor Auguste Rodin. It was in this studio that she met my father, Mario Rocco, a wild and fiery Neapolitan rebel exiled from his country for ten years by Mussolini, then the rising star in Italian politics.

Invited by Baron Empain, the wealthy chairman and principal shareholder of the Katanga Copper Mines, to visit him in the Belgian Congo, my parents left for Africa in 1928. After a yearlong safari on foot, they reached Kenya in time for the birth of their first child, my brother Dorian. I followed eighteen months later and, eighteen months after me, my sister Oria was born.

My parents bought 5,000 acres of land on the shores of Lake Naivasha in the Great Rift Valley and it was here, in this paradisiacal setting, that we grew up. It was

The mosque at Djenne appeared ahead of us.

—Overleaf—
I sighted a Dinka cattle camp spread out on the banks of the Nile.

11

a carefree, fairy-tale existence, filled with animals, wild and domestic, smiling Africans and wilderness sounds. Lake Naivasha was the home of every sort of African water bird, fish and water-lily. We were part of it and shared it with the animals and the birds. We cared nothing for the things that European children did. Our friends were black, our toys were made from bits of stick and string, we played with live animals instead of dolls, and we were looked after by a bevy of laughing black servants who were always there to care for us, amuse us, tell us stories, play with us and clean up after us. We grew up naturally like the trees and the flowers that surrounded us. There was no discipline, no restrictions in our lives. We spoke only Swahili, and when later an Austrian nanny joined us, we added German and then English, French and Italian to our vocabularies.

When the Second World War broke out my father, an enemy alien in an English colony, was taken from us and interned for five years in a South African concentration camp. When he returned, white-haired and toothless, he was a broken man; he never forgave the British for his treatment and never entirely recovered from the ordeal.

At eighteen I left Kenya. We had all been educated in colonial 'white' schools and I was sent to England to a finishing school. I ran away after one year and went to Paris, where, at my mother's suggestion, I took up photography in the studio of a great fashion photographer called Harry Meerson. I never looked back. Photography became my means of expression and I owe many of the important incidents of my life to it. I even found a husband because of it.

I was twenty-six when Lorenzo entered my life. He hired me as stills photographer on a film he was working on called *Dio Nero, Diavolo Bianco (Black God, White Devil)* in Kenya. Three days after I met him he asked me to marry him; we have remained together for thirty tumultuous years, sharing good times and bad, and many many adventures. He became the one man in my life and, although I cannot say the same for him, I am the only woman he could possibly have stayed with for so long. I have never quite understood why. Perhaps it is because we both basically share the same wanderlust, that insatiable thirst for new horizons, colours and sensations that is at the core of all true travellers. Perhaps if I had never met him I would have settled for becoming a housewife, content in the role of a mother, but he injected the elixir of discovery into our relationship and unleashed my inborn predisposition.

My life in Africa has taught me much. It has put me in a position both of advantage and of disadvantage. Because of it I have learned to appreciate and respect the simple formula of survival, and my values have been altered. But with it has

—Previous page—
Cassala, Sudan: people in Africa are in tune with their environment.

16

come a growing inability to communicate, a malaise born perhaps from over-exposure to such varying life-styles. I have now become more of a spectator than a participant. White people born in Africa are foreigners everywhere, a common denominator that somehow seems to link them. Few have understood why, and most develop a self-protective, often arrogantly critical sense, refusing to recognize the importance of tolerance and understanding, and refusing to accept that there is something to be learned from every form of life. I have learned a few things about myself and my fellow humans from a chimp I once had: I recognized in her the animal instincts which exist in each one of us and that cultural inhibitions teach us to control. This is perhaps why chimps endear themselves so to humans. We see in them all that is still instinctive in ourselves and we are touched by it. Primitive people are more in touch with Nature and, when they are not interfered with, the rhythm of their lives is guided by the environment they live in. The Italian author Alberto Moravia once remarked that 'the African does not dance merely for amusement; dance is the expression of a communal spirit.... In Africa everyone dances; one dances like one lives, inserting dance almost casually into everyday gestures. Every art form is an expression of the suppressed and it is perhaps because of this that Africans can dance to any sound ... they guide the music, whereas we Europeans are guided by the music.' The monotonous chanting, the sharing of grief and joy are all part of this same communal spirit, for from it the Africans draw the strength that binds them in their basic instincts.

I once watched a camel herder returning home at the end of the day. He was comfortably perched between the humps of his beast, leading his herd. It gave him an elevated view of his surroundings. He was humming a song as he swayed backwards and forwards in rhythm to the soft, padded gait of the animals. I remember being impressed by the nonchalance of the slow, rhythmic pace, which covered the ground as effectively as any vehicle in the same circumstances.

People in Africa are acutely in tune with their environment and are unperturbed by Nature's sudden changes of mood. A solitary man in a slim dugout, fleeing in front of a dust storm rolling in from the desert in Mali, has left an indelible image; as did one early morning in a Masai *manyatta*, when the sun poured through the branches of a fever tree, bathing the sleepy inhabitants going about their morning chores in an iridescence that removed them momentarily from reality.

It was this fusion of man and his environment that attracted me to Lorenzo's African Rainbow expedition, this trans-African crossing from the Indian Ocean to the Atlantic. I was curious to get closer to the heart of the matter. Travelling on rivers puts one in touch with a less accessible and more authentic world, still uncontaminated by the twentieth century. The further from commercial centres we went, the more hospitable and generous we found the people. Difficult travel communications bring out the best in people, because they create an inter-dependency that binds them together.

LORENZO: I was born in jail. The clinic of the San Vittore prison in Milan was the nearest place to which my mother could be rushed when her birth-pains started. She was on her way to Paris, where I had been conceived and where I should have been born. It was 11 May 1930; I am a Taurian. I am also the only son of an old Neapolitan family, perhaps a baron, probably a count, certainly a vagabond. My birth came nine years after my parents' marriage and I was, oh so very welcome. Years later my father jokingly told me that the only pleasure I had ever given him in life was nine months before I was born.

My mother died when I was seven years old – a doctor had diagnosed her peritonitis as liver trouble and gave her aspirin. Four days later she was dead. I went to live with my maternal grandmother near Genoa on the Italian Riviera. She adored me, but too much adoration does not make a man out of a boy. Luckily she had an old-fashioned maid called Luigina, a tough, leathery peasant woman who could cook better, walk faster and scream louder than anybody I have ever known. She took me on long walks up the hills of Liguria. When I ran out of breath we would stop and sit on the red earth under the shade of the big umbrella pines and I would stare down at the dark sea and wonder what lay beneath it.

I was raised a Catholic from my waist up. At the age of eight I was told I had a touch of the Devil. Often during Mass I would blow my sailor's whistle to kill the boredom; I sang merry tunes at funerals and cried at weddings. Once, after shooting a soldier in the buttocks with an air rifle, I was exorcised with a boring ritual in which I was sprayed with holy water and left for hours kneeling with my hands under my knees on the cold stone floor of the Sanctuary of Divine Love near Genoa.

Quite early on I recognized that the Gambarottas (meaning 'broken leg'), the maternal side of my family, were very colourful, while on my father's side there was the stability and common sense which I never wholly acquired. My father's father retired from the army as a general in 1918 and died at the age of 100, when I was thirty. My father, who was ADC to the Prince of Wales, received a bomb fragment in his neck, a bullet somewhere in his leg and a chestful of medals including the British Military Cross. Wars were common occurrences in my family.

In 1939 I was crossing the railway tracks that cut off the Italian Riviera from the Mediterranean sea-shore on my bike, when I heard Mussolini's imperious and powerful voice from a nearby car radio announcing the outbreak of the Second World War. '*La dichiarazione di guerra è già partita,'* he bellowed. I raced back home to tell my granny and Luigina. 'Oh, my God,' they said together, and my granny added tearfully, 'We have had it.' Everything that was to happen during the next five years seemed to be reflected in her eyes, and yet, still unbeknown to me, was to influence the rest of my life.

Regardless of events, the fishermen of Genoa continued rowing out to sea during the first year of the war and every night, from my bedroom window, I would watch their bright lights flickering in the distance. One wintry night, when it was very cold, I was allowed to go out to sea with them. I stared and stared into the deep, dark water, where the area floodlit by the lamps filled rapidly with sardines that circled madly in the light. Would I ever see a shark or a giant squid, I wondered. When I awoke I was at home in bed, where I spent the next two weeks ill with bronchitis.

During a bombing raid the house next door to ours was hit. We moved to the country, where my great-aunt Carolina had a farm. We were surrounded by acres of wild forests, hills and rivers running through them. My father gave me his shotgun, his cartridge belt and some money to buy fishing nets. Luigina's nephew, Bastiano, a tough eighteen-year-old peasant, became my inseparable companion. I was about eleven years old. From sunrise to sunset we were out shooting, bringing home hares, partridges, quails, fish and river shrimps, which Luigina turned into fantastic dishes for us. We swam across the River Po, slept under the trees and caught fish with our bare hands. I shot my first wild duck and the recoil of the twelve-bore shotgun blackened my shoulder for a week. These were happy days, when I could hardly sleep at night waiting for the next day to dawn. Around us the war dragged on. The house in Genoa was badly damaged, and my father's apartment in Milan totally wrecked. Our beautiful villa in the Tuscan hills near Rimini, filled with family possessions amassed over the centuries, many of them irreplaceable antiques, was blown sky-high by a retreating German army, who gave us half an hour to vacate the premises. My roots were severed. After my granny died, I went to live with my father in his new apartment in Milan. I remember roller skating to school, the speed blurring the ugliness of the city where I was born.

I was shy and clumsy. One day, while eating dinner in the beautiful house of my friend Roberto Gancia, I spilled a glass of red wine on the white linen tablecloth. There was a deathly silence as everyone watched the stain spread across the table. I made a decision then. I would hitch-hike round the world, climb Everest, sail across the Pacific, swim in the Ganges and the Amazon. I would listen to the surf pounding on the reefs in Tahiti and fall in love with a Vahine. Then perhaps I could spill a glass of wine without wanting to shrivel up and die.

Within a few weeks I was off; after a two-year trip around the world I came back to decide about my future. My father bought me a flat above his advertising agency in

Milan, but he might as well have bought me a gold coffin with a silver lining. I could have lived there all my life without leaving the building. I ran away, and wrote to my father begging him to try and understand. He did, and sadly sold off his successful business. I was his only child; it seemed unlikely that I would fit into the 'where-have-you-been-this-summer?' and 'where-will-you-go-this-winter?' society.

I decided, however, that if I wanted to travel, it would have to be with a purpose. A friend of my father's gave me a job with a film crew going to Hong Kong and a few weeks later I set foot in China. On the return journey by steamer I fell in love for the first time. But love came as a shock. Very soon I felt trapped. The lady in question was Pakistani, from Karachi, and she travelled with 365 saris, one for each day of the year. She came back with me to Milan, where I expected the summers of my life would now last into winter; but the sunshine, the tropical scenery, the pounding surf and swaying palm trees remained behind us. I had stripped my dream naked and it died of cold.

I was then hired to film a documentary travelogue entitled *A Trip to Paradise*, and embarked on an ocean liner to New York bound for Haiti, Jamaica and Puerto Rico. I was rather dismayed when I watched the passengers coming on board: 600 American matrons between the ages of sixty and eighty, followed by trunks and trunks full of tropical clothing, bikinis and see-through light-weight blouses. When we reached Port au Prince in Haiti I decided to remain ashore on the pretext that I wanted to film the departure scene. I set up my tripod at the end of the pier and watched with relish as the SS *Atlantic* disappeared over the horizon.

A few years in Rome working as an assistant film director led me to Kenya, where I was to film the flamingos of Lake Nakuru. One night in Nairobi, out of boredom, I went with my film crew to the Equator Club. There were a few charming black whores and a few sleek pimps around, and hanging above the bar some striking photographs of beautiful Masai and Samburu warriors. The owner of the night club told me that the photographer was a friend of his, an Italian girl – who had a phone number in Nairobi, he added, handing me her number on a piece of paper. I picked up the dented phone at the end of the bar and a voice, deep, warm, feminine and intelligent, answered. The next day I met the voice and two months later married it. We had two daughters together, Marina and Amina. Many years later, Mirella's book *Vanishing Africa* was to contain all the pictures I had seen in the bar and which had led me to her.

A fortunate break on the Stock Exchange earned me a large sum of money. I bought a sports fishing boat with diesel engines and a flying bridge, built to catch marlin, sailfish and giant tuna. I shipped the boat, which I named *Samaki* ('fish' in Swahili), to Kilifi, north of Mombasa, on the East African coast, where Mirella and I bought a house overlooking the Indian Ocean. I soon lost most of the money as easily as I had made it, and had to charter *Samaki* for a living. I became a professional fisherman, but after a while I grew restless and knew that something more exciting had to happen.

In Kilifi a ferry crosses the narrow creek which cuts across the road leading to Malindi and the Somali border in the north. Our house, built on a strategic point overlooking the entrance to the creek, was once the residence of the Arab Sultan of Kilifi. Further inland the creek widens to form a large lagoon surrounded by mangroves and coconut palms of a deep green colour. From the sands on the water's edge we dug up ancient fragments of Chinese majolica and Venetian glass, and even some remains of skeletons, perhaps of our Arab predecessors who came to Africa 1,000 years before the Portuguese of Vasco da Gama and the Europeans of the Victorian era.

It was there, on one of those motionless April afternoons, in 1982, when everything is veiled in a shroud of heat, the time of year when the east coast of Africa holds its breath, a period of silence between the monsoons, that the idea came to me to cross Africa from one ocean to the other by boat wherever possible. The purple and white bougainvillaea bushes and the great baobab trees around our house stood out against the pale, hot sky, looking withered and exhausted. I was reading *The Diaries of H. M. Stanley*. Now and again I looked out to sea through the wide verandah arches that frame the outer reef and the passage into the Kilifi creek. A curtain of rain darkened the sky and, as it passed overhead, a rainbow appeared in an unbroken arch stretching towards the far west, where lay the Mountains of the Moon and the Congo basin I had been reading about. At that same moment a small dhow, its sails filled with the monsoon winds, came into the creek, silver bonitos jumping in its wake.

Later that summer my father died of a stroke at his home in Genoa. Only a few days before he had sent me a postcard telling me 'I am the happiest man in the world', because our daughter Marina, whom he adored, was with him. Her lovely face framed by golden hair, her grey blue eyes so like his own, and her slender fourteen-year-old body were the last images he had when he collapsed.

Now I was the eldest member of my family. My father had left me his house, some money and many memories that flooded my mind as I wandered through the empty rooms of his house – my house now – after I had buried him next to his own father and sister in the cemetery on the high hills of Genoa overlooking the Mediterranean Sea. It was then that I decided to make the most of my life and follow any instincts that led me to rejoice in and relish its delights.

I gathered a few things of value – an antique Florentine table, a lamp, my father's desk, some old photographs and books, the painting that had hung above my bed as a child – everything I could not bear to leave rotting in an empty house. I packed them into his car, and together with Mirella and our two daughters, left the place. We have not been back since.

As I was driving away from Italy across France, my thoughts flew back thousands of miles to Kenya, where I had once stood on the ramparts of Fort Jesus in Mombasa, watching the dhows sail into harbour with the last of the monsoon winds. I could hear the sailors chanting as they dropped anchor and unloaded their cargoes of salt, brass coffee pots, water jugs, carpets from Shiraz and Isfahan, carved wooden chests from the Hadhramaut in Arabia. I was sitting on a Portuguese cannon watching Mirella photographing the *nakhodas* (dhow captains). Some sailors sang songs, strangely sad, nasal and dirge-like, haunting and alien to my ears, the songs of men whose way of life was disappearing and of their dhows, the oldest sea-going vessels known to man, which would soon be gone forever, buried by progress and the discovery of oil.

I decided then that I should go and investigate further the world of these disappearing dhows and, after months of inertia fighting the crippling depressions which had set in since my father's death, I left for the Arabian Gulf. I spent a month on a survey trip from Khorramshar in Iran to Basra in Iraq and the Emirates of the Persian Gulf. Then I bought a dhow and with Mirella, two Africans who had come to join me from Kenya, two Arab seamen and a small film crew from Anglia TV in London, we sailed it back to Mombasa, where I moored it beneath my house in Kilifi.

Back home in Kilifi I found *The Diaries of H. M. Stanley* where I had left them, sitting on the shelf by the kitchen door. As I leafed through them again, my thoughts went back to that rainbow in a stormy sky a year before, when the wild idea of crossing Africa by boat first came to me. My encounter with the world of the Arab dhows had sharpened my curiosity and I was eager to find out more about their presence and influence in Africa.

To the Arabs who travelled from the desert land of sand and mountains of Arabia to the East African coast in the nineteenth century, the fertility of Africa appeared like a dream. Helped by the monsoon winds that blow each year for six months alternately from north to south and from south to north, they found in Africa an immense and apparently inexhaustible oasis where they could reap without sowing. Making use of these regular winds they came and went without ever abandoning their country of origin. The discovery of Africa for these men, whose religion and severe traditions had been adapted to their natural waterless environment, was tantamount to finding all that was missing at home. Their penetration into Africa and subsequent colonization of the coastal areas was ruthless, and dearly paid for by the African coastal people, who fled from them, offering little resistance.

The end of the dhow route was the Rufiji delta; Zanzibar and Bagamoyo, north of

Dar-es-Salaam in Tanzania, were the end of the main slave route that led inland to Ujiji on Lake Tanganyika and the Congo Basin.

In February 1871 Stanley himself, on assignment for the Paris office of the *New York Herald Tribune*, had left from Zanzibar in search of Livingstone, who, it had been said, had been eaten by cannibals, taking with him, he wrote in his diary, 'six tons of supplies and equipment, including nearly 350 pounds of brass wire, 20 miles of cloth, a million beads to use as trading currency, 2 collapsible boats, 71 cases of ammunition, 40 rifles, tents, cooking utensils, silver goblets, champagne, Persian carpets and a bath tub'. He hired 200 porters to carry this massive load, many of whom had served with Burton and Speke, as well as two British seamen he had met on his recent travels and a young Christianized Arab called Selim Heshmy, whom he had picked up in Jerusalem, to act as his interpreter. He landed his party in Bagamoyo, saying, 'We are all in for it now, sink or swim, live or die – no one can desert his duty', and to the sound of rifles fired in celebration, struck into the interior at the head of the caravan, carrying the American flag.

Stanley travelled overland and used the boats only when it was not possible to do otherwise. I decided we would travel overland only when it was impossible to navigate. That day I christened my idea 'The African Rainbow Expedition' and turned to studying a detailed map of the area.

I noticed immediately that the ideal itinerary was the Livingstone route of 1857: follow the Zambezi in Mozambique to Tete, then on to the Sciré in order to reach Lake Nyasa, 'the lake of tempests', now renamed Lake Malawi. I would then continue northwards for 500 miles on Lake Tanganyika, and then to the Lualaba river that becomes the Zaire at Kisangani, and finally on to Kinshasa and the Atlantic, a journey of some 5,000 miles. It was difficult to calculate the exact mileage because the rivers I was looking at were winding and formed frequent large loops. I calculated that with lightweight boats I could follow the route by waterway for nine-tenths of the whole journey – an interesting challenge.

I had to take into consideration the serious political problems in Mozambique, with its internal guerrilla warfare. Even with the necessary authorizations this could put my expedition into serious jeopardy. Military-looking craft loaded with equipment and people, navigating in formation towards the interior, could be an irresistible target for any guerrilla on the lookout with a Kalashnikov waiting for a quarry and some glory. 'Sitting ducks,' an English friend had aptly remarked, focusing on my state of mind at the moment.

So I turned my attention to the Rufiji river, whose delta spreads opposite Mafia Island south of Dar-es-Salaam. Two hundred miles inland it becomes the Kilombero, with headwaters in the Mbarara Mountains north of Lake Malawi.

—Overleaf—
To the Arabs who travelled from their desert land of sand and mountains to the coast of East Africa the fertility of the continent seemed like a dream.

Helped by the monsoon winds, the Arabs sailed to Africa, where they found an immense and apparently inexhaustible oasis where they could reap without sowing.

26

Twilight in Muscat harbour, one of the points of departure of the slave trade.

A mysterious woman looked our way.

This ridge of the East African Rift Valley would be the first point at which we would have to abandon the river and portage our crafts and equipment overland, as Stanley had done on the backs of his porters. Africa, Speke had once said, is like an 'upturned plate with its centre forming the high plateaus that run from the Red Sea to the Great Lakes'. Given that the Ruwenzori range is the highest point of Speke's upturned plate, I would have to travel upstream until Lake Kivu in Zaire and then downstream to the Atlantic.

Ideas and observations began piling up in my head. My life in Africa, and the experience of previous safaris there with Mirella, came to my aid, and the idea of navigating across Africa increasingly appealed to me. 'Across Africa by Boat' – I had already imagined the headlines; and why not, if in central Africa there exists such a great network of navigable rivers more or less flowing into each other? But what was most challenging for me was the fact that it had never been done before.

I was especially interested in the Tanzanian southern coast of Lake Tanganyika, an area with difficult overland access at its extreme south-eastern point.

Day after day the idea of this journey increasingly occupied my mind until it became almost an obsession. I decided that the boats would have to be inflatables, large enough to carry passengers and equipment, easy to transport, but hardy enough to resist eventual confrontations with hippos and crocodiles. Then came the question of the engines: 50 h.p. would perhaps be the minimum to move craft of that size. There was also their weight to consider, 200 lbs at least. How would I portage them over the mountains, across difficult areas without roads, and what of the rains, the rapids, the political situation, the permits, the fuel, the money? Who would finance such an enterprise?

A familiar Latin proverb which I learned at school came to mind: '*audaces fortuna iuvat*' (fortune favours the brave), but above all I felt within me an almost mystical impulse to go through with it. I was no longer the adventurous youth who had drifted around the world like a leaf in the wind. I was now over fifty and that detestable sense of responsibility had settled over me, that professional seriousness which usually impedes this kind of enterprise.

I am a great believer that in order to consolidate an idea it has to be put to the test. It is not sufficient to examine it and decide that it is good. Circumstances also have to be favourable so as to guide it in the right direction.

Until one is committed there is hesitancy, the chance to draw back, always ineffectiveness. Concerning all acts of initiative and creation there is one elementary truth, the ignorance of which kills countless ideas and splendid plans: the moment one definitely commits oneself, Providence moves too. All sorts of things occur to help one that would never have occurred. A whole stream of

events issues from the decision, raising in one's favour all manner of unforeseen incidents and
meetings and material assistance, which no man could have dreamt would have come his way.
W. N. Murray – Scottish Himalayan Expedition.

The idea of the African Rainbow expedition met with Mirella's approval. There was a look of patient tenderness on her face as she listened to me tell her of my idea, a bit like one looks at a child who talks of its dreams; at that moment my rainbow was indeed still much like a child's dream, but at least the name stuck and was never changed.

Once I had convinced Mirella and had her on my side, the first hurdle was cleared. The next severe test would be proposing it to the *National Geographic Magazine*, which would give credibility to my project and help my initial fund-raising. 'If they are interested, it could also interest others,' I explained to Mirella. A few weeks later the *National Geographic* reply was brief and meaningful – 'It seems like a rather ambitious project . . . but, yes, we are interested.' I was aware that this positive response was in part because of Mirella's photographic contribution.

The African Rainbow expedition was off to a good start, under a prestigious umbrella and the best auspices. But our friend Bill Garrett, editor-in-chief of the *National Geographic Magazine*, was anxious. 'Don't get yourselves into trouble, you two; be sure and get well organized with at least three boats, some competent assistants and some good long-range radios . . . and good luck,' he added with his broad American smile and firm handshake.

With a letter of commitment from the *National Geographic* and a steely determination that I had not known before in my character, I caught a flight to Milan, where my instinct directed me to look for the equipment and money. It was the month of September; the Indian summer spread across the plains of Lombardy. My childhood friend Roberto Gancia welcomed me with open arms to his home. He had once before been the catalyst when I sailed my dhow the *Mir-el-Lah* from the Persian Gulf to Mombasa.

Without realizing or even planning it, it now dawned on me that, at a distance of several years, this trans-African project was going to be the logical continuation of the voyage of the *Mir-el-Lah*, which had started on the Shat-el-Arab, the 'river of the Arabs' where, legend has it, lay the Garden of Eden, and where in the last few years Iranians and Iraqis have been murdering each other.

Unusual concepts need imagination, but it has always been Roberto who has made them happen. I lay my dreams before him, without any structure or shape, filled with clouds and bright spaces, and he makes them palpable for the industrialists and sponsors. With Roberto's invaluable and constant support it took approximately eight months in Milan to collect the necessary interest and funds and equipment, an exhaustive and dogged undertaking, which would have discouraged and undermined many without the single-minded determination that I was suddenly blessed with. Several major companies – Pirelli, Sabena, Total, Fiat, Mariner-Power Marine, Castoldijet, Gancia, G.F.T. and C.P. Company – as well as forty-two smaller ones became my sponsors. Each one of them had somehow been smitten by the romance of this unusual adventure and were happy to lend it their names and financial support.

I now had in hand a fleet of nine Pirelli boats, nine Mariner 25 h.p. outboard engines, ten Whitehead 6 h.p. engines, two Castoldijet speedboats, three Fiat Panda four-wheel drive cars and three back-up vehicles (one of which we left behind), fuel, aerial transport, three radio transmitters, three generators, C.P. Company clothes for every occasion, medicines, food and much else, both necessary and unnecessary; I also possessed quite a healthy bank account and even a letter from the Hon. Bettino Craxi, Prime Minister of Italy, wishing me well – a letter which opened diplomatic doors and removed much red tape in the countries we crossed. I had enough equipment by now to fill two large containers, which left La Spezia for Mombasa in Kenya.

Now that my dream had taken form, Africa lay ahead of me. There was no turning back. River navigation, even in fully developed countries, is in itself quite an adventure. Rivers often deviate from the beaten paths, zigzagging in fluvial freedom, linked to the geographic and geological lie of the land. In Africa this freedom runs wild.

PART ONE

CHAPTER ONE

GOD HELPS THE DARING

IN THE SPRING OF 1985, I MOVED THE HQ OF MY EXPEDITION FROM
Milan to Kenya and set it up again in two base camps, one in Nairobi, the other at Diani
beach on the coast. For two months the equipment, spreading like a gypsy encampment
beneath the coconut palms, was unpacked, assembled, tested and repacked several times.
Lists were drawn up, new lists were made, then lists of lists, in an endeavour to minimize
weight and the amount we'd have to carry, shaving our equipment down to the bare
necessities. Portaging over rapids and sandbanks was the main consideration, but there still
always seemed to be too much. I couldn't help wondering why white people need so
much when Africans manage with so little.

We took the boats and engines for some trial runs on the Tana river, where we
camped with our long-time friend George Adamson in Kora. He lives there with his
lions, like a mystical man from another age, surrounded by miles and miles of wilderness,
out of touch with but alas not out of reach of civilization, in a world he has created and
which he jealously defends. It is still the distillation of everything pure and beautiful in
Africa. But for how long?

We sat with him during the hot midday hours and later in the cool evenings listening
to him tell us, in his calm, friendly voice, about his life with the lions and the conclusions
he has drawn from his seventy-five years in the bush. 'Overpopulation,' he said, drawing
on his pipe, 'is the greatest problem of the world today. It makes one very despondent
about the future of wildlife, because there is absolutely nothing that can withstand human
pressure. People have to realize that they have got to control their populations, because if
they don't I'm absolutely convinced that nature is going to find a way of doing it and it's
going to be very unpleasant; you can see the symptoms now in the world, everywhere
you look there is strife and that is a symptom of overpopulation.' He fell silent for a

moment and then said, 'Come back and see me when you return from your expedition; I'm interested to know in what condition you found the countries you will be crossing.'

I looked at him for a brief moment; we were men of the same ilk, men who had recognized long ago where lay the real values of life. He offered no advice, but just listening to him was enough for me to understand what true communion between man and nature could lead to. George's life had always been linked to nature, first as a game warden in the northern frontier district of Kenya and then, in the past twenty years, in total absorption in the conservation of wildlife areas and the study of the rehabilitation of lions to the wild. His work, his findings and his experiments with lions have provided a valuable contribition to Africa's threatened wilderness. He is now eighty-five; his elder brother Terence, a few years older than him, died last year, having spent the last years of his life with George in Kora. He knows he does not have much of his life left to live and has come to terms with the inevitability of death with the serene resignation that close communion with nature generally imparts. His last wish is to be buried in Kora, in the dramatic wilderness he so loves, beside his lion family.

As we were talking, Koretta, one of the lionesses George has befriended, ambled up to the tree outside the enclosure we were sitting in and lay down beneath it. She kept her eyes on him as if waiting to hear his voice. He got up from his chair and went out towards her, calling her name. She yawned and rose lazily to her feet, waiting for him to approach. When he was within a foot of her, he handed her the goat's leg he had prepared and stood quite still beside her, pulling at his pipe as she tore at the meat.

I had decided I would also film our adventure and had started some difficult and exhausting dealings with television companies, some of which recoiled as if in front of a madman: 'far too complex an undertaking,' they rightly said; but the footage we shot with George was magical and encouraging.

On Lake Naivasha, Eddie McGee, a survival expert from England, gave us some interesting lessons on survival. He taught us how to check if water is drinkable by 'scooping a handful of water into the palm of your hand, sticking your little finger into your ear and extracting some ear wax, which is dipped into the water. If an oily film appears on the surface of the water it is contaminated. If, instead, it remains clear and the wax drops to the bottom it is drinkable.' He showed us how we could make a formidable pair of floaters by tying knots in the legs of our slacks, placing them behind our head and then jumping into the water, bringing them forward to hit the surface. The air caught in them is imprisoned and the trouser legs turn into floats. He showed us how, by plaiting certain long-fibred reeds and grasses, we could make ropes so strong they could pull a vehicle. He built a sturdy bed with a roof on it by cutting branches from the surrounding bushes, sinking them firmly into the earth and then building a platform and overhead

Before leaving, we took
our boats for a trial run
on the Tana river,
where we met George
Adamson, who lives in
Kora with his lions like
a mystic from another
age.

structure, lashed together with bark and covered with leaves and twigs. He created a pair of tough sandals from plaited grass, and he taught us how to recognize edible plants by their smell and texture, and how to extract mosquito-repellent oil from leaves by rubbing them between our fingers or palms. He was unfortunately not able to come with us, but his lessons were fascinating and added a twinge of danger and excitement to the prospect that lay ahead. We were able to implement his lessons several times along our route, when we got separated from our vehicles for longer than planned and ran out of drinking water or the terrain was not suitable for pitching our tents.

I had collected a mixed bag of volunteers, who joined me without quite knowing what they had let themselves in for, other than the excitement the magic words 'expedition across Africa' ignited in them.

People who live unconventional lives, the way Mirella and I do, take for granted a life-style others find extraordinary. Inertia, and lack of means, imagination or motivation, are often responsible for a monotonous life devoid of the unexpected. People who belong to this category are often content to experience life through others. To them we are special and they have difficulty comprehending how each day can differ from the preceding or the following one.

During the year I spent in Milan setting up the expedition, many of the people I came into contact with expressed a desire to join me, without apparently for a moment considering or imagining what such a request entailed. In this way, one by one, I collected five youngsters between the ages of twenty-four and thirty-five who, after much scrutiny, all persuaded me to take them on: three Italians, one American and one Bahamian. Mirella, who had been absent during my year in Milan and had had considerably more experience of bush living than I, was immediately sceptical about the choice of some of them and expressed her views in no uncertain terms, but her comments failed to convince me; I was already committed to them.

Gianfranco Peroncini, a strapping 6 ft. 6 ins., soft-spoken fellow of twenty-seven, had spent two months with the Mujahiddin in Afghanistan. He was indirectly attached to our main sponsor Pirelli and, as with Lorenzo Camerana, the son of an old acquaintance of mine, who brought me the essential G.F.T. and Fiat sponsorships, he was automatically in a favoured position. Lorenzo, twenty-four years old, belonged to the international jet set. Blond, blue-eyed, with a baby beard sprouting, he looked rather like I had once done long ago. Quick-tongued and sometimes witty, he seemed rather pleased with himself. He lived in London with Shona McKinney, his pretty twenty-four-year-old blonde 'Sloane Ranger' girlfriend from the Bahamas, who had a business creating casual cotton clothes. With her smiling face, friendly manner and easy-going character, she turned out to be the one who adapted best to the conditions we were to encounter. Twenty-five-year-old Marco Fulvi – short, intense and excitable – was outwardly cocksure, but with a chip on his shoulder. He presented himself at my door bearing a red rose and a string of solid reasons why he could be of use to me. His father was a leading sports journalist in Livorno and was very keen for Marco to get some experience of living rough. Byrdine Melton, twenty-eight years old, was an American girl from the mid-west I had met on a yacht in Long Beach, California, where she was working as a deck hand cleaning out bilges and painting hulls. She looked tough and resilient enough, though she had never left the US, despite her obvious taste for adventure. She had joined me in Milan, where, motivated by the enterprise ahead, she dealt with all the boring secretarial work during the year I was setting up the expedition.

Four Kenyans were added later. Twenty-three-year-old Sally Dudmesh, a sometime student of anthropology and alternative medicine, asked to join the expedition hoping to find interesting herbal plants along the route. Her pretty face and gypsy-like appearance would, I knew, add a touch of glamour to Mirella's photographs. Elisabeth Ryeri was born in Kenya. She had been catering in London for several years and hated it. She was at a loose end in Nairobi, looking for something to keep her from returning to London.

We had known her since she was a teenager; her skill in cooking would, I thought, be a definite asset to the quality of our meals. Richard Bonham, a safari guide, also from Kenya, whose main love was bush living, immediately recognized not only a great new safari, but the opportunity of an interesting reconnaisance for his own safari business. The areas we were going to be travelling through were not on the beaten path; difficult and inaccessible, they required considerable organization to investigate properly. He has since set up a successful 'walkabout' base at Stiegler's Gorge on the Rufiji river in Tanzania, from where he takes clients on walking safaris through the Selous miombo wilderness. A fourth Kenyan was taken on to assist Richard on the road.

Left to right: Byrdine, Sally, Gianfranco, Marco, Lorenzo, Lorenzo C., Shona and Elisabeth.

They were all young, friendly, good-looking, healthy and enthusiastic, and were convinced that this was to be the great experience of their lives; but none of us had ever been on a river expedition of this kind and size before and none of us quite knew what to expect. Mirella, who was reading Joseph Conrad's *Heart of Darkness*, nicknamed them 'the pilgrims' after Conrad's fellow travellers who sailed up the Congo with him in search of Kurtz, a hundred years before.

I am basically a loner and have, across the years, developed a philosophy of live and let live. I am often accused of being selfish or uninterested in others, but I rarely inflict my life-style or opinions on others as long as they don't inflict theirs on me. But whoever joined this expedition had to do so on my terms. I had never before found myself in a position of command and did not feel comfortable in this role. I had therefore counted on a trusting camaraderie among my team to see us through the experience. It quickly became apparent that this was an illusion, because I had not taken into account the basic elements of human nature; any group needs a strong leader who lays down the rules, who takes on all the responsibilities and to whom it has to turn for decisions. I did not possess the necessary school-teacher traits and I quickly realized that this mixed bag of young people, from different walks of life, all unknown to one another, several of them in Africa for the first time, would be one of the main problems I would have to deal with.

To carry out an expedition and to film it turned out to be two entirely incompatible undertakings, and this resulted in the worst upheavals among my team; they had joined an expedition, not a film crew, they protested loudly. I did sympathize with them, but I had to contend with the sponsors who had given me the money and the equipment and who were expecting a measure of publicity in return.

Each member of the group had his or her own personality, ideas and reasons for coming to Africa. Mirella was worried, but decided to refrain from interfering and watched them sceptically from a distance. Some wanted to travel fast, others slowly; there were the shy ones, the pessimists and the optimists, each dealing with the experience for the first time and unsure quite how to handle it, themselves or us. I had read the books of Livingstone and Stanley, Baker and Brazza, all of whom had to contend with similar difficulties, and from them I learned that the best way to deal with such situations was to ignore them and go forward regardless, trusting that things would sort themselves out somehow along the way. Or so I hoped. I can now safely say that my unshakeable optimism was one of the main factors that saw us through to the Atlantic.

It is only once an expedition is under way that the real difficulties start appearing and the people reveal themselves for what they are. The crews of yachts, for instance, go to pieces when the yachts are moored in ports, rarely during navigation. Action forces people to deal with reality and with themselves. There is no longer time to worry about trivialities – the unposted letter, the lost shoe, the forgotten binoculars. It quickly became clear that we had too many expedition members and that things would have been much easier had we been fewer – half as many would have sufficed – but it was now too late for drastic changes. Richard's assistant, whose general attitude from the first day was very disruptive, was a negative element we really did not need at this point; it would have been better to lose him before take-off. He was not at all suitable for an expedition of this kind, where an easy-going disposition and a sense of humour are essential. Mirella tried to persuade me to throw him off the team, but my optimism led me to believe he too would change and mellow out once we had set off. Mirella's instincts unfortunately proved to be right; I should have listened to her. What was important now, however, was to get going, to fix a departure date and to stick to it even if it meant bedding-down very soon after we started. After two months on the beach waiting to go, everyone was growing fidgety and tempers were shortening. Endlessly boring and time-consuming customs declarations, permits, visas and road-taxes had to be sorted out, and seemingly interminable red tape had to be dealt with.

Finally the day for departure arrived. 'Tomorrow we go, ready or not,' I solemnly announced one evening, and watched as everyone reacted in their own way, with joy, relief, anxiety. 'D-day is here, no more time for procrastination!' I said as I opened a bottle of champagne, wishing ourselves good luck and God speed. It was an emotional moment and I detected tears in Mirella's eyes. She is an incurable romantic and I knew she alone understood how much this moment meant to me. More than a year had elapsed since I had begun working on this project; finally getting it on the road was an emotional achievement which only Mirella and I could fully relate to. None of our previous adventures had required quite so much effort.

Next day friends and family, dogs and cats, and the usual bunch of curious African on-lookers gathered around our vehicles, which were packed to the hilt, covered with tarpaulins and tied down with ropes for the long road-journey to the Rufiji delta, some 500 miles to the south. Five vehicles, eight boats, eleven expedition members and six African helpers set off for Lunga Lunga on the Tanzanian border in a cheer of joyful farewells, much laughter, shouting and whistling.

I approached Lunga Lunga border crossing with a certain trepidation, imagining all the things that could happen to hold us up, perhaps for a week or more, as our carefully loaded vehicles were unpacked and checked item by item while we awaited permits and official stamps that would never arrive. A bus ahead of us was disgorging a line of African travellers, who all showed some identification in order to cross the border with their goods and chattels. I noticed that it was always with a smile, a friendly greeting, a little joke and a gift that they presented their documents. Some carried a banana, others a pineapple, some oranges, a few eggs wrapped in a cloth, a coconut or a papaya. I stood by the door awaiting my turn and recognized again the importance of a little sweetener in sticky situations. What is important in today's Africa, I quickly learned, is to forget that one is white and to keep an eye on the ways of the indigenous people. Frontier laws were established by the whites and the Africans deal with them in their own way.

It took less than half an hour for our expedition to pass, no questions asked.

CHAPTER TWO

THE MIGHTY RUFIJI

THIS MAD VOYAGE INTO THE UNKNOWN, WHICH WAS GOING to take me back to an Africa I had abandoned ten years ago, left me feeling confused. The warm air rushing through the open car window still felt good. The brilliant colours, the familiar shapes and smells, the tropical vegetation, the smoke and the flowers, the native villages beneath the mango trees, the brown children scattering like leaves before us, revived in me emotions from my childhood, when I was part of this country. Lorenzo's strong profile silhouetted against the open car window was framed by a mass of unruly white hair. His eyes, squinting in the bright light, were fixed on the road ahead. Like a hunting dog, he comes alive only when he is on the move.

Ever since he can remember, Lorenzo has spent most of his time in absent-minded daydreams, talking of adventures with distant horizons, unattainable women, three-masted schooners and coral reefs alive with fish. He is ravenous for the beautiful things of nature – and now he was totally committed to his expedition. He needs places free of crowds, rules and regulations, remote and uncluttered; he has long ago recognized the futility of the crowded places most people of his milieu converge on like St Tropez, Gstaad and the Rivieras for 'fun and holiday entertainment'.

The delta of the four-hundred-mile Rufiji river, Tanzania's mightiest waterway, encompasses an area roughly the size of metropolitan New York. Lying in the sodden embrace of mud and mangrove trees, it is a morass of serpentine creeks and brackish tidal channels, clogged with sandbars, writhing with crocodiles, snarling with mosquitoes, trembling with the crash of elephant herds in the matted rain forest around its banks. The delta does not welcome man; one almost expects to find rubbery prehistoric animals wallowing about in its miasma. It breathes isolation and spawns disease. Even a fugitive would hesitate before seeking asylum here.

I was reading aloud to Lorenzo an excerpt from *The Battle of the Bundu*, which describes the insane Anglo-German war of 1914 that took place in the areas we would be travelling in.

'Is this where you are taking me?' I asked teasingly.

'I've read it,' he answered. 'We'll get through it somehow. The Zambezi route is out, guerrilla warfare is worse, but don't forget that the Rufiji delta is also the end of the dhow route which begins way up north in the Persian Gulf.' It is the final destination of the great wooden galleons that once a year are pushed southwards by the monsoon winds in search of, among other things, the hardy mangrove poles that grow there.

With its massive tributaries the Great Ruaha, the Kilombero and the Luego, the Rufiji river drains East Africa's largest river basin, drawing on an area of nearly 700,000 square miles. Each year its swirling coffee-coloured waters pour millions of tons of silt into the Indian Ocean, creating a hand-shaped delta of mangrove swamps and sand bars fifty miles wide. It is the main artery of the 21,600-square mile Selous National Park in Tanzania (about the size of Ireland), which until recently was considered one of the last untouched natural wildernesses in Africa, 'where a brooding silence pervades the seas of golden grass that stretch endlessly in an undulating landscape to cloud-ringed mountains. It is dotted with steely blue lakes, woodlands, rocky massifs and deep gorges boiling with white water. At night the only lights are those of winking fireflies, coldly brilliant stars and occasional forks of lightning.'

In 1905, when Tanzania was still a German colony, a German cotton scheme along the Rufiji river sparked off the greatest popular revolt against foreign domination in Tanzanian history. It was called the 'Maji Maji' rebellion because sacred water (*maji*) was believed to turn the German bullets to water. 75,000 people lost their lives, and old horseshoes and cartridge cases can still be found amongst former gun emplacements along the Rufiji and Beho Beho rivers; in the south, a huge German-built steam-powered threshing machine still lies rusting in the bush.

From Charles Miller's book we learned that the Rufiji river and its delta are also (and above all) famous for what is known in the annals of history as 'the scene where the most bizarre campaign of the First World War was fought'. 'For in this barely explored wilderness of thorn scrub and dense forest in eastern Africa, the last "gentleman's war" was waged, sometimes under an established code of honour and at other times under guerrilla tactics adopted from African tribal fighters. The legendary German Colonel von Lettow Vorbeck, who was worshipped by his men and respected by his enemies, led a handful of Askaris (native soldiers) against 250,000 Allied troops for four years. The South African, Jan Smuts, perhaps the most able leader of the opposing side, had attempted to encircle von Lettow, but his tiny force escaped his trap.' The sleek German battleship *Königsberg*, the most formidable sea-going engine of destruction in the Indian Ocean at the time, sank in the Rufiji delta and, until recently, was a pathetic landmark to one of history's most unnecessary and futile manifestations of human folly. I faced the prospect of this journey with a certain foreboding.

At two o'clock in the afternoon on a sweltering, airless day in October, our convoy reached the muddy bank of the delta. From a tiny thatched fishing village hidden among the bushes, a bunch of bedraggled natives appeared to greet us and gawk at the unexpected arrivals. Some tired palm trees and a strong stench of drying fish gave the place a feeling of melancholy abandon. Two months late on our scheduled departure, it was now the end of the dry season; the rains were due to break. Everything around hung limp and hot like the weary expedition team itself. An old man in tattered khaki shorts, followed by a naked boy, clambered up the bank. He joined the gathering beneath the only shady tree and was soon followed by an aggressive individual in an official-looking shirt and stained grey slacks who introduced himself as the 'chairman' of the village. He offered a curt greeting and requested to see our papers.

'What papers?' Lorenzo asked smiling.

'Your permit to stop in our village, from the Government,' he replied aggressively. 'We have not been informed of your arrival from Dar-es-Salaam.'

'We really don't need any of this at this point,' I hissed to Lorenzo. It was obvious the man was pulling rank, trying to impress his fellow villagers, but we were prepared for just that and the documents were produced. He was still not satisfied. It was also obvious he was expecting a 'sweetener' before he would authorize us to unload. Lorenzo and Richard followed him to a mud construction, where a worn, decomposing book was produced and reverently placed on a wooden table.

'You must sign your names in this book and explain what you are doing here,' he continued, a false air of authority betraying his own nervousness. The pages of the book were brittle and had turned yellow with the years and moisture; hungry white ants had peppered them with a trellis of tiny irregular holes and the signatures of visitors who had passed before us had faded. Lorenzo and Richard signed their names, the sweetener changed hands and they returned to the tree where we awaited them. An air of defiant triumph on his face, the 'chairman' laughed and chatted loudly with his cronies, ostentatiously punctuating his monologue with his right hand so all could see the plastic Swatch watch he had just received.

Permission to unload having been granted, we started spreading out bags and boxes. Sweat trickling down their flushed, dusty faces and bare backs, our 'young dreamers' from Europe, not yet hardened by the demands of the expedition, were getting their first taste of manual work; they set to assembling the boats, pitching tents, and dividing up the equipment and food, so carefully inventoried during the past year, ready for the morrow's departure.

The heat of the first day faded as the sun disappeared behind the mangroves which spread dark and forbidding along the edges of the delta. The sky, shot with vermilion, faded gently as night crept in. A full moon rose to the east. Lorenzo and I sat on the parched, hardened river bank soaking in the cool of the evening; the earth was still warm and we felt the day's heat seep through our thin cotton trousers, putting us in touch with the rawness of Africa. We watched the river flow silently towards the open sea, where the breakers on the reef were just audible. A rainbird called persistently somewhere in a tree and a flock of white egrets skimmed low over the brown water. Behind us the tents were being pitched for the first time, everyone busy, unrolling bedrolls, fastening mosquito nets, preparing for the first night in the bush; the campfire crackled beneath a large tin kettle still bright and new while the camp boys prepared the evening meal. Suddenly two dhows emerged from the darkness, gliding silently like phantoms in the night, their swollen lateen sails catching the moonlight; the hulls, laden with a cargo of mangrove poles, lay low in the water; ahead of them the Southern Cross hung in the sky. In the poop a kerosene lantern swung gently, throwing patterns across the deck. A group of men, hardly visible, were hunched together beneath it; one of them sang a melancholy song. Lorenzo moved closer and put his arm around my shoulders – he was feeling good; in the bush some cackling guinea-fowl took flight. We retired early to our tents, exhausted and hot but exhilarated at the prospect of having finally got off, and fell soundly asleep, rocked by the sweet lullaby of Africa.

By noon next day the expedition was finally ready for take-off. The inflatables looked impressive lying at anchor, pregnant with air. With some hired hands from the village, we sloshed through the sticky black mud that coated our feet with instant socks, carrying the fuel, the food boxes and the equipment on our heads. As the boats filled up they gradually began to identify with the adventure ahead. Lorenzo filled a gourd with Indian Ocean water; he would empty it into the

—Overleaf—
A flock of skimmers flew low over the water.

47

Atlantic when we reached the other side, he told us, underlining the purpose of the expedition.

The ground-support vehicles were packed and ready for the road; we would meet up with them in Utete, about 150 miles upriver. These vital meetings were programmed to take place at various points along our route, as without their support, our little fleet of inflatables would have been unable to overcome the considerable strategic difficulties of travelling upriver against the current. Then the outboard engines came alive and broke the noonday hush and the expedition took off in a spray of white foam, sliding effortlessly over the water to the excited cheering and waving of our new friends on the bank.

One by one we settled into comfortable positions in our respective boats. Lorenzo, in the lead, stood at the wheel, his straw hat pulled over his eyes and fastened with a piece of twisted cord beneath the chin. I sat beside him, rather grandly I thought, under a yellow umbrella on a soft, plastic-covered seat, both of which he had ordered specially for me so as to ease the strain of such a long voyage. The two sturdy Africans we had taken on board at the village straddled the bow and watched for snags and obstructions, measuring the depths with long bamboo poles. Familiar with the many fingers of the delta, they would accompany us to Utete. Richard followed with the girls on his boat, their heads wrapped in bright African printed cottons, hiding behind sunglasses and aglow with suntan oil; they added a touch of glamour to his craft. He, like Lorenzo, looked very much the part of the African explorer in his green cap and shades, his rifle and binoculars hanging from the steel steering-wheel rod. The remaining 'young dreamers' brought up the rear, dressed in snappy designer safari gear: good-looking, well-built, expensive youngsters, still with cobwebs in their heads, embarking on their first fantasy trip, which they would in years to come be able to talk about at dinner parties. They still had no idea of what they had let themselves in for.

The mangrove marsh, firmly rooted in its liquid bed by great ropey claws like those of prehistoric monsters, undulated heavily as the boats sped by. Goliath herons rose slowly from mounds of dry mud and crossed low over the water in front of us. Imperious fish eagles, perched on the tops of trees, looked down at us, throwing their haunting cries into the hot, still day before swooping gracefully to a tree further on. Small clearings appeared now and again with a hut or two set in the centre, a wooden dugout tethered to a pole on the water's edge. These were the homes of the mangrove cutters, who cut the long, straight poles used in the construction of African mud houses and thatched roofs, and are transported to Arabia aboard the dhows that ride the monsoon winds. They emerged, bewildered

*Bewildered hippos
turned to face us as we
sped past.*

by the unfamiliar sound of our engines, and waved at us excitedly with a friendly
'*jambo*' (hello).

As we sped on, the mangrove swamp gave way to huge trees hung heavy with
curtains of green vines, and then gradually merged into low bush country scattered
with acacias. A few hours later we left the black mud of the delta behind us, and the
sandy banks of the savannah now crumbled and flopped into the water with our
swell. From our maps, bought at Captain Watts in Albemarle Street in London, we
had expected to spend at least two if not three days and nights in the mosquito-
infested mangrove swamps, and this speedy exit came as a pleasant surprise; it also
emphasized once again how misleading even the most zealous purveyors of
information can be.

We spent the first night on a beach of fine, golden-coloured sand that stretched
clean and undisturbed along the right bank of the river. Soon the evening air was
infused with the friendly scent of burning wood from the campfire, the portable
dome tents were erected and the bed rolls unrolled. Lorenzo wandered off down the
river with his fishing rod and brought back a 15 lb Rufiji catfish for our dinner. A
small canoe, with a makeshift plastic sheet torn at the edges for a sail and an old bent

—Overleaf—
*The great trees rose like
monuments on the river
banks.*

51

fisherman perched on the rim, drifted by, silhouetted against the still water. There was no other sign of life until the radio transmitter made contact with the ground-support vehicles a hundred miles upstream to the east.

Africa received us with open arms; she was warm and gentle and extraordinarily beautiful. Our fears of finding ourselves in muddy areas, surrounded by clouds of mosquitoes that would drive us under our nets from twilight to daybreak, proved mercifully unfounded. Instead, the further upriver we travelled the more welcoming the environment appeared to us. Contrary to all our expectations, each evening our campsite revealed itself to be a source of joy. We looked forward to it as to a warm and affectionate mother who treated us like honoured guests.

I stretched out on the gritty river sand and looked up at the black sky and the profusion of stars. The Southern Cross hung brighter and at an angle to the south; the Milky Way spread to its left; Venus, Uranus, the Pleiades and the Plough were all clearly recognizable and brought me back to the first time they were pointed out to me by my father on the farm. I have always been fascinated by the sky at night and never tire of star-gazing. When I am in Europe, where at night people go indoors and never look at the sky, I forget my twinkling friends, but whenever I return to Africa I always feel this same strange affinity with the stars; they are always there in the same place. It is like coming home and finding the furniture, the pictures and the lamps where I had left them, so I never feel lonely in Africa. Now and again a star would shoot across the sky, trailing a tail of white light behind it; sometimes it would keep on moving and I'd know it was the tail light of a passing plane. Things are changing fast in Africa, but here in the silent wilderness of the river I found the reassurance I needed to counteract the insanity of the civilized world I live in. Lorenzo, too, is a different man in Africa. He calms down and becomes one with the universe. People who have an affinity with Africa respond to its magic; they become more mellow; their senses are sharpened; they are at one with nature.

Each evening, an hour before sunset, we would choose a place for our campsite. Invariably the ideal spot presented itself and each time it was different, each time a surprise. We would look at each other across the boats and with a nod and a wink give the thumbs-up signal that we were in agreement. The evening activities turned into a ritual: collect firewood, light fire, make tea, settle down to watch the sun sink on the horizon to the symphony of the African night while dinner was being prepared. These African night sounds, for anyone who has a musical ear, are easily orchestrated. The bass is supplied by hippo grunts, the overall chorus by the insects, the frogs and the water birds, and the melody by the song birds; the doves and rainbirds provide the contraltos. For a musician, here lay the source of an African symphony.

Richard, soft spoken, shy and sensitive, only feels completely at ease when he is in the bush. He shared with us a temperament which rejoiced in Nature's undisturbed vitality, in 'the frozen echo of the silent voice of God' – tiny leaves and blossoms bursting into life after a shower and dead by nightfall; butterflies hovering on a decaying tree; the smell of damp moss in the undergrowth; beetles rolling dung balls; crickets announcing night; the haunting call of the rainbirds. This is our Africa.

We covered approximately fifty miles each day and reached Utete, 150 miles upstream, on the evening of the third day in a state of high exhilaration. Everything so far had gone better than we had expected. None of the hazards we had been warned about had materialized: mosquitoes, sandbars or unpleasant camping conditions. It turned out to be exactly the opposite. All the careful thought Lorenzo had put into the choice of equipment, boats, engines, fuel containers and consumption, tents and the mass of items that cushioned our travel, was paying off. It said a lot for Lorenzo's organizational powers. Given that it was his first expedition of this sort, he proved surprisingly accurate, and this contributed a lot to our general well-being.

The first week would act as the testing period and we fully expected to have to

Each evening before sunset we would choose a spot for our campsite.

make some changes, but this was unnecessary: any alterations at this stage were minimal. If anything, we had taken along too much equipment. The precision and foresight of his organization revealed an entirely new side to Lorenzo, and one I was surprised to discover after thirty years with him.

The Selous Game Reserve was first established in the region in 1905, when Tanganyika was a German protectorate. It was known by the locals as 'Shamba ya Bibi' (the woman's farm) because Kaiser Wilhelm II is said to have given it to his wife in 1912 as a wedding anniversary gift. Constantine Ionidis, a flamboyant and eccentric Greek, known as the father of the Selous, was one of its first game wardens. In 1935 he persuaded the British colonial administration to enlarge the reserve to its present size and to evacuate all the tribal people living around it *en masse* to settlements elsewhere. The geography and climate have combined to form a rare habitat and the dry, sparse, deciduous woodland, known as miombo, has been kept virtually free of human habitation, and cattle, because of the poor soil and the tsetse flies that carry the deadly sleeping sickness, have become the guardian angels of this natural paradise.

The tsetse fly covers the vast woodland savannahs extending north, east and south of the equatorial rain forest, and has spread into the Selous. A bite from a fly infected with this type of sleeping sickness can kill a person within two weeks. In Africa, sleeping sickness has been traced to 5,000 years BC; an outbreak of the disease caused 200,000 people to die on the shores of Lake Victoria between 1902 and 1905.

The tsetse fly is larger than the common house fly and is easily distinguished from any others by its external features: a prominent forward-pointing proboscis (mouth-parts), crossed woody wings folded flat upon its back when at rest, and a unique wing vein. Every eight to nine days the female deposits a fully developed larva, which burrows into the soil to a depth of about one inch and emerges after thirty-five days; each female produces fewer than a dozen offspring. Both sexes consume blood from vertebrates, usually feeding only every fourth day, and both transmit the sleeping sickness. A fly becomes infected when it ingests the blood of a person or animal carrying the parasites and remains infected for the rest of its life. Three of the species are fatal to domestic animals and man, but do not harm wildlife, who after thousands of years have adapted to the trypanosomes. The wild fauna act as reservoirs, storing the minute parasites for later transmission via the flies to people and domestic animals.

The tsetse fly poses a dilemma for conservationists, who agree on the economic desirability of fly control, but believe that human occupation of fly-liberated areas will destroy Africa's well-balanced ecology. Opening up large tracts which are at present the habitats of numerous wild animal species, like the Selous, could be catastrophic to the African biotopes. In retrospect the curse of the tsetse may prove to be a blessing in disguise. Its complete elimination might mean the destruction of one of the world's unique natural regions. Driving or walking through the miombo which covers more than three-fifths of the Selous there is no way of escaping the tsetse fly, who descend quite silently and bore away ruthlessly, even through thick clothing, sinking their probosces like needles into the flesh. Totally fearless, they are not easily got rid of: only strong insecticide spray or violent death by repeated squashing with a hard object on a hard surface can deter them.

In the dry season much of their habitat is destroyed when tens of thousands of acres of the Selous are set ablaze, either naturally by the sun's rays or by bolts of lightning, deliberately by poachers and game scouts or accidentally by charcoal burners. The miombo wilderness, which extends for almost sixteen hundred miles across the waist of Africa from coast to coast, which is of little use except for the gathering of wild honey, is then reduced to blackened, leafless twigs and grey ash, a bleak spectacle the Africans call 'the silver death'. But the tsetse eggs buried in the ground, like the deep, tough roots of the miombo, are not destroyed in the holocaust, and under the first showers of the torrential summer rains the 'dead' bushes and trees sprout tender new leaves and flowers that sometimes have a lifespan of only twenty-four hours, and the tsetse fly begin a new life-cycle.

Although the savannah woodland is still one of the least scientifically researched areas of Africa, more than 2,000 species of plant have been found there; forty of those discovered in the last twenty years are new to science. Clinging to the cliffs of the Luego river in inaccessible patches of forest hang flowers and shrubs still unknown to botanists. 'Butterflies, their wing-tips violet or vivid tangerine, flit among the ghostly trumpets of rain lilies in glades where shafts of sunlight make sunbirds into sparkling jewels and scarlet velvet beetles scurry to the safety of decaying logs on which the diamond-headed praying mantis hovers, hardly discernible, so perfectly has it adapted to the colour of its surroundings.'

To break the river travel Lorenzo would call a halt whenever we arrived at some particularly attractive or interesting spot, where we would spend a few hours or even a whole morning or afternoon in exploratory walks.

When we entered the Selous National Park, we went with Richard into the forests, following the spoor of elephants and buffalo through the undergrowth, watching for lacerated leaves and branches, hoof marks and droppings. Richard enjoyed sharing his knowledge of the bush with us; he knew a lot about the flowers and the trees and had even learned their Latin names. He was knowledgeable about the lore of the bush, for Nature had been his teacher from childhood, when he lived with his father's game trackers, and it was something he was proud of.

We came across the same large golden spider webs we had seen in the garden of James Ash, the snake expert we had visited in Watamu on the Kenya coast. These webs are very tough and act as nets to catch the insects and occasional small birds that feed the spiders. The yellow spiders, named after the yellow splashes on their bodies, build very strong webs that stretch across large openings in the forest to catch anything that flies through it, even insects larger than the host spider.

'They have strange mating habits,' James told us; 'the female often devours the male after they have mated. Some clever males bring along food with which to distract the female; they then wrap her in a length of web, mate with her and flee while the female is freeing herself.'

At night around the campfire Majiji, the tough Tanzanian game-scout we had hired in Dar-es-Salaam, held us spellbound with tales of mythical beings who Africans believe inhabit the Selous – 'pythons 50 ft long that turn into witches when the hyena howls, monster rainbow-tinted tree frogs with diamonds for eyes, and a lake dweller with three heads and the body of a shark'. He told us how each year, when the 'spreading marula trees are in fruit, the elephant go on a colossal spree. They strip entire trees of the greenish-yellow marula plums and then go off to water holes to drink. By then the plums have fermented in their stomachs and the more they drink the drunker they become and reel around boozily.' He went on to tell us, without altering the tone of his voice, how the poachers sometimes fill papayas with battery acid and leave them around for the elephants to collect. It is considered one of the more effortless and efficient methods of extermination. Ironically, it was the President of this very country who once said, 'We will do everything in our power to ensure that our children and grandchildren will be able to enjoy this rich and precious heritage.' Despite the good intentions, which seemingly have gone no further than impassioned speeches, we frequently came across traces of poachers and rarely saw any traces of wildlife and never any conservationists during our crossing of the Selous.

Unfortunately some of our young 'pilgrims' seemed to have difficulty relating to the fascinating life of the bush and betrayed an urgency to return to the river and the boats, as if their main objective was to reach their destination and get back home to talk about their adventure. Was this all that Africa meant to them? They were perhaps still conditioned to living by the watch and had not yet begun to change gear.

CHAPTER THREE

LIONS IN THE SELOUS

A S PLANNED, WE MET UP WITH THE GROUND-SUPPORT vehicles at Utete for the first time. We covered the next 150 miles in just over five days and reached the Rufiji River Camp, kept by a German called Carl, in the early afternoon.

Carl was one of those offbeat eccentrics one only meets in places like Africa or South America. He had been in Tanzania for forty years and had no intention of ever returning to live in Germany. He was obsessed by the Selous and talked about it with the soft reverence and passion usually reserved for lovers.

His camp was closed, with only a few campboys around to receive us. The afternoon heat seemed to have paralyzed everything on land and a blistering glare bounced back at us from the water. The pretty camp, with its thatched verandah and tents set out beneath the trees, hung high above the winding river and the legendary Selous grasslands, quivering in the heat haze. A shiny white icebox behind the bar of the earth verandah was empty but for three remaining cans of frozen beer. We shared them in silence as we watched two male hippos in the river below us in primeval combat. Facing one another, they grappled fiercely for a hold, their huge mouths wide open, revealing vicious tusks. When one slipped and broke the deadlock, they both crashed into the water and disappeared beneath the surface, to reappear moments later and start all over again, emitting awesome sounds that resembled infernal wails from long ago. A dozen uninterested females lay around them like mounds of mud protruding from the water, quite unperturbed by the goings-on, their tiny ears twitching, while a couple of pink-legged tickbirds went about their business of cleaning them of parasites.

When the heat subsided, we moved about one mile further upstream to set up

camp in a flat, shady spot which provided easy access to the road and to the support vehicles which arrived soon after us from Utete. Across the river a line of ancient doum palms with scraggy heads stood like sentries, silhouetted against the sky. An inland lake near our campsite, we discovered, was the nesting ground of several thousand pelicans and a great variety of other birds: Egyptian and spurwing geese, long-beaked African sandpipers, white-crested herons, black-winged stilts, white spoonbills with pink legs, snipe and crested crane. Waterbuck, eland and buffalo came here from the parched backlands to drink. The hippo had accumulated in large numbers at this particular bend in the river. Half submerged in the water, they lay motionless in the cool mud, only their backs visible; snorting and grunting, they spouted water through their nostrils high into the air, adding a primeval atmosphere to the place.

To break the river journey we decided to stay here for a week so we could explore the interior and visit the historic hot springs, where only a hundred years before the slave caravans had stopped to rest on their way to the Indian Ocean. An oasis of bright green palm trees rising high into the sky, sifting the sunlight through stripped leaves, cast shafts of light on the viscous water. We flopped into the hot, sulphurous liquid and gently floated into a world far removed from the arid surrounds we had crossed to reach it.

In the Beho Beho area north of the Selous, which wildlife authorities consider amongst the most magnificent country in East Africa, we came across what must be one of the loneliest graves in the world. Here, 'with the wind for a dirge', lies the celebrated British explorer and naturalist Frederick Courtenay Selous, after whom the reserve is named; he is buried beneath a cracked and weathered slab of concrete at the exact spot where, on 4 January 1917, as a captain in the Royal Fusiliers, he was killed by a German sniper during the East African campaign of the First World War. He was sixty-five when war broke out and the War Office, eager to benefit from his knowledge of Africa, stretched the age limit so that he could join up. Ironically, Selous, whose favourite sport in those pre-conservation days was hunting elephant armed only with a muzzle-loading gun and clad in nothing more protective than shorts, a shirt and sandals, lies where at the time one of the largest known concentration of elephants

roamed; he killed a thousand of them, thirty-three of which are stuffed and stored in the Natural History Museum in London.

Brian Nicholson, the last European warden, told us the Selous had once been one of the few areas open to hunters that had a game population many times greater than it had when the first white men penetrated the country. It was this abundance of animals that attracted wealthy trophy-seekers to the reserve's forty-odd hunting areas in the south. The privilege of shooting an elephant, one of the reserve's lions and a few smaller animals was expensive, but Tanzania had more applications for hunting trips than it could handle. Some of the profits were ploughed back into wildlife conservation, and the professional hunters did the job of strictly controlling culling where the habitat might have been threatened by excessive numbers of a particular species. They also helped deter human predators, poachers whose main targets are elephants for their tusks and crocodiles for their skins. Today, however, the daring white hunter whom Selous personified has been replaced by the African professional, trained at Mweka, the wildlife management college at the foot of Mount Kilimanjaro, many of whom, underpaid and struggling to make ends meet, are secretly in league with the poachers.

We found today's situation very depressing. Despite the dry season, the scarcity of game along the river was quite alarming. Apart from a family of about ten elephants who fled as soon as we appeared on the horizon, obviously terrified by the smell of humans, the only other elephant we encountered was lying half-submerged in the river, dead. When we stopped to examine it we found several machine-gun holes in its hind-quarters. The body was still warm and the immature tusks were no longer than eighteen inches and approximately two inches in diameter. On our walks in the forest we often came upon deserted poachers' lairs; some, recently abandoned, were still fresh and smoking.

'The survival of our wildlife is a matter of grave concern to all of us in Africa. These wild creatures, amid the wild places they inhabit, are not only important as a source of wonder and inspiration, but are an integral part of our natural resources and of our future livelihood and well-being.' So said Julius Nyerere in a broadcast to his nation in 1975, when the ivory scandal, involving the president of Kenya and his family, was first splashed across the international press. In recent years world sales of ivory have totalled thousands of tons despite 'stringent international controls on sales'. Profits finance guerrilla wars and enrich officials. In Burundi alone, where statistics showed that there was only *one* elephant left, 100 tons of ivory – tusks from 11,000 elephants killed in Zaire and Rwanda, for which Burundi is a convenient clearing zone – left the country. Wild animals everywhere vanish, some species forever, cut down by machine-guns, poisoned, snared, run to death with jeeps or killed by starvation and disease as man and his cattle muscle into their last habitats. Ecosystems collapse, taking with them unexamined plant species that biologists say might have helped conquer such scourges as cancer and crippling viruses.

For more than ten years now the international outcry for the protection of endangered species has been echoing globally. Organizations like the World Wildlife Fund print thousands of words and distribute large amounts of leaflets across the world. Men and women of all ages are provided with livelihoods for wildlife protection; they are given heavy-duty vehicles and airplanes, sit in offices, fly around the world to attend seminars, have doctorate degrees in anthropology and ecology thrust upon them, and live in tidy homes with expense accounts in the cities and towns of the stricken areas they visit only sporadically. We never once met any of them in all our months in Africa. There does not seem to be any really useful cohesion of effort or effect on the wildlife they are supposed to, and are paid to, protect; these armchair do-gooders still seem to be suffering from the same debilitating weaknesses as the early explorers: the need for competitive recognition and praise.

An article in the London *Times* dated 2 September 1988 informed readers that:

A controversy over large-scale game poaching in Kenya hit a new high yesterday when a leading conservationist claimed that names of government officials involved had been submitted to a minister. The Nairobi Standard *also published a front-page photograph of two dead elephants in Tsavo National Park with their heads missing, hacked off by poachers using electric saws in their efforts to remove the tusks. Commenting on the picture, Mr Richard Leakey, chairman of the East African Wildlife Society and head of the Nairobi National Museum, asked the Minister of Tourism, Mr Muhoho, to explain how, last week, people were cutting off elephant heads with chain saws in Tsavo National Park, and how, after having removed the tusks, they loaded them into the car and drove across the national park, which has guarded gates. He went on to say that wildlife poaching was economic sabotage that threatened the stability and success of Kenya. The country banned game hunting in 1977, but poaching has continued and threatens to wipe out elephant and rhino. In the past month alone, ninety-two elephants have been killed around the country, according to official figures. Last week poachers killed three game rangers in an ambush in Garissa. Mr Muhoho retorted that, despite these statistics, there were still 22,000 elephants in Kenya, while Leakey claimed there are less than 6,000. The poachers are 'small-timers' working for certain highly placed people whom he could not identify . . .*

Conservation all over the world is no longer something that we can feel magnanimous and charitable about. The changing and decreasing of the natural

—Overleaf—
The only other elephant we found was lying half submerged in the river, dead, with machine-gun holes in its hind-quarters.

65

habitat, the cutting down of rain forests, the pollution of lakes and rivers, the pollution of the very biosphere which creates the climate, the oxygen and all the things that we depend on for life, is now the responsibility of the human race, which has tampered with Nature far beyond Nature's ability to recover on its own. As long as there are individuals, however dedicated in their own way, working separately without any real contact with one another, significant progress cannot be made. Even when one of those people becomes a world figure, such as Dian Fossey or Joy Adamson, once they have been forgotten by the public because they are dead what are the possibilities of their projects continuing? Perhaps the creation of a UN of ecologists, where each individual can contribute his findings and knowledge towards the common goal of conservation, could be an answer to the dramatic situation today.

At the mouth of the Great Ruaha, where the river narrows in the dry season, the passage was blocked solid by hippo. Lined up back to back and beside each other they formed a live barrage from one bank to the other, only the tops of their heads and twitching rubbery ears visible. At the sound of our engines they turned and faced us. Lorenzo and Richard in the lead, their boats low in the water, dropped speed to a minimum and moved forward cautiously. Majiji stood at the bow with his rifle loaded. His job was to ensure our safe passage without loss of life, if possible. He was used to the panic reflexes of wild things and this was a tricky situation we were approaching. Angry or frightened hippo have been known to chew up or overturn boats when all escape routes are blocked, one of the hazards we had envisaged before starting our journey. In his survival lessons Eddie Magee had taught us that beating the water or the side of the boat with an oar is a strong hippo deterrent, as the vibrations have a fearsome effect and they turn and bolt, but here there was no place to bolt to and hardly enough water for cover. Intent on recording the scene on film, I felt no fear; I saw only the savage beauty of the place. As we approached, the hippo sank beneath the surface of the water and suddenly the way was open and clear, but we could not know how deep they were.

'OK, let's go,' Lorenzo shouted back at the other boats, slamming down the throttle as the three boats sped over the submerged animals, bumping and scattering them in a frenzy of churning water. They rose and plunged like dolphins around us as they headed for deep water. We bounced over them so fast there was no time for their panic to turn to aggression and before they knew what had hit them we had passed. Slowly they surfaced to watch us disappear out of sight.

The river widened gradually all the way to Stiegler's Gorge, approximately 100 miles upstream, where the grasslands turn to stone and the current gets stronger as it cuts its way deep into the tunnel-like entrance to the gorge, the steep walls covered in tall, slim trees. From a game-post perched disconsolately atop a white cliff at the mouth of the gorge, two – apparently forsaken – scouts came running down to wave at us. Later they told us they had not seen anyone for the past three months.

We threw our anchors on a spit of fine, dark sand with three huge round boulders on it that looked like a modern sculpture in an ancient world. An eerie silence gave the place a timeless aura. The evening shadows fell in streaks and crept up the opposite face as we unpacked the boats. Then suddenly it was dark; only the tops of the trees were still kissed by the sun's last rays.

Because we were travelling upriver it was not possible to cross the rocky rapids, still very powerful despite the low water-level of the season. We kept in touch by radio with our vehicles, which had reached Stiegler's the day before we did and were awaiting us, before crossing the river on an antiquated cable-car suspended 100 feet above the raging waters. The boats and equipment had now to be portaged up the side of the cliff, a daunting undertaking not only because of the size and weight of our equipment, but because the steep 200-foot-high bank was covered in loose soil, undergrowth and trees. Lorenzo, who had been reading the diaries of Stanley and Livingstone, had learned all about expedition portages and, with Richard's help, pushed the hesitant team forward. There was no alternative. A bunch of Africans recruited from a nearby village at the top traipsed up and down all day with us carrying boats, engines, fuel and camp equipment – the whole river expedition – to the top. When our young 'pilgrims' saw with what zest and dexterity the Africans negotiated their way up the slippery slope they bravely took up the challenge, pitting their muscle and resistance against that of the locals; what started as an ordeal soon turned into a contest of wills and staying power.

By the end of the day every item had travelled to the top and everyone lay spreadeagled on the ground, exhausted but proud. It was too late and we were too weary to move any further, so we spent the night under the stars, comatose amid our scattered loads. Soon after midnight, when we were fast asleep, the first heavy rain of the season fell in a torrential downpour that sent everyone scuttling for shelter. Dawn found us huddled like dejected rats under any available tarpaulins, feigning indifference and sleep, secretly mumbling obscenities; but as is always the case in Africa, sunrise brings smiling solace after a night of discomfort, and soon everyone and everything was spread out drying, the campfire crackled and the uplifting aroma of percolating coffee filled our nostrils and revived our sagging spirits.

All that day we ferried the expedition overland, about fifteen miles through sparse miombo country scattered with giant termite hills to the other side of the rapids. The rain of the previous night had initially cleared the air, but as the day wore on the heat grew intense and the tsetse fly set about boring into us. This was the agony we readily accepted for all the ecstasy we had felt.

The tents were set up under some trees growing on the top of a hillock overlooking the river, and the heat finally subsided as twilight descended on us. After a swim in the river and a cup of blessed, reviving tea we were in fighting form again. It was interesting to notice how the anticipation and then the discovery of new areas always gave us an adrenalin rush that kept us fuelled and helped combat physical fatigue. Human nature is destroyed by repetition and boredom, and this expedition, with its constantly changing scenery and situations, provoked exactly the opposite reaction in us.

While we were asleep that night a pride of lion, attracted by the scent of an impala Richard had shot for the pot just before nightfall, came loping fearlessly into camp. Richard had fastened the carcass high in a tree to protect it from night marauders, but this had not deterred the hungry predators. The black-maned male, whom we saw again next day, had heaved himself without much ado on to an adjacent bough of the tree, from where he could reach the meat, while his female and cubs lay in the long grass around the camp. He lunged at the meat and caught it by the hind legs, landing with it on the pots and pans. The clatter awoke the sleeping camp. Richard and Majiji shot out of their tents, guns in hand, followed in rapid succession by the excited 'pilgrims', hastily tying kangas around their loins and nervously flashing torches in the dark. One by one they appeared in the dark night, wriggling out of their tents rubbing their eyes, their young faces now tanned and healthy; they moved through the trees towards the embers of the campfire like alarmed school kids at summer camp. I watched them through the open flaps of my tent and tried to imagine what each one was feeling, exposed as they were to the rawness of Africa. I had grown up with this sort of thing, but for most of them it was their first such experience and could, I imagine, have been rather chilling; but youth has a wonderful element of bravado and their voices betrayed more excitement than fear.

'What was that?' they called to each other as they groped around in the dark.

'Lion,' Richard's voice, calm and matter of fact, replied from somewhere as he disappeared with Majiji in the direction of the carcass in the tree.

The old lion, less disturbed than our youngsters by all the commotion, had dragged the meat with him into the bushes, where he disappeared with his family, while the dying fire, quickly stoked back to life, lit up the camp and the night was full of excited chatter. Two successive gunshots to ward off the lions instantly silenced the chatter and, moments later, Richard and Majiji reappeared with a reassuring 'all clear'. Over the ritual cup of comforting tea all eyes bathed Richard with envious admiration. Lorenzo and I listened to the commotion from our tent unalarmed. It was not the first time this sort of thing had happened to us. It was part of the song of Africa.

While we awaited the fuel transfer from the vehicles to the boats at the top of the Stiegler Rapids, we explored the wild and rugged landscape of lava rock sculpted by the wind and water of the ages. Dressed only in a straw hat and rubber sandals we walked along the river to the drop-off point. To be naked and feel the bite of the sun, to smell the wilderness on the hot dry air, to listen to the rushing river sloshing against its stone bed, just the two of us in Africa, with not a soul in sight was to taste again the meaning of total freedom.

We walked until our legs and ankles ached and then lay in the pools carved by the water. A great peace and stillness hung about and on the opposite bank a 'kudu' antelope appeared from among the bushes. He stood for a moment looking around, his head high, sniffing the air, wary of prowling poachers, a magnificent young male with perfect spiral horns tipped with ivory. His sand-coloured coat shone in the sun and rippled as the massive shoulder muscles parted and his head dropped to drink. It was one of those uplifting moments when time stands still and one's thoughts turn to God.

The river level was low and around us lay the debris of high water – trees, bushes and boulders – carried downstream on its mad rush towards the sea. As the river-bed widens with each rainy season, the earth is eaten away from beneath the trees and, when they no longer have anything to cling to, they crash; some with their exposed roots hanging like useless tentacles were waiting for the other half to let go. The fallen ones lay like a defeated army where the low water had deposited them, their huge roots now stiff and blackened like the spokes of a giant wheel with the marks of the rushing water still hanging from them. The rounded stones and boulders in their immobility were evidence of their helpless descent in the grip of the river. We bathed and washed our hair, and our shampoo bottle and soap were swept away like the trees and boulders in the brown waters.

Back on the water next day, our inflatables reassembled and reloaded, our team reshuffled – the 'pilgrims' who had been travelling on land in the vehicles swapped with the river team – we moved on towards Shuguli Falls, two or three days and approximately 200 miles upstream, across a stony landscape where only the baobab trees, grave and monumental, thrive in their barren surroundings. We slipped past groups of hippo that plunged around us as they headed for the same deep-water spots as we were, often bumping into us from beneath like rubbery rocks. On the banks of the river the lion family that had paid us a visit watched over the carcass of an upturned hippo as a bunch of vultures picked it clean. Little of the meat remained; just the rib cage and parts of the skeleton still lay on the thick grey skin spread around it. A heavy stench of decay floated on the air.

The sun rose to its zenith and the heat clung to us like a hot blanket, slowly silencing us, as the midday lethargy set in. We slipped into a soporific trance and watched the moving scenery through half-closed eyes, lulled by the smooth mechanical sounds of our Mariner outboards in perfect tune. The hours between noon and four were always the most difficult: we often stopped for lunch and a stretch, beneath a shade tree or an overhanging cliff. It was only once we stopped moving that we really felt the heat and a dip in the water was always refreshing.

We reached Shuguli Falls in the evening, four days later, after another 100-yard portage across some exposed flat rocks that stretched from one bank to the other. Because of the low gradient, we were able to pull the boats over the smooth stones along the water's edge by means of the inflatable rubber rollers we had brought along for just such a purpose. This ingenious invention, when placed beneath the boats, allows them to slide forward easily without causing any damage to the hulls, and needs no more than six people to pull each boat. Once deflated, the rollers are folded away and take up little space. The Pennel and Flipo rubber fuel bladders designed with the same idea in mind greatly facilitated the carrying of large quantities of fuel.

The Shuguli Falls bring into stark focus the size and importance of the Rufiji river for Tanzania, for it is here that its other rivers join up in one of Africa's great spectacles: the Kilombero, which drains the water from the flat valley plains beneath the Mbarara Mountains to the east, and the Luego flowing in from the south. Where the two rivers meet, the water has cut a deep gorge into the rock and passes through it at tremendous pressure, plunging downwards with terrifying, mesmerizing force, forming the Shuguli Falls; hardly 100 yards downstream the water is quite calm again and flows almost imperceptibly.

Here at Shuguli we undertook our next big overland portage around the Falls, thirty-miles east to Malai on the Kilombero river, the only point on this portion of our route where we could meet up with our vehicles. We camped that night at the bottom of the Falls on a small beach on the right bank of the river. Crocodiles

The Shuguli Falls bring into stark focus the size and importance of the Rufiji river for Tanzania.

slithered from the rocks and long-beaked brown hoopoe birds flew off in fright. As we pitched camp, the setting sun enveloped us for a fleeting moment in an aura of light so strange it commanded our attention. Nothing moved other than the reflection of the bushes and trees in the river and the dramatic painted clouds, slowly eclipsed by the descending night. We could hear the Falls pounding upstream.

Lorenzo picked up his fishing rod and with Majiji disappeared downstream. Within the half-hour they had each hauled in one of the legendary giant Rufiji catfish that abound in these waters and can reach 100 lbs. in weight. It was the first big catch of the expedition and caused a ripple of excited chatter through the camp for the rest of the evening. We lay on the hot, flat rocks looking up at the stars for a long time.

CHAPTER FOUR

THE
MYSTERIOUS
KILOMBERO

THE FOLLOWING MORNING THE BOATS WERE PULLED OUT of the water for the second time. Everything was repacked and the exhausting haul over the rocks to the top of the Falls, where we had planned to meet the ground-support vehicles, took up most of the day. Camp was set up again just before nightfall in an open glade beneath some trees; we were now on the Kilombero, which falls here in a series of steps ten feet high, splashing against huge boulders on which hardy river plants cling with roots so firmly embedded that no amount of water force can dislodge them. The tough, dark green leaves seemed made of plastic and moved like strange aquatic creatures beneath the surface of the water.

The discovery of the river at Shuguli offered us a marvellous insight into Nature's perfect ecological balance, and it was fascinating to explore the interaction of the water and the earth. Few people ever came here and the place was relatively undisturbed. Before breaking over the steps and rocks, the river meanders for a mile or two through the trees in a maze of channels cut by hippo who go to eat the long grass growing there. Small islands of tall reeds, with now and again a solitary tree, are scattered in the river bed. They are the nesting grounds for the weaver birds, who build their nests on the reeds, fastening them firmly to the tips so as to prevent access by rodents and snakes. Everything, we found, had a logical function or purpose to it. The ingenious, intricate weaving of the weaver-bird nest is one of

Nature's marvels, for it is built in such a way that the funnel-like entrance is only large enough for the passage of one bird; it then expands into a globe-shaped bag which can hold several eggs or chicks; because of its position, the down-turned entrance is difficult for marauders to enter.

That night we were hit by another torrential downpour, which heralded the beginning of a rainy season we had hoped to avoid. The river rose several feet and next morning we found it lapping at our tents. The falls ahead of us had doubled in force and in size, and it was now no longer possible to climb over the rocks under which we had bathed and showered the evening before.

The thirsty trees and bushes, brittle and flaking the day before, were now suddenly dark and swollen with moisture. Within the next forty-eight hours, minute velvet buds appeared, bringing new life to the apparently dead branches. The parched, powdery earth on the game trails smelled of rain, and butterflies and tiny red beetles like squares of crimson velvet hovered and crawled over it. The fallen leaves lying on the ground were musty and alive with yellow spear-headed mushrooms pushing through the earth and from beneath the bark of trees. The miracle of Nature's cycle was bursting out all around us, but there was still no sign of our vehicles. We had lost radio contact with them; our supplies were almost out; in another two days we would have to depend on gun and reel for our food.

On the sixth day after we arrived, Lorenzo decided to send Richard on foot to Malai, our next meeting point, to find out what had gone amiss. It had rained every day for several hours and we had run out of everything, even the basics: no more salt, or cooking fat, matches, paraffin or sugar. I was down to a dozen Sweetex tablets. There still remained half a packet of black tea and some dry beans. I was the only one in the group who had experienced fasting and its beneficial effects and so was not bothered by the circumstances; Lorenzo and the 'pilgrims' had never before found themselves in this situation. It was interesting to observe how each of them dealt with it in their own way; for the first two days the strange, yet unidentified, 'malaise' which we had noticed beginning to manifest itself earlier on among some of our 'pilgrims' was aggravated by the lack of food, but the hunter instincts were sharpened. Everyone was out fishing and Richard and Lorenzo kept the camp supplied with game meat and birds, but cooked on a wood fire without salt or fat this food was not very palatable and the black tea without milk or sugar was strong and bitter. The least affected were the Africans and Richard, hardened bush people, but for Lorenzo and the 'pilgrims' it was quite an experience, which they took like veteran soldiers. We became aware how spoiled our palates have become in the western world with our need for refined tastes, sugar, salt, etc., which kill all natural flavours and make our foods so unpalatable when they are missing.

Richard and Majiji left next morning before sun-up carrying with them the roasted leg of an impala, a blanket, a lightweight tent fly, a rifle and a flask of drinking water. They expected to cover the thirty miles in two days. The rest of us settled back to thinking of our empty stomachs and comparing our weight loss. For Lorenzo and myself, this forced interruption to our journey presented a wonderful pretext for delving further into the area. We wove through the bushes following the game trails that sometimes took us way inland, far from the river. At other times we were confronted with surprising aspects of the river, which seemed to wander like a raging free spirit over the land and the boulders, through the trees, sometimes soft and quiet, other times loud and violent, filling the air with spray that smelled of the wild. Our 'pilgrims' seemed to appreciate less this temporary lull in the momentum of the expedition and often looked bored, despondent and obviously hungry. Some feeble attempts at making the most of the situation in exploratory walks or fishing forays did not seem to alleviate the tedium; it was obvious they were not enjoying the unexpected interlude, for which none of us was really prepared.

The two men were back in camp the following evening with one of our vehicles. They had met it a few miles out of Malai: it had been lost for four days, stuck in the bog of black cotton soil that stretches from the river to Malai. When it rains the tenacious sticky mud can keep one prisoner for days. A case of fresh provisions soon brought the involuntary fasters together around a plate of spaghetti, while the new arrivals struck camp and loaded up. Surprisingly, we found that our bodies had already adapted to the spartan living and we felt the better for it, lean and energized; and we all had a bout of indigestion after our first meal.

The thirty-mile journey to Malai was an adventure in itself. We got stuck in the mud six times and each time needed a major excavation job with logs and rocks and branches to dig ourselves out, leaving a trail of debris and deep ruts behind us that scarred the gentle, soaking landscape.

Malai, once a wildlife game-post in colonial times, was now an abandoned, desolate place. By a stretch of the imagination one could picture it set out neatly beneath the great mango trees on a rise above the river, with white-washed stone buildings and painted tin roofs, perhaps some flowers and white stones bordering the path, a flag perhaps and some well drilled and scrubbed rangers in starched khaki, perhaps some battered bush vehicles. Now the buildings, except for one, had lost their roofs, their doors and their windows. The plaster was cracked and scarred with words and slogans scrawled with charcoal in Swahili and English. A few trees still grew, offering some welcome shade. The heavy rainfall of the past week had temporarily brought back life to the hardened, stony earth, through which tender blades of grass were pushing.

Half a dozen stragglers who said they were park rangers, in faded bush-green army fatigues, still lived there, hanging about, bored and despondent, with nothing to do. The government of Tanzania had not paid them for several months and they informed us they would not be there much longer. Morale was at its lowest and they asked to join our expedition. We spent two days with them, drying out, regrouping and resorting; they seemed happy to have us and one could feel their pathetic need to talk to someone new. They brought us firewood and water from the river and we sat on the crumbling steps talking of the old days. We left them some provisions – tea and sugar, some dried milk and some mouldy biscuits – and bade them a sad farewell. I can still see their laughing faces as they waved us goodbye from the banks of the river, happy to have momentarily been part of us, as they helped reload, reassemble and refloat boats and vehicles. These were the real victims of independence, people who had lost their identity during the colonial era, now no longer able to re-adapt to an independent state, where no one cared or worried about them. How many we were to meet along the way.

Here in Malai a passing Landrover picked up Elisabeth, our first defector. The malaise which had been creeping in among our 'pilgrims' now suddenly came out into the open in the form of a goodbye note from her, with no explanation for her decision. It was clear she had had enough and didn't want to make an issue of it. I folded the note away in my pocket and was secretly quite relieved, as were some of our diehards; it was like losing a piece of luggage on a heavily overloaded cart. We had been on the river for approximately one month and each time we met up with the land-support crew I was aware of this strange, indefinable uneasiness that existed between the river crew and the land crew, despite the care we deliberately took to arrange frequent exchanges so that no-one would feel left out of the river experience. It was difficult to pinpoint the cause, but each time we met up on the river it became more apparent. The expedition had had its shake-down and had taken on a shape of its own; there was little we could change at this point and any grievances were, perhaps purposely, kept from us. Like Livingstone and Stanley before us, we decided not to make an issue of it and ignored it, conveniently dismissing it as character clashes; our 'pilgrims' were perhaps beginning to feel the pinch, as they began relating to the real meaning of a transafrican expedition, with its good and its bad days. I felt several of them were realizing that they had not embarked on a joy-ride and were not enjoying the experience as we were, but were still loath to admit it.

We lost two more a week later: Gianfranco, who left without a word of farewell, and Richard's troublesome assistant in his vehicle. By the time we reached Mbeya, our team had dwindled to six: Richard, Sally, Lorenzo C., Shona, Byrdine and Marco – finally the right number. As in all things balance was crucial. Until this point we had been vastly top-heavy, something that had worried me from the start, but that Lorenzo had thought was necessary because of the portaging and the possibility of people either getting sick or dropping out. Our lack of experience had made it impossible to be more precise on this issue; it is always easy to be wise afterwards, but at the time we were facing *terra incognita*.

To us, back on the water after ten days on land, the river looked good. The familiar sound of the engines, the breeze on our faces, the passing scenery all brought back that wonderful sense of freedom which moving always imparts. What a relief it was. Like taking flight and leaving beneath one the problems and worries of daily life.

About forty-five miles from Malai the river is barred by rocky ledges. We had therefore to portage the boats and our task was greatly facilitated once again by the very useful inflatable Eurovenile rubber cylinders.

LORENZO: The place was picturesque and we decided to spend the night on these rocky banks of the Kilombero. I threw a line, with a solid hook I had baited with a piece of dried meat, into the water. It had hardly disappeared in the current when the cork reel, on which I had wrapped 100 yards of nylon line, was violently wrenched from my hand. I had never before been caught so unprepared by a fish; it must have weighed at least 20 lbs. It was my last line and catching that fish would have spelled the difference between an excellent supper and a tin of meat. I had to make up for it. It was four in the afternoon; there were still three hours of daylight ahead. I heard the 'kekekeke' of some guinea fowl and grabbed my twelve-bore and some buckshot. But approach was difficult: the bush surrounding the river and stretching inland was sparse and scattered, with groups of leafy trees thirty feet high. I watched about twenty birds running fast along the dried bed of a small stream, which was now covered with a green velvet moss that managed to grow and flower apparently without water. Fire-red insects no larger than horse flies hovered over the green carpet on which they fed. There was never a dull moment in our journey.

There was not much point chasing the guinea fowl; I therefore wandered off down the little waterless stream, happy to be alive, to be where I was, to be the way I was. In the African wilderness, sudden movements catch the eye. Way ahead, about two hundred yards from me, a dozen antelope crossed the sandy river-bed where it was wider and covered with tufts of dried grass. Impala, I thought, but I was not sure. At that precise moment I became a hunter with half a dozen people to feed. I suddenly felt that real hunting instinct again within me, not that of the sportsman or the trophy hunter, but that of the provider of food. I knew that to try and bag an impala with a twelve-bore shotgun in such open grassy country was virtually impossible, but I decided nevertheless to give it a try. I would not fire unless I was certain of a kill; I had therefore to get to within roughly thirty yards of my quarry.

Thirty strides are not many in Africa. It is the distance a lion springs on its prey. It is a dangerous distance, over which the antelopes can 'feel' even without seeing. Hunting an animal with a rifle and perhaps a telescope is quite easy. The animal has not much leeway, it does not even have the time to become nervous, to sniff the air. My twelve-bore was an old gun my father had picked up as a souvenir in a destroyed house during the Italian retreat at Caporetto in 1917.

I began walking with considerable difficulty, my body bent low in front of me. After about fifty yards I stretched out on my stomach and, abandoning the river-bed, crawled up the bank among the roots of the grass, spiky and sharp as razor blades. In the distance I spotted a dozen fawn backs, in the middle of a meadow. Their heads were hidden beneath the grass tufts they were feeding on, but of the dozen, a couple of them kept lifting their heads and could have seen my movements. The wind was favourable for me to attempt an approach, so I crawled towards a tree that would have prevented the antelopes from seeing me as I gained terrain. I never lifted my head until I had reached the tree, which was about 100 yards from where I had been lying.

I knew that to bag an impala with a twelve-bore shotgun in such open grassland was almost impossible.

To crawl for 100 yards dragging a gun with the left hand and using the right to advance without making any noise or breaking dried twigs is not only difficult, it is exhausting. To avoid detection along the way I had to slither over fresh, fetid buffalo dung which was lying about. After half an hour of effort and with growing determination I watched the impala from behind the tree. They had moved away from it and were now closer to the point I had crawled from, about 100 yards from me. It had got cooler. I looked at the time; it was almost six o'clock. In one hour the sun would be dropping behind the horizon with equatorial velocity. I rested a while on my back, scraping the buffalo shit from my face with a twig. Two squirrels chased each other on a branch above me. Out of the corner of my eye I caught a movement to my right. Slowly I rolled back on to my stomach and grabbed the barrel of my gun. Three impala were returning towards the tree under which I was hiding. I thought they would come round full circle. The wind was changing direction and had they moved too much to my left they would have sensed me. I tried rapidly to interpret, to evaluate, to sense the next moves that would bring me to 30 yards from my prey. I felt like a primitive man, covered as I was in buffalo dung. The acrid but vital scent was beginning to excite me, penetrating my nostrils, making me feel wild as an animal. The vision of an empty-handed return to camp, the humiliation of failure, spurred me to absolute immobility. I shall shoot at 30 yards and only at 30 yards, I repeated to myself, keeping the animal in my sights, my finger on the trigger. The sun was low now, tinging the sky with red and orange and yellow, silhouetting the impala in a golden field of light. Total silence preceded the half-hour before nightfall, when all the birds seemed to be thanking Nature for having created them, free, in a marvellous world. I was afraid that the low rays of the setting sun would bounce off the barrel of my gun and attract the impalas' attention. They were now at 40 yards. The light in the sky was fading. Thirty-five yards. I had difficulty holding my breath; I was shaking. I also thought of that poor innocent animal, that lamb of God, victim of our sins, who was about to die in order to feed our bodies, the way other impalas feed other animals, tunnies feed sharks and sardines feed tunnies. My cracked lips were burning, though I was not aware of my thirst; my skinned knees hurt. Thirty yards. I squeezed the trigger with the sights on the chest of the impala. One dry shot. The animal crumbled as if hit by lightning. The others lifted their heads, momentarily undecided before bolting. This was a hunt, not a massacre; one animal sufficed for the sacrifice.

As I approached the dead animal, I noticed the blood stains on the soft white fur of its underbelly. On its breast there was a well-concentrated rose of buckshot. It was seven o'clock. In ten minutes it would be dark. I grabbed the impala by the horns and began pulling it behind me. It weighed 100 lbs, maybe more. I had to stop every ten yards to catch my breath. My bones ached, a terrible thirst was upon me, my lips were dry like the earth of the parched river-bed and yet I smiled, thinking of our supper in that beautiful camp on the banks of the Kilombero river amid the grey streaked rocks. I thought of Majiji, our Tanzanian tracker, who would be proud of me. I dragged the impala with the sheer strength of my will. Would I find the camp? I could no longer see anything, not even the sky. I heard a shot. They were looking for me. I let go of the impala, inserted a cartridge into the barrel of my gun, lifted it skywards and fired. I lay on the ground, my head propped on the soft belly of my prey. I looked up at the stars and searched for the Southern Cross, my favourite constellation. A zebra barked, a jackal replied in the distance. I heard a human voice. It was Majiji. Suddenly he was there standing over me

At midday we would stop for lunch on a sandy spit.

speaking of his satisfaction. '*Misuri, misuri*,' he said; good, good. He was carrying the .375 Magnum. There were lions around, he told me, he had heard them earlier on.

I left Majiji with the dead animal and walked back to camp, from where I would dispatch two men with a *panga*, the long African sheath knife, to dismember it. I went down to the river to wash. The red eyes of lurking crocs watched me. I was tired, no longer hungry; the hunt was over.

The five-day trip along the Kilombero Valley was full of unexpected surprises, as little is known of this great river. The words of Stanley came back to us: 'An enduring pleasure is derived from exploration of new, unvisited and undescribed regions, the morrow's journey is longed for in the hope that something new may be discovered. For the traveller who is a true lover of "wild Nature", where can she be found in such variety as in Africa, where is she so mysterious, fantastic and savage, where are her charms so strong, her moods so strange?' This 'enduring pleasure' was becoming addictive; each morning we could not wait to get going, such was the anticipation of discovery within us. For those of us who had these feelings it was a very unifying element throughout the whole journey; but it left us frustrated and

:MIRELLA

disbelieving when we realized that some of our 'pilgrims' did not share them with us.

An interesting psychological metamorphosis was taking place: things which before had seemed so necessary to our daily existence we now dispensed with. Food, for instance, became purely an element of combustion, sleeping was reduced to a mattress on the ground and a bedroll, ephemeral things like mirrors, hairbrushes and combs were put aside, clothes needed only to be comfortable and functional, style and look no longer mattered. The only absolutely essential items for the journey were the mosquito net and the insect spray can, for without a good night's sleep Africa is unbearable and insects in Africa are everywhere; if they don't kill you they can drive you mad. Africa's wild nature is potent and invasive, and has to be dealt with; then it becomes warm and gentle, making material discomforts acceptable and endurable, and one's spirit soars.

Encounters in the wild, be they with man or bird or beast, turn into events because of their rarity. On rivers one can travel for miles and hours without encountering anything; one moves through a silent world of colours and shapes where the earth and the sky are in primal evidence and one's awareness is stretched to its limits, so that a sudden movement or appearance jolts one from reverie, and a

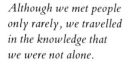

Although we met people only rarely, we travelled in the knowledge that we were not alone.

*Encounters in the wild —
be they with man, bird
or beast — turn into
events because of their
rarity.*

*Buffalo, startled by our
passage, offered us a
fleeting glimpse of
themselves standing like
ebony statues.*

fleeting moment can sometimes develop into an exhilarating new experience. Everything and anything is possible in these circumstances, where time no longer holds any meaning and your whole being becomes receptive. This, for true lovers of Nature, is what Stanley was referring to: a canoe slipping silently through green rushes leaving a delicate wake of light behind it; a heron rising in flight, drawing in its long neck and legs to fit the streamline of its airborne body; the native family clustered around a couple of huts perched on a protruding mound of mud, enveloped in a reflection of white clouds and surrounded by miles of floating reeds, beckoning and calling, eager for contact; the sparkle of fast-moving fish in the water; the solitary fisherman waist-deep in water fixing his trap, offering us his catch; the naked youth weaving a rush mat on the mud; a pelican with a broken wing unable to fly; a flock of egrets gliding through light and shadow as they wind their way downriver ahead of us.

From dawn to dusk our days were bathed in expectancy and our travelling punctuated with visions and sounds that belong only to the world of the river. Although we met people only rarely, we travelled in the knowledge that we were not alone, for here on the Kilombero river, where life is harsh and demanding, man does not compete with it but has learned to live in harmony with it. Had anything happened to us we felt sure that these marsh dwellers would have come to our help. When we stopped for the night in a clearing cut out by them on the banks, they would appear silently from among the reeds, poling a canoe, to throw us a rope of twisted fibre in a gesture so simple and friendly no greeting could have been more appropriate. Some would come bearing freshly caught fish, still alive and shining pink and silver. They refused the money we offered them, but gladly joined us for a cup of tea and usually left with a packet of tea leaves, some sugar or some maize meal, which was always much appreciated. What would they do with money in a place like this?

A herd of buffalo, startled by our passage, crashed into the surrounding rushes, but not before offering a fleeting glimpse of themselves standing there like ebony statues, their massive horns framing ominous heads, water dripping from their mouths like quicksilver in the harsh midday; with nostrils distended they looked at us, defiant and arrogant, before turning and charging into the rushes that closed behind them in a heavy protective curtain. Further downriver a delicate biscuit-coloured cob peered at us through the long grass and then leapt like a ballet dancer into the water, followed by its offspring, and swam, completely submerged except for the head, across to the other bank with hardly a ripple.

For days we wound our way through the Kilombero marshes in a labyrinth of channels that often brought us back to where we had started from. Sometimes the channels were so narrow we had to hack our way through rushes that at times were ten or fifteen feet high. We finally got so lost that we had to retrace our steps to some of our marsh friends, who came on board and guided us with the same ease as we moved around the streets of our home towns. They bade us farewell with much laughter and wished us a safe journey at the junction of the Mpanga river, another large waterway, equal to the Kilombero, which we had never heard of and was not marked on the map. Our friends returned to their homes on foot, swimming the channels when there was nothing solid to step on. The going now was much easier and we were able to plane at full throttle without weeds and roots to choke the propellers.

We reached the Mpanga mission, set high up on a 100-foot bank overlooking the river, in the early evening. We could proceed no further because here the river cascades in a series of falls and rapids for several miles back to its source in the Mbarara mountains, plunging over boulders and fallen trees as it begins its massive journey to the Indian Ocean. A tree trunk several feet in diameter lay across the river bed, forming a natural barrage from one side to the other beyond which we could now no longer proceed; this tree marked the end of the first leg of our river journey. It was not dead. Half its roots were still embedded in the bank and it went on living in its horizontal position, allowing all sorts of parasites to grow into and over it, while the river tumbled hardly three feet beneath. The trunk was smooth and yellow in colour; all sorts of mosses and different kinds of mushrooms were drawing life from it, and in the branches some birds had built their nests. It was cool and dark in this part of the river, a place I could imagine coming into from the hot sun to rest; a very peaceful place; a fitting punctuation mark in our long journey.

The Mpanga mission had been built many years ago during colonial times by Swiss missionaries and was now still run by a young Swiss padre and two young Irish nuns. They were not there when we went to call on them, but had left the day before by Landrover, we were told, for Ifakara, a day's journey from there.

Here we were, in the middle of Africa, having travelled for almost two months without sighting anything European. Time seemed to have slipped by so fast we had difficulty in believing the date when at the mission they told us Christmas was not far off. How easy it now was to detach ourselves totally from the world we had come from. Our lives were now regulated by the sun, the days and the nights no longer had names, the months had no age. It no longer mattered because other elements relating to our surroundings had replaced them, elements that had to do with our daily welfare, our survival, our spirits, where the trivialities of civilization no longer fitted; each day we were moving closer to the chimps, and we were loving it.

Around us now suddenly spread a perfect little Swiss compound, swept clean and neatly laid out. A main tree-lined avenue led to a red-brick church with a tall steeple and a weather-vane at the top. The surrounding buildings looked like mountain chalets, with steep snow-drift roofs covered in locally-made sun-baked clay tiles. Tropical creepers hung from wooden flower-boxes and filled the air with heady scents. In the church tower the bell struck twelve as we walked up the avenue, its chimes strangely foreign in this hot African setting. A bunch of rowdy schoolgirls in blue and white cotton uniforms, clutching their books, poured out of the buildings and walked past us down the avenue to a shaded clearing where several large tin saucepans were cooking on open fires. They invited us to join them for lunch and lifted the saucepan lids, covered in hot coals, to show us the day's menu— baked rice with curried fish and banana stew. It looked delicious and we accepted the invitation.

The hospital doctor called us over for a chat; he was treating a woman who had just been bitten by a green mamba with the legendary black stone the White Fathers

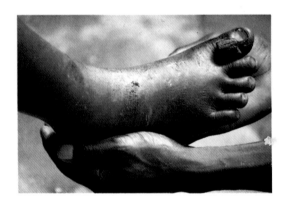

The black 'stone' is made from a special chemical formula kept secret by the White Fathers in Belgium and, when applied to snake bites, extracts all the venom.

had brought to Africa long ago for snake bites. We had heard a lot about this stone, made of a special chemical formula, kept secret by the Fathers in Belgium and which, when applied to the afflicted area, absorbs the poison within a few days; once it has all been extracted, the stone detaches itself and falls off. It is laid in milk for some hours to purify and is then ready for use again. This positive interaction between the blacks and the whites here at the mission was reassuring, the fruit no doubt of years of patience and devotion on the part of the dedicated missionaries. It would have been nice to talk to them about this quiet, little-known haven lost in the Tanzanian wilderness, but they were returning from Ifakara only after we had moved on.

Before starting on the expedition we had been to see James Ash, the snake expert living in Watamu on the Kenya coast. Our meeting with him came to mind as we examined the woman's painfully swollen foot. 'The most dangerous snake', he had warned us, 'is the puff adder. It relies on its camouflage to catch its prey and only the anti-venom can save its victim from death. The spitting cobra is dangerous because it can spit from four or five yards, and if the venom gets into the eyes, milk is the best

immediate remedy, for the conjunctiva of the eye is very absorbent. The green mamba is a deadly snake, recognizable because of the "smile" on its face and its small, beady eyes. The boom slang', he added, 'is one of those fearful snakes that always tries to get away. It is rare that people get bitten by them; if they do, the effect of their venom is very slow. One usually has time to fly to South Africa, the only place where the anti-serum is available, because there is so little of it in the world. At first the bite is not very painful, but then one comes up in bruises all over the place, big navy-blue bruises, and one begins to haemorrhage from one's gums and sometimes from the corners of one's eyes, and one actually begins to die of loss of blood, as the blood leaks through the capillaries. It is important', he emphasized, 'to learn how to distinguish the vipers from the mambas and the cobras, so as to administer the right antidote in time. One can feel the bites from cobras and mambas as the venom travels up the stricken area; it feels like a hair being dragged up or across it. In the case of a puff adder the local pain is very severe.'

The symptoms of snake bite and of fear are quite similar. Dilation of eyes and pupils, pains in the stomach, involuntary evacuation of the bowels, dry mouth, sweating are all symptoms of fear and also of snake bite. It is often not possible to see the snake that strikes, for it scuttles off into the bush or grass; but the black stone has been proved to withdraw venom regardless of its source. In out-of-the-way places it is the best and safest medication to administer.

We camped for two days beneath some ancient mango trees beside the river about half a mile south of the Mpanga mission, while we packed up the expedition for our long cross-country haul to Mbeya, 200 miles away. We cleared the ground and cut all the low bush around our campsite to deter any lurking snakes. The rains that had hit us at Shuguli had wrought havoc with the river here and the level was still high. Freshly-uprooted trees lay about in the brown water and, as everywhere, a little crowd had gathered on the banks waiting for us, dabs of bright colours on the green backdrop.

Dozens of eager hands grabbed the anchor ropes we threw to them. They helped unload the boats and like little ants carried our goods and chattels to the nearby campsite. As we settled down to the tea-before-anything ritual, they formed a circle around us with skinny limbs entwined, dozens of pairs of eyes solemnly fixing our every move.

An old man with a small boy in tow carrying a yellow puppy appeared. He was wearing a large straw hat and a peacock-blue and silver lady's dress, whose hem reached his knees, over a pair of faded army fatigues. The boy had on a long khaki shirt that badly needed to be washed. The two stood motionless in the shadows and said nothing until we offered them some tea in a mug. They took it with shy humility, a knobbly hand tipping the hat. One by one the forest people came out from the trees, funny little people carrying their belongings and their tools. One, with a long, homemade shotgun, asked for some cartridges. The disarming smile on the lined face, the clothes hanging in tatters around the emaciated body, instantly endeared him to us, and we invited him to share our evening meal so he could tell us about his hunting prowess with that antiquated gun. He hunted birds and monkeys to supplement his family's meals, and cartridges were hard to come by here; he had been using his old cartridge cases filled with salt and nails and some explosives stolen from the Chinese bridge-builders on the TanZam railroad. We examined the weapon and the ammunition and asked him how many times the hunter rather than the hunted got shot. He laughed. 'Not very often, just sometimes,' he said.

On the path behind him two women, with heavily-laden baskets on their heads and bundles of firewood strapped to their backs, joined the party. After a stare and a few words of greeting they went on their way down the narrow foot-path that followed the river for miles through the trees.

As night descended everyone shrank back into the trees, but by sun-up they had doubled in number. The children told us they had been let off school for the day so they could come and look at us; their teachers apparently thought there was more to learn here with us than on their benches with their books. The old man with the shotgun returned with a bottle of palm wine – in exchange for the cartridges, he

*The two stood
motionless in the
shadows and said
nothing until we offered
them some tea in a mug.*

explained. He took us to see how he gathered the sap from the palm trees in small bottles fastened with a shred of bark to a gash in the trunk. The sweet, sticky substance oozed into a little bamboo gutter about three inches long and half an inch wide and trickled into the bottle. Some golden bees were feasting on it and the whole contraption was an ingenious example of wilderness technology. Mixed with honey and left to ferment in the sun, it turns into a potent alcoholic beverage.

The village chief at Mpanga sent a runner with a message he carried in a split stick, inviting us, in broken English, to report to him; it was the custom, he explained, for new arrivals in the area. We spent an hour with this gracious, gentle man, who showed us proudly around the village and told us with a tone of regret that during the colonial days it had been a government administrative outpost; the crumbling remains of law and order were still visible in the court house, where some chickens scratched and picked on the earth floor. People sat on wooden chairs chatting outside the mud and brick buildings lined up in the shade of huge planted trees. A mixture of melancholy abandon and African indifference hung in the air. Did it really matter, I thought as I walked down the avenue, that the white 'benefactors' were no longer there, did the people miss the amenities brought to them, had they really been necessary? On the surface it looked as if the loss was only minimally felt and everyone had quite naturally reverted back, with African resignation, to their ancestral way of life. This was, of course, Africa's salvation and the reason for her survival. The white man's presence had never been considered more than that of an invading army, after whose retreat life resumed its natural course.

A five-ton lorry took us to Malimba station, twenty miles away, where we caught the TanZam train to Mbeya. Our vehicles had driven straight to Mbeya from Malai; the railway at Malimba was closer to the river and therefore easier for us to reach. The train had just left and the next one was not due for two days. On the empty station platform a man with a wooden cart was selling oranges. After several hot hours on the road, two days in this godforsaken place felt like a long time.

We camped for the two nights in a clearing at the bottom of a high hill just above the tracks. We walked through the forest to the top and came across clear evidence of charcoal burners destroying the trees. The presence of the railway had opened up the country and the inevitable consequences were beginning to appear. A stream of crystal-clear water fell over some huge boulders into a natural basin, providing us with a splendid mineral-water shower to wash in.

After several false departure announcements we finally got ourselves ready to board the train in the late afternoon of the third day; but the stationmaster informed

Shona would sometimes teach English words to children who flocked to our campsites.

us, after we had lugged all our equipment from our camping ground, that we could not take it with us, for this was a passenger train; our equipment could only travel on the goods train, which had not yet left Dar-es-Salaam. It should be arriving in the next forty-eight hours, '*Inshallah*' (God willing), he reassured us. Back in the clutches of African government administration we were now no longer masters of our destiny. There was no alternative but to adopt their methods of dealing with such inconveniences, namely a shrug and a laugh. We left a discontented Majiji behind to guard the equipment and joined the hordes of black bodies on the station platform, struggling beside them to board the overcrowded train with our bags and bedrolls. Every inch of space was taken. The wagons and corridors were packed to capacity and the journey was to last through the night for eighteen hours. The good humour and friendly laughter of our fellow travellers could nevertheless not dispel the overwhelming claustrophobia and odours of urine and hot sweat. I tried once to use the toilet, but recoiled in disbelief at the door. Flush toilets are not an African amenity and few know how they are operated. The urine-soaked toilet tissue and excrement on the floor and over the top of the bowl instantly paralyzed my kidneys and banished any necessity to relieve myself until I left the train next morning in Mbeya.

CHAPTER FIVE

THE CROCODILES OF LAKE RUKWA

T HAT NIGHT WE CLIMBED 4,000 FT IN THE 200-MILE TRAIN journey and when we reached Mbeya, at 10 o'clock next morning, the air was cold and crisp, and we could see mountain peaks through the low clouds still shrouding them. These were the Mbarara mountains, the birthplace of our rivers. The move from Mpanga to Mbeya was like moving from Africa to Europe in the winter. Our ground-support team had arrived a couple of days ahead of us and had set up camp in the compound of a French road construction company on the outskirts of the town. It was early December, sixty-five days into the expedition; here matters took a sudden turn when three more of our 'pilgrims' withdrew from the expedition after a confrontation in which the 'malaise' which had accumulated all along the journey was finally aired and we could no longer ignore it.

Lorenzo sat stoically through the onslaught and said nothing. After each one had had his say it was still not clear what really lay at the source of the disruptive feeling that had hung over the 'pilgrims' virtually since they met. It was evident that there was a clash of individual egos but also, and above all, many of them had now come to the realization that an African expedition can seem quite different in Europe than it does in Africa. The magic words lose their glow when the grind sets in, unless there is a sufficient motivation to propel one forward and eliminate the sometimes inevitable monotony.

Our 'pilgrims' were obviously not cut out for this sort of adventure. I looked across at Lorenzo sitting opposite me beneath his frayed straw hat; his face was blank and I knew he was not listening, thinking no doubt already of the morrow's journey and the discovery of new ground. As is often the case in these sorts of situation, I move in like a mother hen and try to smooth the ruffled feathers. For the first time since the expedition transferred from Milan to Kenya, I now felt it was my turn to say something. Rather touchingly they turned their attention eagerly to me, almost as if they expected me to wave a magic wand to right things; but in a few short sentences I was, alas, only able to tell them that things could not and would not change. None of us had known what to expect and if some now felt disappointed it seemed pointless to continue if they were not enjoying the experience. City life, which most of them had been born to, evidently still held them in its grip and they had not been able to change gear and adjust to the new rhythm that such an expedition imposes – impossibility of planning more than a day or two ahead, tentative fixing of times and dates, dealing with unexpected circumstances, changing plans, diverging – all elements to be contended with when breaking new ground. Did Stanley or Livingstone or any of the great explorers know when, if at all, they would reach a given point, what they would find and where they would go from there? They followed a loose and flexible direction. This is what exploration is all about. One cannot be bound by elements that belong to another world. Above all, we concluded, they lacked the motivation that propelled Lorenzo and me and were not satisfied just to ride along with us.

Richard, Sally and Marco had understood this and did move along with us without any difficulty, enjoying the experience almost as much as we did. I understood how the 'pilgrims' felt and much appreciated the efforts they had put into the expedition, but there was nothing to be done and because they were young, inexperienced and seemed confused I felt we owed it to them to eliminate any further illusions. I believe in confrontations in such circumstances even if they seem brutal. If they felt unable to adapt to the demands of the expedition, now was the time to turn back and go home, I explained simply to them. All except Marco, Sally and Richard bailed out.

Next day we left, with the three remaining diehards, for Lake Rukwa, a little-known lake that had a good ring to its name, ten hours to the east. Luckily a private light aircraft returning empty to Dar-es-Salaam from Mbeya airport took our last defectors on board, facilitating their rapid departure. What was interesting in this situation was that their absence went absolutely unfelt, and as soon as they left it was almost as if they had never been with us. If anything we all felt much more comfortable, perhaps because we were more in tune with each other.

The rough road to Rukwa took all day and offered us a vision of an Africa long forgotten. This was the Africa I had been born to, of my childhood, before electricity, roads and airports; the Africa about which books were written, behind whose gentle contours and heart-stopping views still lay the enigma that draws white men to her.

Lorenzo had been more affected by the showdown in Mbeya than he cared to reveal and only I was aware of his deep disappointment, but the ten-hour drive across the gentle landscape, over which the rains had spread a pale green mantle, put things back into their right perspective and when we sighted the lake everyone was feeling better.

The expedition to Lake Rukwa was to take us into a region where absolute autonomy was indispensable. We had foreseen that even by maintaining radio contact with the 'contaminated' world we were leaving it was not going to be possible to request any help in the form of evacuation, fuel or anything else. Our old Bedford 4X4 military lorry was going to have to perform miracles in the next weeks.

Rukwa looked forbidding from the top of the escarpment and not at all what we expected from the descriptions we had been given. Rimmed by mountains, it is typical of the chain of Rift Valley lakes that stretches from Lake Victoria to Lake Nyasa. The track down the steep escarpment to the shores, 300 ft below, was rough and covered with loose stones which we had to clear away. Vehicles rarely passed this way and people here travelled on foot. From Mbeya the road climbed to over 11,000 feet and dropped to less than 3,000 at the level of the lake. The African Rainbow convoy had to proceed with extreme prudence. We had to keep remembering that the most important thing was for the expedition to reach its end, and the end was still far off. All the equipment, therefore, had to last us for the whole route. It was not so much the difficulty of the descent that worried us but that of returning back up from the lake. In Africa one sometimes has to abandon a vehicle, and if we had lost our Bedford lorry it would have dealt a nasty blow to the expedition.

From the mountain tops one could clearly see the marshy bays, the tortuous course of the hidden river that descended from the plateau, the great dark green

trees around whose roots the lake gently lapped. This was crocodile country.

The crocodiles on the lake had multiplied greatly and had claimed the lives of several people who lived beside it: the Game Department in Mbeya had begun culling and they asked if we would help them as they were short of guns and ammunition and needed to eliminate approximately 400. How they were going to do this, and indeed who was going to do it, was still unclear. The culling had been suggested after a study *in situ* by Professor Hills of Arusha, a zoologist I imagine, sent by the government of Tanzania. But that was all they told us. The rest we had to find out for ourselves.

We set up base camp at the bottom of the road, floated two inflatables and left next day for Rungwa, a two days' journey to the north, where the crocodile infestation was especially acute and where only a few days before a child had been

The crocodiles had multiplied greatly and had claimed the lives of several people who lived around the lake.

95

'This is Abeli, the best crocodile hunter. He has his own gun and has killed many, many crocodiles,' Wellington told us.

taken from its mother's side as she was washing her clothes. The savage beauty of the lake added another dimension to this unexpected adventure, where the concept of killing did not fit the scenery. Apart from the rare encounters with civilization, the further we travelled inland the deeper we entered the real heart of the continent. Here in Rungwa the last white man, an Italian padre, had passed on foot four years before on his way to a mission station 300 miles away.

Wellington was sitting with his friends under a large mango tree when he saw our boats pull up on the black volcanic beach. They came down to meet us with a jubilant welcome punctuated with much laughter, and soon everyone was talking about crocs. Wellington was one of the old inhabitants of the area, and, like his friends, had been born at the mission station about seventy miles to the north. They had lived in Rungwa with their families for many years, cultivating the fertile soil along the lake edge with basic crops that kept them alive – manioc, wild tomatoes, sweet potatoes and corn; chickens provided eggs, and the wild mango trees offered an abundance of the best and biggest mangoes I have ever tasted. Totally self-contained, here was a wonderful example of people living in harmony with Nature, where the presence of the white man and his amenities seemed superfluous. The stories of cruising monsters lurking by the shore awaiting an easy prey – a fat baby, a goat or a dog – grew more and more outrageous as the prospect of a kill spread an instant wave of excitement, turning our arrival into a major event. It is at night with torches that crocodiles are hunted, they explained, because it is easier to creep up on them in the dark and their eyes shine like red beads.

Wellington turned to one of his friends and pulled him closer. 'This is Abeli,' he said, proudly presenting him to us. 'This man is the best crocodile hunter,' he told us in English, a large grin illuminating his shiny round black face. 'He has his own gun and has killed many many crocodiles.'

Abeli, a cool, laid-back fellow, acknowledged the accolade with a hesitant smile. He fixed us with steely eyes and put out a hand to greet us; we noticed that the left one was missing, severed just above the wrist. He had lost it hunting crocodiles, he told us, pointing at the stump, when the gun he had made himself exploded.

That same night, after we had finished setting up camp, a dozen men presented themselves to us, led by Wellington. They said they had canoes and wanted to be part of the hunt. Our boats, they explained, were no good as they were too big and made too much noise. Wellington had been in the Tanzanian army and had acquired a sense of command which he now used to select four men and two canoes. He called out the four names, touching each man on the arm, and introduced them as 'reliable people who knew . . .'. Gaudens Kilimanjaro, Stanislaus, Denzio and Abeli straightened up and beamed, proud and excited as their names were called. The others looked on crestfallen and moved slightly to one side. Wellington, in the black and white *pied-de-poule* woollen overcoat he never took off even in the heat of midday, became our go-between and everything we did from then on somehow quite naturally seemed to pass through him. He stayed with us all the time and left us only to go home to his family for the night.

The canoes were subsequently inspected, guns and torches checked and an appointment made to meet after the moon had set. Richard and Lorenzo would go in different canoes and directions, it was decided, each with two men, as it was not possible to know where the large crocs would be cruising.

:LORENZO

The few fishermen families that live along the sombre shores of this lake pay a tribute of blood to the crocodiles almost every week. The children, in all their innocence, are the most frequent victims. Playing along the lake shores, swimming among the tufts of giant grasses, they forget any lurking danger and suddenly the steely jaws of these giant antediluvian reptiles tear them from their carefree lives.

Prompted by the fishermen who had come to our camp in their canoes, I accepted their invitation to go out with them that very same night to have a look at the crocs and to study their movements. Abeli came with me, proudly holding his home-made gun in front of him. He explained to me that he had manufactured his new barrel from the steel casing of a steering-wheel rod.

I had chosen to ride in Stanislaus's canoe because it was wide, a good twenty foot long and well hollowed out. With the weight of my borrowed rifle on my knees, a .375 Magnum, I precariously squeezed my backside into the prow of this floating tree-trunk in which I was to pass the long hours of the night. So that I could bend forward to aim and shoot, flash the torch or grab the container of drinking water I had placed between my legs, Stanislaus had piled a bunch of humid leaves beneath my body, bent now in a most uncomfortable foetal position. Wellington and four of his men had to hold on to my canoe, now floating in shallow water, so that I could get into position without capsizing it. The idea of overturning in deep water in the dark night flashed vividly through my mind. In view of this I had fastened a nylon string to the butt of my gun with an empty plastic bottle at the other end. In this way, had we overturned, I would at least not have lost the gun, which did not even belong to me. With God's help, I would have kept afloat by clinging to the sides of the canoe.

My hunting companions took me to meet a witchdoctor, a thin old woman with sunken, shining eyes who received me in front of her hut.

After this bewildering rehearsal, my hunting companions had taken me to meet the witchdoctor, an old, thin woman with sunken, shining eyes who received us in front of her hut, which stood on a clearing between the lake and the forest. She pronounced some magic gibberish as she squashed a handful of reddish leaves in a mortar. She rubbed some of the mixture on my forehead and some on the barrel of my gun and then tenderly took my hands in hers and turned the palms outwards as if to read them. After having deposited some magic potion in each of them, she asked me to squeeze my fists tightly and keep my eyes closed for a few moments. Then she spread some white ash on my eyelids. Now, she told me, I was ready to battle with the man-eaters of Lake Rukwa.

I have always had a great respect for witchdoctors and their magic. I have never submitted to their ceremonies in order to please them, but have always accepted their invitations so as to adhere and show respect to the local traditions. More than once in my life I have seen magic work and witnessed surprising results. And even this time the seemingly magic nonsense I had just performed was to have a most unexpected consequence.

Squashed into the bottom of my canoe, I listened to the faint lapping of the water and the quiver of the long pole with which Stanislaus edged us delicately forward. I was barely able to distinguish the great bunches of water reeds through which Stanislaus would pass to take me to the inside of the lagoon. It was not the crocodile hunt that excited me, but rather this silent foray into the night in this timeless primeval setting. Fortunately I had with me a powerful flashlight with which, every now and then, I scanned the lagoon, the trees and the bulrush reeds. The wide cone of light lit up the ruby-red eyes of the many crocs floating around us or hidden beneath the roots of dead trees rising from the marshy waters, creating strange, monumental shapes in a play of countless shadows, transforming branches and exposed roots into eerie, contorted tentacles of hidden monsters. In those sublime primeval moments I felt I was in a Dantesque world: hell or paradise, it did not matter, filled with the shapes and sounds of invisible nocturnal creatures alarmed by our presence and occasionally framed by the beam of my flashlight. Most frequently I was able to follow the herons that rose slowly and disappeared into the darkness beyond.

Abeli, my gondolier, now and again bent down to whisper some information about

As we moved towards the canoe, we could see the crocodile that filled the whole length of it.

99

Wellington already had eight children, but he was worried that his wife might have no more.

the crocodiles. He told me in Swahili how to distinguish the big from the small crocs by the reflection of their shining red eyes. Abeli wanted me to shoot and was quite surprised at my reticence. The truth was that I was loath to rip apart that special night with the loud report of a rifle shot.

Any conservation expert could see that there were too many crocs around. The recommendation of Professor Hills to kill 400 was obviously not going to change matters on Lake Rukwa. However, it would give a boost to the sagging morale of the villagers of the region – a wise political move.

MIRELLA: After a long and uncomfortable night, Richard and Lorenzo returned in the early hours of the morning with two small dead crocs draped on the bow of their pirogues. The big monsters had eluded them: to get them into shooting range was proving far more difficult than our optimistic croc hunters had predicted. Subsequent nights were unsuccessful and finally the men decided to set up a bait with a hide on a spit of sand that stretched into the lake.

A waterbuck was shot to feed the hunters and for bait. Richard left with two men as the moon sank behind the black horizon. He was to conceal himself in the hide and wait. He had not been gone an hour when two successive gunshots, followed quickly by a third, ripped through the night and echoed like thunder in the surrounding hills. After a long period of silence we saw the torches flicking about on the dark water and we knew they were returning.

Richard jumped out of the canoe, barely suppressing his excitement.

'Got him right between the eyes,' he blurted out, hardly able to contain himself. 'We just had time to settle inside the blind when we saw all those eyes, about ten feet from the bait as we swept the torchlight over the water. We didn't have to wait long before one of them moved towards it and stealthily slid out of the water, grabbed hold of the carcass and started pulling it into the water, but we had tied it firmly to a stump. I flashed my torch and saw this great head with the blood-red eyes framed by the horns of the waterbuck. I fired, aiming between the eyes, and I knew my bullet had hit home. There was a great splashing as all the crocs turned and made for deep water. We rushed forward and saw my quarry slither back into the water; I let him have another in the back of the head and that did it . . .'

The words came tumbling out at us, painting such a vivid picture of the incident we could have been there beside him.

'What did you do with it?' I asked.

'In the canoe,' he answered off-handedly, trying to regain his British cool.

We moved towards the canoe and there it lay, filling the whole length. When we measured it next morning it stretched out on the pebbly beach for fourteen feet. People came to see the dead croc; some of them brought presents into the camp.

Next night was Lorenzo's turn to sit alone by the bait.

While we were paddling to the hide, about a mile from the camp, a strange thought came to me, that of Pope Julius II, who blessed his enemies before killing them with his bow and arrow. In the name of conservation I was now on my way to destroy crocodiles, yet the old hunting instinct was taking hold of me. :LORENZO

As a civilized man in wildest Africa, I was now able to recognize more and more the conflict, the clash, that exists between our natural instincts and our self-imposed disciplines.

Watching Abeli's expression, I could read his inner peace and the tranquillity of his soul. He does not know or care what happens beyond the confines of Lake Rukwa. He knows so little, yet his ignorance seems more like purity than a lack of knowledge. And I, who know so much, am here suffering guilt, denying my primeval instincts, fighting them, yet allowing them to guide me. Yes, I would shoot a crocodile – for Abeli, for his family.

101

With steady movements, Abeli paddled the pirogue forward, three strokes to the right and one to the left. Each dugout has a natural trunk shape that requires different stroking rhythms to steer it straight. He jumped into the water and for a second I thought he had gone mad. He stood knee-deep in the lake looking around in the dark. Low on the water I was able to recognize the shape of a dead tree stained white with bird droppings. This night seemed especially black. The silhouette of the tree gave me a sense of direction; until that moment I had been lost in the darkness. I got out of the canoe and stood on the beach; I could not light the flashlight now as it would disturb any of the big reptiles that might be lurking around. I knew where the hide was and I followed Abeli to it, twenty steps into a familiar darkness: I could visualize the beach as I had been there before with Richard.

I settled in the hide while Abeli returned to the canoe. A man alone makes less noise; he is not tempted to talk and moves less. It would now take a while for the nocturnal waves we had broken to settle.

The mosquitoes were there, but my Autan spray kept them at bay. Out on the spit of sand, surrounded by bunches of reeds rising from the water in tight clusters, nothing stirred. The stars shone so bright they seemed artificial.

I sensed a movement behind me. A hand touched my shoulder. It was Abeli. It was time to flash the torch. I swallowed hard. I had longed for that moment but hated it now. My star-gazing would not protect Abeli's fishing nets. I pointed my long black six-battery flashlight in front of me and lit up the marshy area around me. The scene was fantastic, awesome, intimidating. I saw first the red eyes of many crocodiles pinned to the still, shining surface of the lake, the driftwood scattered around, tall, dry trunks of dead trees silver-grey in my beam. I checked the bait, still securely fastened with ropes to a tree stump ten yards in front of me on the sand by the water.

What at first I believed to be a semi-sunken log I noticed had ruby-red eyes at the end facing me. This was, no doubt, a huge croc. I did not yet know what its reaction would be. Should I wait for it to emerge further and come closer or was this the best chance I would ever have to cull a man-eater fifteen feet away from the muzzle of my .375 Magnum? Abeli gently squeezed my shoulder. I lifted the rifle, lined up the sights between the shining red eyes and pressed the trigger.

At that distance I could not miss. But easy shots are tricky shots. The shattering explosion was followed by a turmoil of splashes. I reloaded and fired again into the convulsive mass of foam and scaly bodies, but this time without the red eyes to direct my shot. I clutched my torch and the barrel of my gun in my left hand. I should have tied the torch to the barrel.

Suddenly there was nothing where the croc had lain – just a ripple in the water where the commotion had taken place. I reloaded and got to my feet. Abeli was brandishing the long punting pole and we both rushed to the beach. I kept flashing the light, keeping my finger on the trigger. Crocs in action can spring suddenly like steel coils. Abeli probed the water with the pole, which sank into the soft sand a few steps from the shore – the water was deep. I tasted the bitterness of defeat. I now had a wounded animal on my hands which I had to track down and kill. But how and where? A croc in the water leaves no spoors, no blood trail. Abeli kept probing the water with his pole but he never hit anything scaly and hard. I flashed my torch again and again.

Out of the corner of my left eye I suddenly saw my crocodile swimming drunkenly away towards the deeper waters of the lake. I could just discern the top of its long head, the thick scales on its back tracing a thin line over the still water surface. It moved slowly, and was clearly wounded, but it headed for the open lake. I aimed again, fixing my sights just below the slightly protruding turret of its head, held my breath, trying to suppress my excitement and my rage, and fired. Reloading immediately, I fired again, more out of frustration than conviction, and that was that. Had I hit it once more, my croc would now sink, dead or wounded, into deep water and I would have to wait for daylight to do something about it.

I swept my torch beam one last time across the marsh. The ruby eyes had gone. Only the silent, liquid stage now remained, the dead tree-trunks, the clusters of reeds and the shadows; the actors had all made their exits. I switched off the light and returned to camp in the black night nursing dark dreams. Abeli remained silent and expressionless. He accepted life as it came. I didn't.

After Lorenzo and Abeli had left, we all sat up around the campfire, drinking tea, :MIRELLA waiting for the tell-tale shots, but for several hours the night hung silent about us, and one by one we retired to our tents and went to bed; our hunter friends curled up in their blankets beside the fire and fell asleep. In the early hours of the morning, when the Southern Cross was low in the sky, two successive shots woke me from my sleep; two more followed in rapid succession and then silence. Impossible to know what that meant.

I stepped out into the star-spangled night. It was very dark but the starlight made it possible to discern the tents, barely visible beneath the great black trees. Some crickets, a croaking toad, and the soft lapping of the water on the beach broke the stillness outside. I looked up at the sky; the stars were crisp, like diamonds hanging in space, and the horizon was just visible; one of those magical African nights.

I did not notice the returning canoe until it was quite near; a long dark shape moving like a shadow over the surface of the lake, the four men just discernible silhouetted against the night sky. The torchlight swept the shore as they looked for the little beach where we were camped.

I went down to the water's edge to meet them. 'Well?' I asked.

'I got a huge black croc,' Lorenzo said, shaking with excitement, his blue eyes shining like headlights at me. 'I hit it twice, right between the eyes as it was coming out of the water towards the bait, but it got away. I saw it disappearing beneath the surface of the water. Before it sank I shot it again; but it never surfaced, it got away. Don't know where the hell it went; must be badly wounded or dead by now; not possible for it to go far, we'll probably find it tomorrow somewhere in the rushes nearby. I hate this culling business.' Lorenzo's face was drawn as he looked at me from under his tattered straw hat, disappointment, rage and frustration written in his expression.

I knew what was going through his mind. To create a healthy balance among wild animals living in one congested area, culling – read 'slaughtering' – some of them is often necessary, yet people involved in conservation know that culling is a most unnatural way of 'conserving' wild life. Moreover culling can be a messy business; shooting in difficult conditions means that, inevitably, some animals get wounded. When this happens, the hunter must track them down to finish them off.

CHAPTER SIX

LOVE, MANGOES AND WITCHCRAFT

L ORENZO'S FRANTIC THREE-DAY SEARCH FOR HIS CROC LED
nowhere, and a frustrated fury crept into his sentences each time he talked
about the unfortunate monster. I was rather surprised at the importance this
loss meant to him and tried without much success to analyse it. Having grown up in
Africa, one croc more or less in the lake did not seem that important to me, but for
Lorenzo it was almost a point of honour. He was tormented by the idea of a
wounded, suffering animal, bleeding to death somewhere. Richard, Marco, Sally
and I returned to base camp to collect provisions and fuel, as it was becoming
increasingly evident that we were going to spend more time on Lake Rukwa than
originally planned. We left Lorenzo surrounded by his croc hunters on the
blistering black beach, promising him we would be back on Christmas Eve, four
days ahead. As we pulled away from them, the little group made an eerie picture,
reminiscent of the early explorers. Lorenzo's metamorphosis was quite in keeping
with the wilderness around him. In his faded knee-length khaki shorts and frayed
straw hat, barefoot and sunbaked, he looked much like the characters in the books
on exploration of Africa we had been reading. I knew he would not rest until he had
found his croc.

LORENZO: It was the first and only time during the expedition that I remained on my own, totally cut off from the rest of the 'civilized' world, in one of the wildest of African regions. I felt I was now one of the villagers, with all the advantages of community living, but exposed to a life I was not ready for, either mentally or physically. I was down to basics. The easy relationship with the people who lived here was my best asset. Because I knew that Mirella and the others would soon be back, I was really happy to be alone. I thrive on solitude; I fish and hunt best when no one gives me suggestions.

It was five days before Christmas. The fuel Mirella and the team would be returning with would allow us to explore the northern part of the lake, where the crocs are so hungry that they snap at the paddles of the fishing canoes. So, with a pile of ripe mangoes outside my little dome tent, I now had four days to find my wounded leviathan before the others returned.

MIRELLA: Richard, Sally, Marco and I arrived back at our base camp an hour before dark. A storm was building up on the far side of the lake and the wind was whipping the water in angry patterns. I was thankful to be back on *terra firma*. Kirubai, one of our men left to guard the camp, was surprised and smiling to see us back. We had left him behind regardless of his feelings and told him to wait until we returned, the way one does with Africans, I hate to say. Without a murmur of protest, he had quickly made friends with the local fishermen, who supplemented his rations with the fish they caught and smoked. He told us that he had been sick for three days with malaria but had dealt with it by taking some quinine and aspirin he had found in the medicine chest. Two small boys hardly five years of age had looked after him, fetching water and cooking for him. The camp looked cool and inviting under the spreading flame trees in full vermilion bloom. The Bedford lorry and the two Fiat Pandas parked beside each other gave the place a familiar feel. It was like coming home. How quickly a piece of wilderness can become familiar.

Although we were on the same lake, the contrast between our two camps was extreme: one stark, hot and basic like a hunter's bivouac; the other, with its large tents and vehicles beneath the flowering shade trees, was cool and almost luxurious, with a sense of permanence about it.

The storm that had been gradually gathering hit us minutes after we had unloaded the boats. I sat in my tent and watched the fat raindrops explode as they hit the earth. For a while everything was obliterated as the thunder and lightning boomed and cracked above us. Storms in Africa are often violent and intransigent and there is nothing to do but sit them out. I was thankful to be in my tent and not on the open lake. The hot air was suddenly cool and fresh as the rain rushed up the steep mountain behind us. The sun's last rays filtered back through a heavy mist, igniting the bulrush heads in front of my tent, delicately etching them as in a Japanese watercolour. Slowly the dark, menacing sky became streaked with red and orange and the black clouds, tinged with mauve, evaporated. For a brief moment the sky and distant hills were aflame and then gently faded as the night crept in. African sunsets can be spectacular, but I had yet to see one quite so dramatic.

I curled up inside my sleeping bag and dived back into Garcia Marquez's *One Hundred Years of Solitude*, from whose pages unwound a story wild and violent as the nature which now surrounded us. The flame inside the hurricane lamp beside my campbed and the soft pattering of the receding raindrops on my tent kept me company. There was a strange link between the story I was reading and the life we were now leading. I thought of my two daughters left behind in misty England, of my parents dead now for ten years, and of the exploits that lay ahead. Life itself was an adventure and we were born adventurers. Almost sixty years before us, my father and mother had had a similar experience when they walked for a year in the Belgian Congo – only then Africa was still the unknown dark continent. I slipped from one to the other until I drifted off to sleep in a kaleidoscope of visions and sensations that belong to the realm of dreams.

It was Christmas Eve when we returned to Lorenzo and our little hunting camp four days later. The sun was setting in a dark crystal sky as we pulled up on the black beach again. Our boat, heavy with fuel and provisions to last a month if necessary, was low in the water. Lorenzo and his ragged croc hunters were waiting for us on the water's edge where we had left them. He was thinner and scruffier, with a stubbly beard, but he had a mad glint of such contentment in his eyes I knew at once that he was finally back in his element. The hard living and spartan diet of dried fish and mangoes, his simple companions and the obsessive search for his missing croc were obviously agreeing with him. Every day and all day since we had left they had combed the shoreline for some tell-tale signs of the elusive monster, but had come up with nothing. We sat around the fire that night and decided to enlist the help of another witchdoctor. He had, we were told, powers that could guide us in the right direction.

A little before midnight, some children appeared from among the trees, pattering softly along the path. They stopped a while with us around the fire and told us they were on their way to Midnight Mass in the nearby village. Midnight Mass on Lake Rukwa, deep in the belly of Tanzania, sounded interesting, and we followed them into the night.

Lake Rukwa is fringed with tall, feathery bulrushes.

The little village was silent and empty as we wound our way among the trees and palm-thatched huts towards a wooden barrack with a cross above the entrance door silhouetted against the clear night sky. Inside, hurricane lamps hung along both walls and filled the interior with an orange glow. Familiar Christmas carols seeped through the walls into the night. The place was packed. Everyone in the village had squeezed in and sat in dabs of bright colours on the wooden benches. The women in their cotton dresses wore kerchiefs on their heads, their babies, scrubbed clean and shining, strapped to their backs or suckling a breast. The men, in their Sunday best, wore once-tailored jackets, misshapen hand-downs of assorted European vintage and clean open-necked shirts. School boys and girls in their green and yellow uniforms sat together to one side. The Roman Catholic teaching brought to this remote area by the missionaries long since gone had left its mark, and now, years after they had departed, the Christmas ritual was still alive. Respect and discipline had survived in the humble village school. When we entered everyone turned and looked at us, squeezing up tighter to make room beside them on the benches. The carols had a wild African beat, provided by three drummers, two guitars and some South-American-type maracas made from sun-dried squash gourds with seeds inside. The voices were strong and rich and wonderfully melodious, and the sounds made us want to dance. At midnight exactly, the village padre in a grey suit and a stiff white clerical collar took up his place behind the little wooden altar at the end of the room; he began his sermon in the local dialect, which we could not understand. The room was hushed and silent as he talked of God and Jesus and Mary and the Holy Birth. He led the congregation in prayer with a clear, almost beseeching voice. When the service was over the singing started for real, and quickly the Christmas hymns slipped into a jungle beat as the crowd moved out into the night. The drumming got louder and then stopped dead as the high-pitched female voices took over, pure and strong, piercing the air. The deep male voices intoned to the clapping of hands and then the drummers returned, leading the congregation in a full-blown medley of voices that followed us for a long while after we had left the scene.

The witchdoctor appeared next day at noon. We gathered around him in the shade of a tree and watched as he unpacked his tins and feathers and magic stones from an oily leather bag. He was a thick-set man of about sixty-five with an orange knitted cap on his head, soiled khaki shorts and a checked shirt under a sleeveless woollen sweater. A wooden stool was brought over for him and we sat on stones in a circle around him. He laid out his tools carefully on the ground in front of him, poured some water from a tin on to a smooth piece of carved wood about four inches long, and began rubbing it with a round white stone which he withdrew from his pocket, mumbling incantations and spitting on it now and again. He looked up with his rheumy, bloodshot eyes and asked Lorenzo questions, and then returned to his rubbing. He repeated this half a dozen times and then closed his eyes.

We watched in silence. I could hear the birds chirping in the trees and the flies buzzing. Perspiration beaded our foreheads and trickled under my cotton shirt. Then he opened his eyes and looked straight ahead of him.

'The crocodile is still alive, it is dying somewhere in the grass over there,' he said, pointing over our heads with sweeping movements in the general direction of the shooting. 'Go now, right away, before the night comes, you'll find it.'

He gathered up his bits and pieces, got up and stretched his arms above his head. Lorenzo put some money in his hand, thanked him and moved away. The croc hunters remained a few moments with the old man, chatting quietly with him, and then shook his hand reverently before he turned and wandered back down the path through the long grass to his village.

We piled into the inflatable sitting hot and bloated on the lake edge and headed towards the hide where the shooting had taken place. Here we transferred into two wooden dugouts that had been abandoned on the sand and punted through the long golden bulrush clumps, typical of the area, into an inner pond carpeted with dark green floating vegetation on which pale mauve flowers with delicate, almost transparent petals sat like exotic butterflies. It was very still and hot in there. The dark wooden canoes cut effortlessly through the vegetation and twice we saw the ripples of crocodiles scuttling in the water beneath us towards the safety of papyrus clumps. We sat very still on the bottom of the dugouts so as not to rock or capsize them; the water was only inches from the edge and I did not much fancy being dumped into its forbidding depths. A Goliath heron swooped low in front of us and landed like a ballet dancer on a tree.

We touched ground on the other side and, as we got out, sank knee-deep into the soft black mud. We fell into single file behind each other, Abeli in the lead with his homemade rifle on his shoulder followed by Lorenzo with his .375 Magnum cocked and glinting in the sun. The little path was flanked on either side by shoulder-high grass that spread in a solid wall of pale yellows and greens along the flat land between the water and the hills. If the witchdoctor's predictions were right, our dying croc was there somewhere in the grass. We moved forward cautiously beneath the biting sun, our clothes clinging with perspiration to our bodies. The tough blades of grass slashed at our bare legs and arms and made them itch unbearably.

We touched ground on the other side of the lagoon and, as we stepped ashore, sank knee-deep into soft black mud.

We walked in silence for an hour and then stopped and gathered beneath a clump of dark, thorny trees. I was beginning to feel weary; thoughts of turning back crept into my mind. How would we ever find our croc in these surroundings — if indeed it was there at all? But our African hunters, fired by the words of their magician, ploughed on, fanning out through the grass in different directions. They disappeared out of sight, leaving Lorenzo and me alone.

Despite the discomfort and heat we could not ignore the omnipresent silence, broken only by the quiet buzz of invisible insects. What other living creatures dwelled beneath these long, daunting stalks, watching us as we moved beside them — snakes, wild boar, antelopes, rodents, wild fowl, crocodiles perhaps? All the sounds of the African night were now stilled by the heat of the day. Only the crickets with their shrill incessant buzz could be heard, and they too fell silent as we passed beside them.

Then we heard Abeli's whistle, that piercing sound made by forcefully exhaling over two fingers placed on the tongue, that unmistakable call that carries loud and clear for a long way. We all converged towards it and there he was with his missing hand, his rifle propped on his shoulder, looking down at the huge grey carcass, the elusive croc that had given us such a run, dead and swollen at his feet, with the gaping bullet wounds behind its skull and above the right shoulder suppurating and covered in green flies. The tiny eyes on either side of the long head, with its cavernous mouth and vicious teeth, were open and clouded by death. How long it had been here was anyone's guess; to have come so far, almost four hundred yards from the water's edge in a last effort to survive, was awesome and commanded respect. The witchdoctor had been right; we stood in silence looking down at it, and then the excited chatter broke out. It measured fifteen and a half feet from tail to snout tip. Abeli and Denzio, Gaudens Kilimanjaro and Wellington turned the beast over on to its back, revealing the belly of tiny milk-white scales, smooth and shiny, in such contrast to the tough black scales of its back, and the skinning knives came out. The intense heat was subsiding. I sat on the ground propped against a tree and looked up through the dark leaves, listening to the sounds of Africa's fever and the excited comments of the croc hunters going about their gruesome task. We returned to camp in the cool of the evening with the skin rolled into a bundle and tied with a long blade of grass, ready for salting, leaving behind us the skinless white carcass of our brave croc, which by tomorrow would have fed an assortment of Africa's carnivores.

We were awakened that night by loud voices coming from the direction of the campfire. I listened for a while, trying to catch some words that would explain the commotion. Through the thin nylon walls of my dome tent, I saw two figures approach, silhouetted in the moonlight. They stopped in front of the net entrance. From my bed I could distinguish only two pairs of dark legs to the height of the knee. They stooped down and called my name.

'*Shauri gani?*' I said in Swahili; 'What's the matter?'

'Come, we need you. There has been an accident.'

I pulled on my *kikoi* and crawled out of the tent. As we walked towards the fire, now stoked back to life, they explained to me that there had been a drunken brawl in the village and that a man had been badly slashed by a panga on the head. He was squatting by the fire holding his head wrapped in a dirty white *shuka* (cloth). Beside him stood another man and a young woman, her face swollen and tear-stained.

Lorenzo and Richard joined us and together we listened to the violent tale of

The huge grey carcass of the elusive crocodile that had given us such a run lay dead and swollen at our feet.

115

In Africa, when twins are born, God has been generous.

jealousy and betrayal. The standing man clasped the young woman firmly by the forearm as if he was afraid she would bolt. He had caught the two lovers, he explained, *in flagrante delicto*, and the woman was his wife. He had suspected them for a long time and that night set an ambush. Unable to contain himself, he jumped them, slashing the unfortunate Romeo several times on the head and shoulders; now he was terrified the man would die, could we help?

I looked down at the wounded man and gingerly removed the blood-stained cloth. The great gash gaped up at me, stretching from the centre of the forehead to behind the right ear. The head was soaked in blood. As I put the torch to it I thought I saw the brain pulsating. A wave of nausea rushed through me and I put out a hand to Lorenzo to steady myself.

'Put some water to boil,' I told Wellington, 'and bring the medicine chest, then make some tea and prepare a campbed.'

Lorenzo held the torch as I swabbed the wound with warm water and Dettol disinfectant until it was clean, removing bits of skull, bone, sand grains and grass. The cuckolded husband and his terrified wife watched wide-eyed and silent, totally trusting my basic knowledge of first aid. The wounded man made no murmur, he just sat there hunched over his knees, propping up his head by the chin. I covered the wound with some sterile gauze and bandaged it lightly. Then I turned to the gashes on the back and shoulders; an hour later it was done. I handed him a cup of steaming tea in which I had dropped two Disprin tablets. There was nothing more we could do but wait for morning, when we would arrange for a canoe to take him back to base camp, where he would pick up a fisheries vehicle that would take him to the hospital sixty miles up the road to Mbeya. We laid him on the campbed and covered him with a blanket to wait for daylight. The husband and wife sipped their tea by the fire. They were calm now; soon they got up and left us, disappearing into the night with a simple gesture of thanks and farewell, promising to return at daylight to look after their wounded friend. Africans hold no rancour. Rage, violence and forgiveness are emotional kin which they handle without much ado.

The parents of the wounded man came next day with a small basket of woven palm fronds containing six magnificent yellow mangoes. They lay at the bottom of the basket smooth and tight and succulent, a tropical still-life fitting the surroundings. 'A gift,' they said, with touching grins that wrinkled their old, weatherworn faces, 'for having cared for our son last night.' Together we bundled him into the waiting canoe and cast them off into the open lake for their long journey to our base camp. The wounded man's face was horribly swollen and he could not open his eyes. Limp and resigned, he was in obvious pain now but no sign betrayed his feelings. The loaded canoe slid away from us amidst lively farewells and good wishes for a safe journey. We watched them diminish into a black speck on the sparkling lake, then turned away to start the day. We never heard of them again.

Wellington told us he knew of a place nearby where the trees were heavy with mangoes like those we had been given and he offered to take us there so we could acquire some more. On the way, he asked me if I had some fertility pills for his wife. She had had two miscarriages and was now unable to conceive. I asked him how many children he had. 'Eight,' he answered proudly.

'What d'you want more children for?' I asked.

'My wife is still young and she can go on giving me children for several years,' came the simple and logical reply.

'But Wellington, surely eight children are enough, you are already complaining that you have difficulty clothing and educating them, would it not be better to stop now and concentrate your efforts on them rather than have more?' I continued with European logic. 'Life today is no longer what it used to be. You have to decide which path you want to follow. If you want to adopt the modern way and have your children educated and westernized you just cannot go on having so many. If on the other hand you want to go on living like your forefathers did, then you have as many as you can and they will take care of you when you are old and will help you look after your land and go fishing, but the two just don't go together.'

He laughed and agreed that he had understood, listening attentively as we walked along the path through the small cultivated patches of maize and beans and manioc growing around the huts scattered among the trees; but he was not convinced, and said that his wife could never accept this theory and would leave him if he talked to her like that. What I was implying was still too distant for these simple-minded people, uncontaminated by the march of the century. Wellington had been in the army and had evolved but his people, living on the shores of Lake Rukwa, had remained mercifully protected and were now trying to amalgamate the past with the present, an impossible equation which would take them a long time to solve.

We passed an old man sitting wrapped in a blanket on a wooden chair in front of his hut. His wife was sorting dried beans on a mat beside him, her legs stretched out straight in front of her. She was humming quietly to herself. We stopped to greet them; the woman looked up at me from her bean sorting.

'Mama,' she said, 'can you help my husband, he is very ill and must go to hospital, but we have no money to pay for transport.'

'What is the matter?' I asked.

'He is bleeding from the intestine and has difficulty urinating,' came the direct, alarming reply.

'How long has he been like this?'

'One month.'

It sounded serious enough and, if true, immediate assistance was needed, a prostate operation perhaps. I pulled out the 300 shillings I had brought along to buy the mangoes and gave them to her. 'Take this,' I said, 'and go to hospital tomorrow, you must not wait any longer.' I emphasized the urgency, trying to explain the gravity of the symptoms. His son, Jonas, a young man of about twenty, ambled over and thanked me, assuring me they would leave at daybreak.

Accompanied by Jonas, we left in search of the mangoes; he told us he had some himself and I struck a deal with him. 'Now that I have no more money you give me 300 shillings-worth of mangoes in exchange for helping your father get to hospital' – a kind of old-style barter I thought he would understand. He hesitated for a moment, half expecting me to give him more money. 'I help you, you help me, OK?'

He laughed and said, 'OK,' but he did not have 300 shillings-worth of mangoes. 'I'll bring them to you tomorrow.'

'OK,' I said, and we turned to begin our return journey back to camp.

Three days went by and no mangoes appeared, so we wandered back in the cool of the evening to see how things were proceeding and get some news of the old man. We found him still sitting there by the door of his hut where we had left him but with a new blanket.

'Well, what happened, you didn't go to hospital?' I asked surprised.

Jonas came over and said, 'Oh, my father is better, we decided he didn't need to go to hospital after all so we bought him a new blanket.'

'The money has suddenly made him better,' I said, half irritated at having been taken for a ride. After all my years in Africa I was still a sucker for their sly ruses. 'What about my mangoes?'

'Oh, your mangoes. I haven't collected enough yet, I'll bring them tomorrow.'

*Small children
accompany their mothers
wherever they go and
suckle the breast until it
is dry.*

Not very convinced, I moved on, resigned to being hoodwinked yet again. A *musuungu* in Africa is always a target: every possible ruse is employed to give him nothing for something. It is normal, after all; they have so little and we have so much.

Next day, however, Jonas arrived in his canoe with a mound of yellow and green mangoes piled in front of him. He counted them one by one as he unloaded them. 600 mangoes, two for every shilling I had given his father. Legend has it that these succulent tropical fruits, now growing wild on the shores of Lake Rukwa, have grown from pips discarded by the slave caravans on their way from Zaire to the Indian Ocean. If the legendary slave route had indeed passed along these shores then we were reaping the fruit. I kept my negative generalization to myself, thankful that I had made no comment, and reiterated that his father had to go to hospital if he didn't want to die.

Ten days had already slipped by since we dropped anchor on these wild shores. We kept hearing stories of croc attacks from passers-by, for our camp was set along the main footpath that joined the villages along the lake shore. We decided to break camp and move north to Rungwa, where the crocs, we were told, were even bigger, less disturbed and in far greater quantities. As we were packing up and loading the boats a croc victim who had survived wandered up and stood quietly watching the activity. His right leg was badly scarred with tight, shiny laceration marks and one foot was quite deformed.

'What happened to you?' I asked him.

'I was eaten by a croc,' he answered nonchalantly. We moved over to the shade of a tree and he told me his story. 'I was visiting my sister on the mainland at that village over there,' he began. 'I left her to return to my own village before dark but when I got to that spit of sand where you shot your croc it was already night so I decided to sleep on the beach, because I knew it was too dangerous to walk in the water at night. I was very tired and I went to sleep on the sand. While I was sleeping a croc came out and grabbed my foot. I began shouting and hit it as hard as I could on the head with my *rungu* [knobkerrie]. Each time I hit it, it opened its mouth and grabbed me further up the leg, pulling me towards the water. I hung on to the reeds but it was a big croc and my grip was not strong enough to resist the pull. The villagers heard my cries and came running to help me. When they arrived I was already half in the water, but the croc let go immediately when it saw all those people and disappeared into the water. It was very dark and I was in great pain, bleeding badly. My friends wrapped my leg in a *shuka* and carried me back to the village. Next day a fisheries Landrover took me to the hospital on the road to Mbeya. I stayed there for four months, looked after by a good Italian doctor, until I was well enough to return to my village. It took me another six months before I could walk properly again. That was one year ago. Now I am all right again. God was good to me, *Mungu Iko* [God is present].'

He told me his story dispassionately as if he were talking of someone else.

By midday the boats were loaded and everything was strapped down tightly. The 600 mangoes, carefully packed in baskets and cushioned with grass so they would not bruise, had pride of place. The lake was very still; it shone like a mirror, reflecting the strong midday light. All our new friends gathered around, sad to see us go. Wellington and Abeli, looking a bit crestfallen, took the last basket from me and watched as I rolled up my trousers before wading into the muddy water. We had all been suffering from infected insect bites on our legs which never seemed to clear up because of our constant contact with the water. Mine had turned particularly nasty and in an effort to keep them dry and allow them to heal I asked Abeli if he would carry me to the waiting boats.

'No problem,' he said smiling.

Straddled on his back, we churned through the water and he deposited me gingerly in the boat. I could not help thinking of the image we must have cut on this wild and beautiful shore surrounded by our crocodile hunters, on one of whose backs the white 'memsahib' was being carried to her waiting boat! I thought of a similar situation my mother had once told me about, when, in 1929, she arrived in Ujiji at the start of her year-long walking safari in the Congo, and was transferred from the lake steamer to dry land astride a sturdy, half-naked African. With his strong black hands grasping her thighs and the acrid odour of his hot sweat filling her nostrils, his muscular body moved like a potent steed through the water. For a young lady from the decorous sixteenth *arrondissement* of Paris, in which she grew up, the experience had remained memorable. Much had changed in Africa since then, but sixty years later, for different reasons, the scene was now being repeated.

We had shared a part of our adventure with our new friends and several begged to come along with us. But there was no room on the boats, so they stayed behind and waved from the shore; tomorrow the pace of their lives would take up its monotonous beat again.

We reached Rungwa several hours later. The mountain range that until now had flanked us receded from the lake shore and seemed to peter out in the distance to make way for the Rungwa river, which spilled into the lake where the shore curved towards Sumbawanga and the mountains on the other side. The landscape, with its

*Vlasinka, Costansia and
Gaudencia, damsels of
the lake, brought us wild
mangoes.*

trees bleached white by the sun, had a pristine texture to it. Hippo lay in motionless
mounds among the trees, twitching their ears and spouting water. We cut our
throttles and moved slowly forward so as not to disturb the silence. Some fish eagles,
perched on the desiccated branches, hurled their haunting cries into the steamy
afternoon; crocodiles lurked like menacing logs, navigating slowly on the water's
surface, their beady eyes and scaly backs just visible until they sank without a ripple
at our approach. Pink-legged spoonbills, water tits and Egyptian geese stepped
gingerly on mudflats, sifting through the soft black lake sludge near the river
mouth. A floating island of pelicans drifted by, plunging together after transitory
fish brought downstream by the river flow. There was no sign of human habitation;
an eerie hush permeated the slightly sulphurous air. We remained mute and
subdued, feeling like intruders into a secret world; only the soft purr of our friendly
outboards disturbed the quiet as we weaved through the hippo channels where the
water was deeper.

We entered the river mouth from the lake. The banks were only a few feet high
and everywhere, on the grassy green flatlands and on the sand banks, crocodiles
were basking in the afternoon sun. They crashed from the banks with great splashes,

writhing like prehistoric ogres into the safety of the water, escorted by a trail of ripples. Flocks of white egrets winged downriver to roost on the trees for the night and orange-breasted skimmers raced with incredible speed in formation, low over the water surface.

Our campsite, about a hundred yards up the Rungwa river, was soft and inviting, with shade trees and short green grass like a garden lawn. We pitched our tents on the banks of the river flowing only a few feet below. What a difference from the harsh, blistering, fly-infested camp we had left behind that morning. There was plenty of dry wood around, and soon the campfire was crackling gaily, infusing the air with its familiar scent; very quickly our new bush-dwelling, with our belongings strewn about and the empty inflatables parked and anchored beneath us ready for action, became a functional abode. After the ritual reviving mug of tea we set off on an exploratory walk before dark set in. A hundred yards behind us, an arm of the lake stretched inland for about half a mile, forming the promontory on which we were camped. The land was flat and sandy and the water shallow. More pelicans and flamingoes and a variety of water fowl gathered here for the night. The white egrets we had met earlier on had now roosted with the ibis on the trees, perched immobile and delicate like exotic flowers silhouetted in the sunset. As we wandered back to camp the moon was rising to the east and the sun was setting behind the mountains to the west. Tiny white butterflies and fireflies whose transparent wings were dabbed with velvet brown fluttered around our feet, escorting our footsteps across the tender grass. For a brief moment an iridescent opaline glow swept over us and then faded. It was dark before we arrived back in camp.

The croc infestation at this end of the lake lived up to what we had been told further south. When we returned to the dead trees next day to investigate the area, we found crocs floating about everywhere, grey and immobile like dead wood.

So that we could observe them at close range, we built a hide on a protruding mud flat with some dry palm leaves and Richard bagged a *puku* antelope (which looks much like an impala) for bait. We secured the carcass firmly to a tree stump about thirty yards from the hide, and to attract the crocs we spread the blood and entrails about in the water, and then withdrew inside the hide to wait. I propped my camera on a Y-shaped stick in front of me with the lens peering through a hole in the leaves. Lorenzo sat beside me with his binoculars and Richard, Sally and Marco moved the inflatable some fifty yards away among the dead wood, where they waited, carefully concealed behind a bush. The heat was oppressive and made us sweat a lot, the doum palms hung limp and heavy and the water was very still.

From our vantage-point we could just discern the backs of some crocs above the water. We did not have long to wait. 'Here they come,' Lorenzo whispered without lowering his binoculars. They were beginning to circulate, and we could see the first ripples on the water. Through the lens of my camera I watched them converge slowly towards us like silent submarines, hardly disturbing the water's surface. Then they stopped dead about fifteen feet from the bait and froze. We counted three and then seven, ten then fifteen. Moving in close, they parked beside each other, their long snouts pointing in our direction, their beady eyes fixed on the bait in a deadly stare. I could now pick out the scales on their backs through my lens. My pulse was throbbing in my ears, sweat trickled down my forehead into my eyes, momentarily blurring my sight, and I was breathing short and fast. Lorenzo beside me remained motionless, glued to his binoculars. We waited for the next move. It did not come for a long time. Then suddenly one of the backs gradually rose out of the water, detaching itself from the others, and very slowly crept forward, moving like a giant lizard on its short webbed feet until it was entirely exposed. It froze again about three feet from the bait, pausing to listen and perhaps to ascertain the validity of the magnetic force pulling it forward and out of the protective cover of the water. Then it lunged forward; its great mouth opened and shut like a clamp on the carcass. As if this was a signal, the others converged in a frenzied amphibian crawl on to the bleeding meat.

We watched incredulously as they tore it from each other, their grotesque heads pointing skywards as they devoured enormous chunks. Crocodiles have no tongues and do not use their teeth to chew. The food is swallowed whole and then digested by strong gastric juices. The vicious teeth serve only to kill and tear. They were quickly joined by more monsters, who appeared from everywhere as if drawn by a magnet. Within fifteen minutes we counted sixty, all crammed into the limited space around the bait. They climbed on top of each other, slithering and slipping about in their frantic endeavour to lodge their teeth into the meat, their great tails guiding them like rudders. There were several seventeen-footers and some perhaps even larger. One particularly dark one had lost its bottom jaw, probably the result of a bullet or a fight; the jaw still dangled grotesquely from the unsevered hide, giving it an even more demonic appearance. They were totally oblivious to our presence and the clicking of my camera shutter, but were obviously nervous at remaining uncovered for so long. They tried pulling the carcass into the water but it was securely fixed by the horns.

Three rolls of film and half an hour later Lorenzo crept out of the hide and very slowly moved towards them, shielded by a doum-palm leaf. When he was about half way between them and the hide, the emergency signal within them was suddenly triggered and like a flash they turned and swung around in wild panic, slithering back into the water, churning and flaying the mud in a savage reptilian rondo. Within minutes the fiendish scene had dispersed and the concealing water became tranquil again. Only the severed antelope head, fastened by the horns, remained. It was a memorable moment, this insight into the rawness of Africa, almost as if we had gained right of passage into the inner sanctuary of a forbidden world which few are privileged to enter.

Next day we returned to try another of Lorenzo's experiments.

'What would happen,' he asked us, 'if we fixed a piece of meat to a large hook and tried to fish a croc the way one does a marlin?'

It seemed an interesting idea. We climbed into a tree, fastened a rope with a hook embedded in a hunk of meat at one end to the overhanging branches and threw it into the water. We waited in a fork of the tree about six feet above the water. Sure enough, this time a touch more cautiously, the floating logs began converging towards us. We remained very still, allowing them to approach until one was directly beneath us. It fixed us with its beady eyes, its mouth half open for a long time without moving. Suddenly a thrashing in the water nearby made it sink. We had hooked a croc. We jumped out of the tree and grabbed hold of the rope under the illusion that we would ground the beast, but this was no marlin at the end of the line. It was like trying to bring a lion to heel. The rope thrashed about and was impossible to hold on to. We were like puppets attached to some superhuman force until the meat and hook were finally yanked free, which put an end to the ill-fated experiment.

Back in the boat we steered our way cautiously through the water, fearful that the disturbed crocs might be a little nervous now; our rubber inflatables were easy to lacerate. We had been watching one particularly large fellow who had been circling in ever tighter circles around us, disappearing and reappearing beneath the water, always a little closer. Suddenly we felt a jolt beneath us as if we had gone aground or scraped a stump and from the prow we saw the long grey shadow emerge only inches beneath the water surface and then sink again out of sight with a slash of the tail.

'Let's get out of here,' Richard advised, 'it could be stalking us.'

Bewitched by this strange, enigmatic behaviour, Lorenzo was loath to leave. 'Let's wait and see what happens,' he insisted.

A canoe with two fishermen appeared among the white trees. They pulled up beside us and after an exchange of banalities we told them about the circling croc.

'Yes, we know that croc,' they said excitedly, 'it's an old wounded male that has taken two of our children from the village and several goats, we have been hunting it for a long time, but it is very fast and we have been unable to kill it. If you can help us we would be very happy.'

We were exchanging information in low voices when it reappeared, navigating surreptitiously close by. Lorenzo picked up the .375, cocked the trigger and aimed at the head, following the moving target in his sights.

'Don't try and kill it now,' I pleaded. 'You'll never hit it like this.'

The words had hardly left my lips when Lorenzo fired; the unexpected report made us jump.

A distinct dull thud told us the bullet had struck home and for a brief moment the water around us exploded. As it settled only a smudge of red blood was visible, but no croc. It had sunk to the bottom or got away, there was no telling. We waited for it to surface, guiding our inflatable at minimum throttle among the trees. For two hours we hung around scanning the water and finally gave up and returned to camp leaving the fishermen on watch.

'We have sprung a leak,' I said, trying to remain calm. 'The boat is full of water.'

Our sandals, hats and oars were floating in inches of water on the bottom. We had been so engrossed by the goings-on around us that we had not noticed we were slowly sinking.

'We'd better get home fast,' Richard said. 'I don't much fancy being stranded in this place.'

We all agreed. If the croc was dead we'd find it in the morning. It was late afternoon when we got back to camp, thankful for the end of the day. We had been out since daybreak and were burned up by the sun, aching all over. When we pulled the boat out of the water and turned it over we found an eighteen-inch gash caused by the impact with the sharp croc scales.

The two fishermen came at midnight to tell us they had found the beast, dead in shallow water not far from where we had hit it.

We repaired the inflatable and returned next day with the skinners. The croc measured fifteen feet six inches; when we slit it open we found the half-digested scales of a water turtle, two baby hippo tusks about four inches long and half a red rubber sandal.

The rains broke a week later and one night the river rose right up to where our tents were pitched. The brown water rushed by in a mad torrent, carrying branches, debris and muddy foam in its wake. The sky was overcast and grey for most of the day and all around us the saturated ground was inches deep in water. We sloshed about barefoot and flecked in mud. For several days it rained almost around the clock and, when the sun broke through the clouds for a few hours around midday, we hung our damp bedding and clothes and maps on the bushes to dry, and moved our tents to higher patches in the grass. We had to soak the firewood with kerosene so it would burn: meals were reduced to a minimum. Our spirits began to sag when after a week there was no change in the weather; finally we decided to pack up and pull out before the river broke its banks.

We spent one last relatively rainless day exploring the Rungwa river, now in full spate, and travelled upstream for several hours past clusters of hippos revelling in the high water. A large herd of _puku_ antelope grazing on the river bank around a bend scattered and fled in panic among the trees at our sudden approach. Long-legged storks picked at frogs and insects in the soaking grass, and ducks and geese and waterfowl floated contentedly past on the current and then took rapid flight. The great trees rose dark and resplendent above the lesser vegetation. Several times we had to manoeuvre our inflatables around the fallen ones floating unencumbered towards the lake, their roots and leafy branches awash in the brown foam from the falls further upstream. The force of the river flow was evidence enough of the heavy rainfall further north, and there was no telling how long it would last. We switched our engines off and floated in silence back to camp, riding the flux with the debris and the waterfowl, moving fast through this soundless world pregnant with moisture, at one with the pulsating nature still so mercifully undisturbed by man.

We broke camp and the next day travelled the whole length of the lake back to our first base camp. Three weeks had gone imperceptibly by since our descent into this surprising, little-known lake of the Rift Valley.

Back in Mbeya, dogged by heavy rainfall all the way, Lorenzo came down with high fever and lay for forty-eight hours shaking on his campbed. We dosed him for malaria, which put him back on his feet again, but he looked suddenly tired and drawn and very thin, with a marked loss of energy and appetite.

Here in Mbeya we decided to call our first halt. There was no point in going on in the rain. Our friends at the French road-construction compound offered us a container to store our boats and equipment in; the first leg of the expedition ended. Richard, Sally and Marco and our team of four Africans from Kenya drove the Bedford lorry back to Kenya. I went back to London and Lorenzo to Milan. We would resume the expedition again in March, when the weather improved.

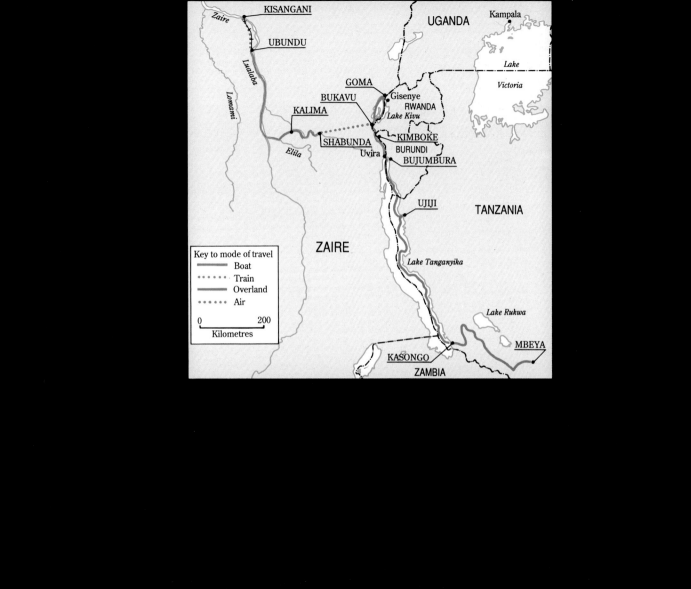

KISANGANI

Zaire

UGANDA

Kampala

UBUNDU

Lualaba

Lomami

GOMA

Gisenye

RWANDA

Lake

Victoria

BUKAVU

KALIMA

Lake Kivu

SHABUNDA

KIMBOKE

BURUNDI

Elila

Uvira

BUJUMBURA

UJIJI

TANZANIA

ZAIRE

Lake Tanganyika

Lake Rukwa

Key to mode of travel

Boat

Train

Overland

Air

0   200

Kilometres

MBEYA

KASONGO

ZAMBIA

CHAPTER SEVEN

THE LAKE OF TEMPESTS

LORENZO'S MBEYA MALAISE PERSISTED IN MILAN. HE SAW A doctor, who recommended he have a malaria blood test. The test was negative. 'It's probably "La Philippina",' the doctor told him, naming a particularly virulent form of Asiatic flu that was sweeping Europe at the time with symptoms much like his. He gave him some pills and told him to rest.

Each time he rang me in London Lorenzo complained of his condition, always reassuring me, however, that he was not ill enough to have me come over. As it was not malaria, it would probably pass, he insisted. It persisted for a week; I was concerned, though not overly worried yet. His condition in Mbeya kept haunting me. Then one day the phone call came.

'You'd better come, I'm losing control,' I heard him say, faint and shaky.

Roberto was away in Iraq and was not due to return before the evening. That was enough; I caught a plane to Milan and a few hours later was by Lorenzo's bedside. He was lying in the semi-dark, perspiring heavily, his mouth was dry and he complained of severe pain in his head and neck. How could this not be malaria, I wondered? I decided to take him back to London to the Hospital for Tropical Diseases and waited for Roberto to return that evening.

When he saw him, Roberto took me out of his room and said, 'I have never seen him like that before.'

'Nor have I,' I answered.

He telephoned the doctor; I felt a bit reassured now he was back. Roberto is the sort of man who, in a crisis, takes control immediately and with his gentle, soft-spoken manner takes decisions without hesitating, communicating confidence to those around him, characteristics I admire most in men.

The doctor assured him there was nothing to worry about, it was certainly not malaria, and, with time, would pass. I sat on Roberto's bed with him listening to the phone conversation; he stretched out a hand and reached for the railway timetable while the doctor was talking to him.

'OK, OK, thank you very much,' he said, running his finger down the page. He hung up and turned to me. 'OK, you're taking him to the Kantonspital in Zurich, right away.'

He dialled the hospital number while he was talking to me, introduced himself in German in his gentle, polite way and asked to speak to the *primario* who had once saved his own father's life ten years before. There was no bed available.

'I am sending him anyway, he's dying and he's my best friend, he's like my brother, please do what you can to accommodate him,' he said firmly. 'Don't worry about the bill, I'll look after it. Thank you very much, I know I can count on you.'

He hung up and immediately dialled another number in Zurich.

'I would like a double room for tonight, the name is Gancia.' He was told that the hotel was full. 'Please find a room, it's for my friend, he is very ill and will be entering the Kantonspital tomorrow morning. Do what you can. Thank you very much, send the bill to me.'

He hung up and took a quick draw on his cigar. 'Come on, Mirella, we have no time to lose, your train leaves in half an hour. Get Lorenzo out of bed and dressed. Manuel will take you to the station.'

Ten minutes later we were in his car. 'Drive quickly,' he said to Manuel, his chauffeur, and slipped a million lire in cash into my hand. 'Here, take this, now go, quickly, you'll miss the train.' There was no time for thanks or kisses. 'I'll call you tonight,' he shouted as we rolled away from him.

As soon as we were comfortably installed in a first-class compartment of the Milan–Zurich express, Lorenzo slumped into a semi-conscious heap in front of me. The possibility that he might be dying hit home. Until then I had never yet associated death with either of us. Roberto's speedy actions fired the alarm bell. The five-hour journey seemed endless. Lorenzo slipped in and out of consciousness mumbling incoherently, his eyes wide open but apparently seeing nothing. He did not answer when I spoke to him, just swallowed the water I gave him. He had an insatiable thirst.

When we arrived at the hotel the phone rang as I was signing in. It was Roberto; he wanted news of the trip and said he'd call the hospital again at midday tomorrow. We slept fitfully beside each other in the little hotel room; Lorenzo thrashed about in the bed complaining that he was suffocating, his head hurt and he was covered in perspiration. I tried to remain calm as the battle raged inside his body.

Early next morning we were at the Kantonspital. The head nurse was waiting for us as we checked in. She took one look at Lorenzo and said, 'Leave that for now, we'll do it later.' Lorenzo collapsed into the wheel-chair and we charged down the shiny corridor to the lift; in no time he was lying in a bed so white and crisp we could only be in Switzerland, I thought. The *primario* arrived immediately, a good-looking, neat man of about forty, sun-tanned and healthy; he exuded self-assurance and confidence. I instantly felt we were in good hands and began to relax as I moved to the background and let the professionals take over. Three *professori*, specialists in tropical medicine, joined us as the nurses busied themselves with test tubes drawing body fluids and blood for the lab. A glucose drip was fastened to his arm and he was left to rest until the diagnosis was reached.

'He is very sick, but don't worry, you are in good hands,' the *primario* said to me. 'Is he a heavy drinker?' he added.

'No, he never drinks alcohol,' I assured him, perplexed at the question.

'Well, that's a relief,' he replied as he left the room and moved on to his next patient. Roberto's phone call had put Lorenzo on the top of his list of patients that day.

I returned to the hospital at three for the verdict. 'A severe case of cerebral malaria,' the *primario* said gravely. 'It's a killer, but you got him here just in time,' he added. 'No one dies of malaria in the Kantonspital,' he assured me, smiling, 'but he had only forty-eight hours of life left in him, perhaps less.'

God bless Roberto, I thought, you've done it again. It's not for nothing that we call you the godfather; without you he would be dead. I thought in panic of my intention of flying him back to London to the Hospital for Tropical Diseases; he would never have made it. Several of my friends had died of this. The virus travels fast once it gets to the brain, blocking the blood vessels; it turns into a race with time. For ten days Lorenzo lay in semi-torpor with quinine drips in his arms around the clock; very slowly he recovered. I had never thought of life without him, and although we spent a lot of time apart he filled that all-important space that allowed me to live alone and independent without fear. Our sojourn in the hospital battling the malaria virus was an important milestone in our thirty-year relationship; it served as a reminder that whether we liked it or not we were terribly important to one another.

Special dispensation had been accorded me so I could share his room. I slept on a narrow stretcher bed wheeled in each evening by pretty, efficient, white-starched nurses who became our friends, fascinated by the stories of our adventure. Lorenzo slept most of the day; I sat beside him in front of the tall French windows that opened out on to a pretty wrought-iron balcony. Through the crisp white organza curtains I watched the helicopter ambulance flying past several times a day, ferrying wealthy patients to the hospital, a bright red spot on a wintry canvas. From the fifteenth floor the pretty town of Zurich, with its tall church steeples and quaint roofs under a mantle of snow, looked like a picture postcard.

When Lorenzo left the hospital he had lost twenty pounds and had aged alarmingly; the disease had taken its toll. His hand shook so much, he was unable to sign himself out. For the first time since my father's death I had lived again the distressing days spent in the Nairobi hospitals during the last years of his life as he slipped slowly from us. Lorenzo looked like him now with his thin, bent body and shaky walk. He had been well looked after in the luxurious hospital, which resembled the Ritz, I thought, in comparison to the more spartan hospitals I had been used to. From the banks of the Rungwa river in Tanzania to the luxurious white room of the most famous hospital in Europe, the passage was brief, but the chasm that separated them was more than material. It had to do with civilization and the pristine worlds of our ancestors.

Roberto lent us his chalet in Gstaad for the convalescence. We travelled through the Swiss Alps in a quaint little train used by skiers and local inhabitants of the Lehman Valley. A month in this golden nest, strolling among some of the most spectacular scenery on earth and eating the finest foods, brought Lorenzo back almost to his old self.

We returned to Kenya later than planned, at the end of April, just as spring was breaking out all over Europe. I caught the plane back to Nairobi a bit half-heartedly, but the demands of the expedition tugged at our fibre and there were no alternatives. It was back to Africa.

Before leaving Nairobi we paid a visit to Dr Reese, the head of AMREF, the flying-doctor service for East Africa, to talk to him about Lorenzo's malaria experience. Reese has been practising for many years in Kenya and knows a lot about this silent African killer.

Cerebral malaria, clinically known as *Plasmodium falciparum*, he told us, is the worst kind of malaria and, if not rapidly detected, kills you. The malaria parasites travel to the blood vessels in the brain and block them, giving rise to cerebral and mental symptoms which eventually cause death. Since about five years ago, there has been a major change in East Africa in the response of the malaria parasites to drugs. Chloroquin used to be very effective in the treatment of the disease and also as a prophylactic, but now the parasites have largely become resistant to chloroquin, and quinine has to be administered in its place. The best way to avoid getting malaria is, of course, to avoid getting bitten. Nearly all malaria transmission takes place late at night and in the early hours of the morning; mosquitoes which bite during the day usually are not the sort which give malaria. Those that do, bite between ten o'clock at night and five or six in the morning, so if one can get under a good net during those hours and take a prophylactic like Paludrin, which is the best in East Africa – two tablets every evening while one is in the risk area and, all-important, for two weeks after leaving the area, which is what Lorenzo did not do – the chances of contracting the disease are minimal.

The two main types of mosquitoes that transmit malaria in East Africa and Zaire are known as *Anopheles gambi* and *Anopheles funestas*. Although malaria is probably one of the most common ailments in Africa and many people have either had it or will get it some time in their lifetime, it should not be regarded lightly because more and more cases of deaths from a cerebral form of the disease are occurring; we should consider ourselves very lucky, said Dr Reese, that Lorenzo's symptoms were caught in time and that we were within easy reach of hospitalization.

We now had to face the fact that the last remaining members of our team had withdrawn from the expedition. Time had run out on them; they had grown bored with waiting for us, and their own personal demands had forced them to pull out. Richard began setting up his foot safaris in the Selous, Sally went to the Yemen to buy silver beads and jewellery for her planned new business, and Marco returned to Italy for his military service. Only Lorenzo and I were now left to continue into the second leg of the expedition and we had to gather a new team. Losing Richard was the worst. Where would I find a replacement who had the multitude of talents he had brought along with him? – his total commitment to the expedition and to Africa, his knowledge of the bush, his mechanical expertise, his boundless enthusiasm for Nature and above all, like Lorenzo, and Henry Morton Stanley before him, the adrenalin charge that fed on the discovery of new and unknown wilderness.

A month in Nairobi chasing up all my contacts and old acquaintances brought Hugo Douglas-Dufresne to my door, and, by the time Lorenzo arrived, I had put together a new crew: Charlie Babault, twenty-one years old, the son of a hunter friend of mine; Hugo's cousin, Adam James; and Juliette Westlake, a pretty, dark-haired Canadian nurse who had adventure in her blood. This was a far more likely group than the previous one, though to them too the romance of such an adventure seemed irresistible. Twenty-five-year-old Hugo, a brilliant young engineer, was on holiday in Kenya from the North Sea oil rig he had been working on. Charlie was looking for adventure. Adam, twenty-four years old, had returned to Kenya after two years on a farm in northern England. Juliette, thirty-two, had been working as a nurse among the Samburu tribe in northern Kenya and was at a loose end; her visa had run out and she was awaiting a more permanent work permit.

Our suave and worldly Italian friend Ludovico, who was reshaping the Nairobi International Casino, invited us to set up our HQ at his sumptuous house. He lived there alone in true old-colonial style while the owners were abroad, tended by a bevy of immaculately trained servants in white starched uniforms. I don't know what we would have done without Ludovico at that precise moment. His Italian charm and wit, his boundless energy and ready solutions to every problem, the delicious meals served in great style and accompanied by a selection of vintage wines, kept our spirits high as day after day we slowly got the expedition back on to the road.

A new team of three Africans was hired: Michael, a cook from the Casino lent to us by Ludovico, who had never been on safari in his life; Mwangangi, a lorry driver, lent to us by Charlie's family; and Wainaina, his camp assistant. The Bedford lorry was serviced, new camping equipment was tested, and we left again one bright morning at the end of May for Dar-es-Salaam and arrived back in Mbeya a week later, revived, reshuffled and raring to go. Our French friends at the road-construction site were still there, waiting for us, our boats and equipment safe and intact. After a few days checking, revising and reloading we set our sights on Lake Malawi, sixty miles to the south. It was not exactly on our route, but after the experience on Lake Rukwa we were loath to leave it unexplored.

The day before departure, while in the grubby town of Mbeya doing last-minute shopping, my camera case with all my cameras was lifted from my car. I was in a crowded African *duka* (shop) paying for the provisions when, unbeknown to me, a hand imperceptibly entered the pocket of my safari jacket. Instinct made me swing round and I saw a tall youth hurrying for the door. I lunged at him without thinking and managed to grab him by the shirt, ripping it in half as he recoiled from me and bolted. I checked my pockets and to my relief realized my money was in the other one. I chased after him and I saw him disappear down the crowded main street. When I returned to my car I found the camera case was missing and in a panic rushed to the police station to report the theft and the incident in the *duka*. Within minutes we were back in the crowded street. The youth was still there; I recognized his torn green and white shirt. The policemen in plain clothes quietly climbed out of the car and crept towards him, following him to the market-place, where he joined two of his partners in crime. The police jumped them and caught hold of one; the others bolted and disappeared among the crowd.

Back to the police station we went for the statement and details of the lost equipment. The collared man was roughed up a bit by the inspector, who whacked him hard with a stick on the shins, making him holler. 'You tell us who your friends are and where they live or we'll beat you to pulp,' he said calmly. I felt suddenly sorry for the fellow; the old guilt of those-who-have-and-those-who-have-not engulfed me and made me nauseous.

'Don't worry, madam, we'll get your cameras back, it was lucky you acted fast,' the inspector reassured me. 'We know these bastards, they've been here before. Check back with us in the morning.'

I left unconvinced and panicky. How would I now retrieve my equipment in time for tomorrow's departure if they did not find it tonight? Constantly on the move, it would be impossible to have a new batch despatched to me and what would I do in the meantime? When I got back to camp I was feeling almost hysterical. The middle finger of my left hand was painful and throbbing and when I showed it to Juliette she said it was broken. Everything had happened so fast I never felt the pain when the thief I grabbed had torn himself from my grip, but the jar was so violent it broke my finger.

Next morning, when all was packed and ready to go, I dropped in at the police station on our way out of town. 'Is this your equipment?' enquired the smiling inspector, pulling out one camera at a time from his desk drawer. I stood gaping at him for a full minute at least before words came to me. I could have kissed him, but refrained, trying to keep my cool. 'Thanks for a job well done,' I said, handing him a fat reward, after he had told me how they had ambushed the thieves in their huts at three in the morning, led by the youth they had collared.

Few important geographical features in the world can have been 'discovered' so many times as Lake Malawi (formerly called Lake Nyasa, the lake of tempests). Dr Livingstone was the first man to furnish an accurate account of this inland sea, but long before his time many other pioneers had stumbled upon it. Bronze-skinned pygmies were the first men to find the lake. They were followed, centuries later, by black men from the Congo rainforests, and by Arabs from the red sands of Oman. Almost certainly the first European eyes to see Nyasa were those of a Portuguese trader in 1616, but his countrymen failed to exploit his discovery. Thereafter a long silence settled over the lake; it lost its flavour of authenticity, and joined the company of other myths and travellers' tales. Then, just over a hundred years ago, Livingstone revealed it again to Europe and his genius made it something almost personal to himself, while the lake in return illuminated his own character for us. Today his spirit more than any other man's broods across its waters.

It is a starkly jaded, tawny-coloured land and it has a spell that is all its own. The whole lake shore is drenched with the heavy linden-sweetness of flowering trees compounded with the musty antique odours of bats, wood-smoke and wet earth. The lake itself is never out of sight for very long. With its spume-splashed rocks and golden beaches washed by gentle, sleepy waves it seems more like a sea than a lake. Nyasa is a singularly alien and exotic thing; there is an elemental and undisciplined quality about it that makes it stand outside the range of ordinary experience. Hot springs boil up along its shores and hiss like angry reptiles as they pour into its cooling waters, and when the clouds descend a battalion of dervish-dancing water spouts leap 500 feet into the air to meet them, as though the very water was trying to escape from some demon hidden in the lake. There is no tide to mix and intermingle the waters of Nyasa, but something similar although stranger – a seiche – continually sets the lighter oxygenated surface water skidding to and fro across the useless, stagnant layer below; as though the lake was being rocked like a gargantuan bath tub. No life could possibly exist in this deeper water, which stretches down nearly half a mile to the lake's bed, yet such is the impression of enigmatic mystery emanating from Nyasa that after listening to the natives' stories of the monsters seen emerging from it, one wonders uneasily what abysmal fauna do in fact live there. The fickle way the lake's level fluctuates periodically through twenty feet or more changes its shape from year to year. Only quite recently has it been realized that the Nyasa is nothing more than a dammed-up river whose narrow overflow into the Shire blocks up periodically with sudd, until the weight of water piling up after a few years bursts through the barrier and roars away towards the Zambezi.

I read aloud the passage from *Livingstone's Lake* by Oliver Ransford as our little convoy headed towards Lake Malawi. In 1967 Ransford had for six years been a Government medical officer of Nyasaland, where, on Lake Nyasa (as Lake Malawi was then called), he found a freely growing shrub *Tephrosia vogelli*, a natural snail poison whose powdered leaves when sprinkled on infested pools killed the snails that produce bilharzia. In this way he eradicated bilharzia from the area and fell in love with the lake.

From the incision of the Great Rift Valley to the present day, Lake Nyasa had a turbulent, exciting and colourful history. For a long time it remained a myth to the outside world but slowly information accumulated. The Arab and Portuguese intrusions added greatly to knowledge of this remote continent but each degenerated into a squalid hunt for slaves. David Livingstone is, of course, the great hero of the lake and his Zambezi Expedition is still of absorbing interest, especially when in 1862 the expedition was joined by five women, including Miss MacKenzie, who brought with her into this wild and unexplored country a pet donkey, two broken-down mules, her housekeeper and her maid. After Livingstone the lake shore saw the founding of missions of many denominations, which brought with it the religious rivalry that so baffled the natives; then came the continent's partition in the most gigantic landgrab in history for 'jingo frontiers drawn by frock-coated diplomats of Europe'. Finally independence was granted; Dr Banda took the reins and Lake Nyasa became Malawi.

The night before arriving on Lake Malawi we had our first unpleasant encounter with African bureaucratic rule since the expedition started, when a drunk and aggressive District Commissioner forced us to leave the beautiful campsite we had found beneath a cluster of spreading bamboo on the edge of a little river that spilled into the lake, because we had not reported our arrival prior to setting up camp. This was a strategic zone on the border of Tanzania and Malawi, he emphasized. It was obvious that he was pulling rank. For the first time since setting out on our journey we felt the difference in our colour. Who knows what previous humiliations and frustrations he was venting on us? No manner of persuasion, no ministerial passes, no invitation to tea made him budge from his stand. Tightly ensconced within the secure confines of his government Landrover, surrounded by his subalterns, he found the setting ideal for a show of power. Bloated and self-important, he reminded me of a strutting turkey, and it was all I could do to keep my ex-colonial antagonism at bay and remain calm and polite. It was six o'clock in the evening, a light drizzle was falling and we had just finished erecting our tents and floating our inflatables with the intention of remaining put for several days while we explored the lake. With our expensive equipment, vehicles and radio transmitters we did not look like mere tourists – more like Russian spies or CIA agents in disguise.

'You have half an hour to leave the premises, I don't want to see you here when I return,' he told us stiffly, mimicking who knows what colonial overseer of his youth.

'So be it,' I said to the team as he sped off down the road. 'Let's pack up and get the hell out of here before it gets dark and we get soaked.'

Lorenzo took Hugo, Adam and Juliette with him in the boats and headed towards the open lake, leaving Charlie and me and our Africans to dismantle and fold the camp and repack the lorry and other vehicles again before nightfall. A group of villagers, incensed by the DC's unfriendly behaviour, offered to come along and show us the way to the mission station, a convenient place around the lake to meet up with Lorenzo and his team on the boat. The rain broke all over us as we were stuffing the last things into the back of our lorry but, because it was the first day in the bush of our expedition's second leg, our spirits remained high despite the sudden, unpleasant change of plan.

—Overleaf—
*The Livingstone
Mountains rose dark
and majestic.*

The hasty departure in heavy rain at seven in the evening from the camp at Itungi had not disturbed me unduly. It was important, I knew, to descend the Kiwira river just sufficiently to be out of reach of the hostile police and find a place to spend the night. The Kiwira, with its huge bunches of bamboo rising from both banks, giving it Asiatic characteristics, is a small river, and in the narrower sections the tops of the canes on the banks touch to form a tunnel. The sun's rays filter through the yellow-green leaves of these plants, which are sacred to the Japanese.

After some hours' navigation, the vegetation and the tunnels disappeared from the river banks. From my calculations we had now reached the estuary and were not far from Lake Malawi. It was decidedly time to stop. The Tanzanian borders with Malawi are imprecise here. It was now no longer possible to stumble on a soldier patrol at this point. In the dark, broken now and again by shafts of light from my torch, which I kept low, level with the water, I had detected the presence of canoes and human voices. Reassured by an initial offer of cigarettes and courteous greetings, they told us in Swahili that we were about a mile and a quarter from the river. In order to attain deep water it was necessary to follow a natural dam of sand and weeds to the *melango*, the passage into the famous 'lake of tempests'.

It was the first time we had to sleep in the inflatables: perfect to transport us and our equipment, which at this moment was impossible to unload, but sleeping four in one boat was another matter. The impossibility of protecting ourselves from the mosquitoes disturbed me most; if sleeping curled on top of the equipment was not really a problem, the mosquitoes most definitely were. It is no good wrapping oneself in the net because, as it brushes against the skin, one is bitten through it. With the help of the oars tied together in a cross over the centre of the boat, the net tucked in wherever possible, we managed to spend a reasonably satisfactory night as we awaited the light of the next day. As I lay listening to the high-pitched buzz of the mosquitoes trying to get at us, I recalled the warning words of Dr Reese, in Nairobi, that malaria mosquitoes are especially infectious late at night, between ten and the first hours of dawn.

Mosquitoes aside, the African night spent on the estuary of the Kiwira river had a particular fascination. The Livingstone Mountains, named after the first man to give us an accurate description of this inland sea, were visible in the distance. I don't remember having slept much that night, but a journey like ours prevents any feeling of fatigue. The fishing canoes had begun moving before dawn, bumping into each other with the characteristic sound of hollowed wood. The oars caressed the water surface, adding yet

another note to the gentle concert offered by the birds at their awakening. I remember the pastel colours of this melancholic region, the oyster greys of dawn, the soft greens of the rushes, the successive flights of white egrets passing low over the river and veering suddenly to avoid our boats. The fishermen preceded us; we waved to each other to show we were not hostile; it was all they desired. Everything was extraordinarily clear; each stem, each flower stood out before us as if it were etched in crystal. It gave me the impression that my eyesight had suddenly improved, that I was younger, more vital, filled with renewed energies from an unknown source.

Fortunately our engines were not noisy, and we were able to descend towards the lake without disturbing the nature that surrounded us. Through the bunches of thinning reed canes we saw a tongue of black sand covered with the debris of high water. We followed the edge of the sand dam, passed some returning fishermen and gently floated into Lake Malawi.

A look at the maps told me we are at Itungi Port, at the northern end of the lake. A name on a map, a point to load and unload merchandise, a long beach, ten miles in length, joining the mouth of the Kiwira river to the Livingstone Mountains rising over the lake, which at that point is 2,000 feet deep. At Matema, another name on the map, we were presumably going to meet up with Mirella, the vehicles and the rest of the team. The lake was calm and flat that morning, the mountains, lit transversely by the low-lying sun, were covered by a veil of mist painted from below by the refracting blue of the lake. The summits were mauve and the deep ribs leading down the mountainside towards the lake deep green tinged with gold.

From where I was on the lake, I was able to pick out the little square brick houses with corrugated iron roofs in the village of Matema, but there was no sign of our vehicles yet. We approached the black shore. The water lapped over it gently in small rotating wavelets, more like those of a sea than a lake. The sun beat down fiercely on us as we stepped off the boats. Mirella appeared through the bushes, barefoot and dishevelled but happy indeed to see us.

We had travelled slowly for several hours through water-filled potholes on a deeply rutted track, and despite our efforts finally slithered off the road and remained hopelessly stuck for the rest of the night. Morning found us stiff and dishevelled and tightly mudbound in the midst of a luxuriant banana plantation, surrounded by a group of gaping Africans who had crept out of the leaves to check out the nocturnal arrival. With the help of some of them we lifted the lightweight Pandas back on to the road; but the heavily loaded seven-ton Bedford would not budge and required considerable digging and jacking up to free the wheels.

I drove on down the road in one of the cars towards the meeting-place on the lake so as to reassure the others, and left Charlie behind with the other car, to deal with the lorry. The two-hour journey to the lake shore was a delight. All the way, on either side of the road, the banana plantations intermingled for miles with palm and cocoa trees through which could be seen neatly swept compounds surrounded by palm-thatched bamboo habitations. Great tropical plants with wide-webbed leaves and creeping sweet potatoes paid homage to the rich black cotton soil in a symphony of green. Little wonder this area was known as the bread-basket of Tanzania. It is the most fertile and highly cultivated zone in the country. One could almost feel the vegetation breathe and grow.

It was almost midday when we finally made contact with the others. That night we all sat on the beach and drank the three bottles of champagne brought along to baptize the second leg of the expedition.

We spent a week at Lake Malawi camped on the steel-grey sandy beach that fringes the northernmost tip. The Livingstone Mountains rose dark and majestic to one side of us and on the other the water shimmered to a lost horizon where it blended with the sky. A dilapidated mission station, struggling to keep alive the teachings of missionaries since the days of David Livingstone, has eradicated all signs of authenticity. Wearing shorts and shirts, the people were nondescript and westernized, without any particular identity. We could have been anywhere in the black- skinned world.

During the next few days we explored the lake, pulling into little mud and thatch villages beneath spreading mango trees, chatting with the inhabitants and watching them manoeuvre through their simple days as they dealt with the essentials of their existence. They brewed banana and coconut beer and pounded maize flour to a soft, white, pungent powder; they moulded and fired round clay pots which they finger-painted with white chalk paste, and carried away to market piled high in canoes or strung together on a pole, balanced on strong shoulders; they sat for hours on the beach or beneath the shady trees engrossed in endless conversation. On the terraced slopes of the hills they cultivated manioc and maize crops. We were the only Europeans around and many requests for money came our way. Far from being destitute, the people here were well versed in the art of trade: everything had a price and was for sale.

When we left the area a week later, we came upon a funeral gathering spread beneath the mango trees beside the road. About 200 wailing women in bright coloured cottons sat, with legs outstretched in front of them, on the leafy ground

The grieving mother with her tear-stained madonna face looked down at the body of her tiny child lying in a finely woven shroud beside her.

144

around the grieving mother. The dead body of her tiny child, wrapped in a fine woven fibre shroud, lay on the ground beside her. We stopped and wandered over hesitantly. A group of men sitting around a smoky fire nearby greeted us and asked us where we came from.

'Could I take some pictures for my story?' I asked them, a bit embarrassed at my request.

'No problem, madam, if you pay,' they answered.

'We would be happy to make a contribution towards the funeral expenses,' I replied, trying to soften the pecuniary edge.

One of them got up and went over to the mother, with her tear-stained madonna face, to deliver the message. All eyes instantly turned in our direction, and interest was momentarily deflected from the dead child. 'Go ahead, it's all right,' the man came back to tell us; we put some money in his hand. The wailing recommenced and suddenly the grief-stricken father exploded from the trees and came at us brandishing a panga, shouting at us to go away. Tears streamed down his face. He was immediately subdued by two older men standing by him and he fell on his knees sobbing in his hands. We moved quietly away.

A short time later the palette of bright colours rose and moved into the sunlight for the funeral procession, which wove in a long line towards the burial ground, where the little bundle was deposited in its earthen resting place. The grieving father walked by himself at the back, a pathetic, solitary figure, like a black punctuation mark at the end of the colourful line.

We stopped at a cheerful, buzzing market along the road and for a brief moment lost ourselves in a mass of humanity hawking produce of the fertile land we were crossing. Huge bunches of green bananas and baskets of oranges sat beside heaps of chillis and beans and potatoes, bottles of vermilion palm oil stood on wooden tables next to pungent heaps of dried tobacco, fish and manioc and a variety of African delicacies still unknown to us.

Ten miles outside Mbeya our Bedford lorry and the two Fiat Pandas veered westwards and crossed the Mbarara Mountains in heavy mist. The air was cold at the top and a strong wind was blowing, whirling the clouds in and out of the valleys and down the steep escarpment to the boiling plains below. We were suddenly on the Scottish moors, it seemed, the mountain sides covered in long golden grass instead of heather. A variety of wild flowers grew haphazardly along the road; tall-stemmed and elegant, they thrust their petals skywards, drinking in the mist, or crawled in disarray along the ground and spilled in brilliant showers over the road banks. It was the azure morning glories which struck me most, so incongruous in

Lake Tanganyika is unpredictable; one can never take it for granted.

this African mist. Our little convoy appeared and disappeared as it snaked along the ridges and down the winding road to the hot flatlands several thousand feet below.

Our next big stop was now the shores of Lake Tanganyika, an important milestone in our expedition. The famous lake had seen many explorers before us and had taken its place in the annals of Africa's tortuous history. The anticipation with which we approached its shores helped us bear the long, hot and exhausting two-day journey over corrugated roads in the dust to Sumbawanga, the last small town before the steep descent to the water's edge. We crawled in first gear over great volcanic stones littering the track and had to clear them by hand when it became impassable. Our new Kenyan team did us proud, negotiating the difficult passages with care and great expertise, and when, after several hours, the lake suddenly appeared through the trees, they let out a great whoop of joy. There, finally, was the lake beneath us, a patch of molten glass spilling to the horizon, an inland sea whose distant shores lay out of sight, sparkling in the afternoon sunlight. It was so bright it made us squint, and we dived behind our sunglasses as if we were shading our eyes from some enticing sorceress.

We unloaded and set up camp on a small beach beside a palm-frond village nestling beneath a coconut grove. The land all around was parched and barren and fell in great ribs, depleted of all vegetation, but, in the deep gulleys in between, tall trees grew with apparent ease in the topsoil washed down by the rain. It was soft and cool under there and the lake-dwellers welcomed us with touching delight, visibly surprised at our appearance. Few white people came this way now or ever, it was so remote a place, and difficult of access.

We had to park our vehicles on a rise about 100 feet above the water; the usual group of curious onlookers traipsed up and down with us on a crooked path, transferring the equipment to the little beach, an unexpected ideal launching-pad just big enough to accommodate our camp. In the evenings and in the early mornings a welcome mist rolled in from the lake and bathed us and the valley in a sheath of moisture that soothed our burning faces and chapped lips. Long, sleek canoes emerged at these times from the reeds and bulrushes; propelled by long-poled punters, they slid delicately on the still water.

It took five days for us to reach Ujiji, the historic meeting-place where Stanley found Livingstone. Adam and the Africans arrived with the vehicles a few hours after we did. We followed the ribbed, barren coastline from dawn to dusk each day, stopping for the night on open beaches or in sheltered rocky coves when the lake got choppy, as it often did in the afternoons when the wind rose. Lake Tanganyika is an unpredictable lake one can never take for granted. Many people have been drowned on it, surprised by a sudden change of mood. As on the open sea, the mornings are still, with no sign of turbulence, but as the heat of the day escalates the air rising from the hot plains rushes down the mountain slopes and sweeps in great gusts across the immense sheet of water, rousing it into white-capped waves that sometimes reach eight or ten feet in height, making it difficult to get back in the frail, unstable dugouts used by the lake-dwellers. Travel here is confined mainly to the lake, and the inhabitants have become wary of its fickle moods. The coastal scenery bears witness to its violence. What little vegetation survives here has adapted to the harsh climatic conditions. Grasses and reeds are hard and uninviting, clustered tightly in protective walls, cactus and euphorbia cling with ropy roots to the rocks, and the sandy beaches are often covered in flotsam and aquatic debris. Canoes are pulled well out of the water, fastened to stones at night, huts are robust and well-constructed lattice frameworks, thickly plastered with mud and stones and thatched with hardy grass or palm fronds. The larger villages spread along the great bays where the shore line curves inland and the water is calm, protected by rocky

Long, sleek canoes
emerged from the reeds
and bulrushes; propelled
by punt poles, they slid
delicately towards us
over the still water.

headlands that provide useful points of reference to the traveller and are clearly marked on the maps.

Our uncapsizeable rubber inflatables, each propelled by two 25-h.p. Mariner engines, rode the waves with remarkable dexterity. It was not always pleasant travelling in choppy conditions and the days seemed very long and unending, but Lorenzo, Juliette, Hugo and Charlie seemed to prefer a bit of action, revelling in the spray and the tricky negotiation of the waves. We often pulled in for the night, wet and exhausted, thankful to be back on land. Some days were smooth and idyllic and allowed for more intense observation of the coastline. These were the days I preferred, soaking in the sun or shaded beneath my umbrella, picking out the images of a pristine Africa with my camera. It was an ever-changing picture show that kept us entertained and erased monotony. At times the scene became dramatic and almost theatrical with giant boulders, smoothed and lashed by the waves, rising 100 feet from the water, with sometimes a solitary tree perched on the top; one of those miracles of Nature: how and where did they draw life from these lifeless monoliths?

The water here was deep and cold, and the people bottom-fished with large hooks fastened to long lines. The lake codfish had large, bulbous, protruding eyes –

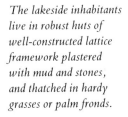

The lakeside inhabitants live in robust huts of well-constructed lattice framework plastered with mud and stones, and thatched in hardy grasses or palm fronds.

ugly inmates of a sombre world where light rays are dimmed and deflected. All our efforts at fly-fishing led to nothing. Despite the array of fancy lures and tempting morsels with which we courted them, we did not catch a single fish. Night fishing with nets and kerosene pressure-lamps does, however, provide necessary protein for the inhabitants in the form of great shoals of tiny silver sardines and whitebait which are laid out to dry on the hot sands each morning and gathered up in baskets in the afternoons. Cooked with palm oil and wild tomatoes and herbs or roasted on flat irons they are consumed once a day with a manioc *polenta*, the staple, monotonous diet of the sturdy lake-dwellers, whose harsh living conditions have made them as tough and resilient as the hardy plants that live beside them.

Not many outsiders come this way, as roads are few and far between and life here is governed by Nature. It seemed astounding to us, with all our material necessities, how content and undemanding the lake-dwellers were: simple, whole-some people who, everywhere, greeted and welcomed us with touching enthusi-asm, always ready to help or just sit and talk endlessly, eager for news and information. Each village has its own little infrastructure – a chief, a group of elders and a school teacher. Children are taught elementary lessons, reading, writing, spelling and arithmetic, under the trees, squatting on stones on the ground, or in

Children here are taught elementary lessons in a 'classroom' beneath a wild mukuyu *tree clinging to a boulder; the smooth side of the rock serves as a blackboard.*

rudimentary mud and reed classrooms with rough-hewn wooden benches. One such classroom was particularly imaginative and decorative, beneath a wild *mukuyu* tree clinging to a boulder about fifteen feet high. On one side the rock surface was smooth and flat and served as a blackboard. The overhanging branches provided shade on a fragment of beach that had been swept and pounded hard. The pupils, aged from six to ten years, sat on stones with little slates on their knees, mouthing the words of the teacher as he pointed them out on the rock with a long stick.

They were in mid-lesson, their backs to us, when we pulled up on the beach. We watched for a while not wanting to disturb them, but then a dog began to bark and gave us away. That was the end of the lesson for the day. The teacher asked us over and introduced us to his dozen pupils, who in unison bade us good morning. We joined the class for a while, and then were asked to give a little talk about our journey. Lorenzo stood up beside the teacher and for a half hour kept everyone engrossed and amused with his tales; he then offered to take them for a spin in the boats, and became their instant hero. It was not easy to leave them at the end of the morning; we promised to return, but of course we never did as we had to press on; how else could we leave these lovely, simple souls? Perhaps one day we shall go back; for both of us it is an appealing prospect.

Our campsite that night was one of the few unfriendly ones. The setting was alluring enough, with its soft golden sand fringed with rocks and trees, but hardly had we alighted when an invisible army of dreaded sandfleas burst from the sand, buzzing in our ears and noses, our eyes and mouths, driving us insane.

'We can't stay here,' I implored, 'let's find another place.'

But it was getting dark and we had unloaded the boats. We wrapped our heads and faces with *kikois*, the colourful African *sarongs* we always carried with us, and for the first time pulled out our gnat hats, an ingenious invention for just such occasions: fine mosquito netting sewn around cloth hats and tied around the neck, which made us look like creatures from outer space. Thank God the invading army withdrew with the daylight and we had a peaceful, gnat-free night; but next morning they were back again with the sun. I had never before been so eager and relieved to hit the water again, and extracted a solemn promise from the team never to allow a repetition.

CHIMPS AND BABOONS

THE BEACH AT UJIJI, WHERE STANLEY FOUND LIVINGSTONE in 1873, was as inconspicuous as its name was notorious, with canoes pulled up on the sand and a mêlée of people going about their business, buying and selling fish, washing clothes, repairing nets; it had a look of windswept abandon about it. Although it is clearly marked on the map, we sailed right by it and had to retrace our wake when we found ourselves arriving at Kigoma.

Kigoma is one of the lake's main ports, about fifteen miles beyond Ujiji, which scars the countryside with its cement wharfs, petrol tanks and great steel ships at anchor. Ujiji, in contrast, because of its association with the great explorers, is swathed in romance, but now, just over a hundred years after the historic meeting, it is merely another beach.

Two eccentric-looking Englishmen standing beside their donkeys among a little group of Africans came over and introduced themselves gleefully, surprised at our unexpected arrival and quickly identified with us. John Tardios and Adrian Cantor, a dark-haired Mediterranean from Malta and a redhead from Lincolnshire, had arrived in Ujiji a week earlier after a two-year trek across Tanzania following the Stanley route. Toughened by the trek, bouts of malaria, dysentery and sunstroke, their leathered faces and faded clothes bore witness to their strange ordeal.

We loaded our bags and equipment on to the donkeys, and together followed the path that led inland from the shore to the little dusty town and the spot where the historic meeting had taken place. The legendary tree beneath which the two explorers first shook hands had since died and been replaced by a huge mango tree. The whole area had been fenced off by a stone wall with two wooden slatted doors fastened together by a chain and a lock. A cardboard sign, pierced through one end and hung from a wire, read 'Livingstone Monument – Closed'.

—Right—
We loaded our bags and equipment on to donkeys and followed the path that led from the shore inland to the dusty little town of Ujiji.

—Below—
Mary Anne Fitzgerald, African stringer for the International Herald Tribune, *joined us at Ujiji. 'Where are you?' she had asked over the radio. 'In the middle of the lake,' came Lorenzo's reply.*

Henry Morton Stanley was sent by the Paris office of the Herald Tribune *to find David Livingstone in Africa.*

We banged on the doors and after a few moments a delicate white female hand appeared and handed us a key through the slats. The doors swung open and revealed the owner of the hand standing between two more donkeys. She was tall and slim and dressed in olive-green army fatigues and a khaki shirt, her hair pulled back from her hollow, suntanned face. It lit up with surprise as John introduced us to her, but the strain of the long journey was still very evident in her anxious pale green eyes. She was Christina, the wife of John Tardios. Gentle and soft spoken, it was difficult at first to associate her with so strenuous a voyage, but, as we got to know her, it became evident that beneath her fragile appearance lurked a tough lady with a calm, uncomplaining disposition.

A simple stone and cement monolith with a cross engraved into a contour of Africa stood beneath the mango tree, with 'David Livingstone 1813–1873' inscribed on a brass plaque at its base. To the right of it was another plaque with the names and dates of Burton and Speke. We stood together in front of the three names recalling the now familiar exploits of the legendary explorers. It was very quiet all around; the sunlight through the mango leaves cast a dappled pattern on the grey monument and the donkeys nibbled at the bushes that had been planted around it.

John, Adrian and Christina had set up camp in a small two-room stone building inside the compound, which served as a travellers' rest. Built by the Tanzanian Government, it was a nice memento to the three men who had first traced the route. We brewed tea on camping-gas burners and sat for some hours in the shade of the great tree exchanging stories and letting our fatigue drain away. It seemed a fitting place for such a break.

When the heat subsided, we wandered through the little town on earthen streets flanked on either side by earthen houses with rusty corrugated-iron roofs. The main street was tarmac, but pitted with holes because of the surprising amount of through truck traffic that kept a constant haze of dust in the air. The shops were laden with coloured cloth, mattresses, tin pots and pans. People stood around talking and children followed us everywhere. Outside the mosque, Arabs in long white *kanzus* sat in clumps playing African dominoes or immersed in eternal conversation. From a nearby schoolroom, a chorus of young voices, reciting the Koran and singing Muslim songs to the accompaniment of tambourines with brass bells, floated out through barred

'Livingstone was a character that I venerated, that called forth all my enthusiasm, that evoked nothing but the sincerest admiration,' wrote Stanley in his journal after their meeting in Ujiji.

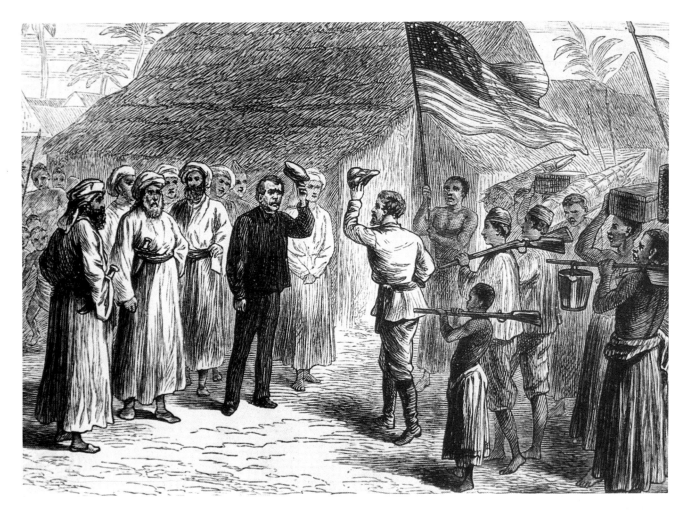

windows, underlining a past of Arab slave-traders. Two huge trees with gnarled, exposed roots still stood as silent witnesses of a grisly scene, in what had once been the slave market, for here in Ujiji the captured slaves were herded together before beginning their long journey to the Indian Ocean and the Arab dhows awaiting them in Bagamoyo. Ujiji, for those familiar with Africa's history, conjures up a multitude of such dramatic images, traces of which are still apparent everywhere.

In Kigoma we met up once again with our vehicles and spent a few days sorting, repacking and reshuffling. The next rendez-vous was set at Bujumbura in Burundi, the northernmost point of the lake. We moved on by boat to Ngombe Stream, about one hour north, to Jane Goodall's chimpanzee sanctuary, where she has been studying and monitoring chimp behaviour for the past twenty-five years. She had

When Stanley and Livingstone finally met, Stanley had been on the move for more than two years and Livingstone had arrived in Ujiji just over a week earlier.

157

Slaves who tried to escape were severely punished in public to deter others.

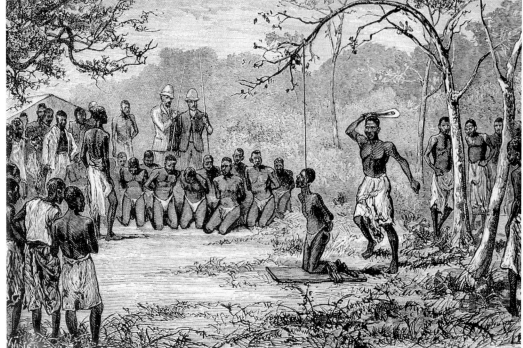

— *Above* —

Hamidi bin Muhammad, a Zanzibari Arab known as Tippu Tip, was to become the greatest slave trader in Central Africa.

— *Right* —

A slave caravan on the march.

Stubborn passive resistance was often the only recourse of captured slaves.

159

*Fleeing slaves were
hunted and, like wild
animals, captured with
sturdy nets.*

Gorillas, like slaves, were also hunted in the forests, but killed afterwards.

161

just completed the first really comprehensive book on the subject, entitled *Chimpanzees of Gombe: Patterns of Behaviour*.

By a wonderful coincidence Jane, who now lives in Dar-es-Salaam, had just come up to spend a week with her chimps to collect the data gathered by her team over the past year, and so we spent several fascinating days with her and her chimp family. Despite a few grey hairs, Jane has changed little over the years. The beautiful Botticelli face and quiet green eyes, the silky hair pulled back in a pony tail, the neat, trim figure and elegant bush clothes gave her an air of cool serenity, a lady in total control of herself, her life and her environment. It was both reassuring and intimidating, subtly demanding respect and imparting quiet confidence.

I had not seen her for twenty years, but had followed her rise to prominence in the wildlife world through her books and films. The usual bitchy rumours had labelled her difficult, arrogant and elusive, and we were unsure how she would receive us in her little kingdom. We had left messages for her in Kigoma, but these remained disconcertingly unanswered, until we spied her in her motorboat chugging past our camp several hundred yards out on the lake on her way to Ngombe.

'OK, let's go after her,' Lorenzo said, jumping into an inflatable.

The water was choppy and she did not slow down at our approach, just kept going. She sat under a large straw hat beside some of her fellow-workers, an Indian, two Africans and a white man, looking aloof and distant, a Mona Lisa smile on her face. We shouted our greeting to her over the noise of our respective engines, informing her of our intended visit next day to Ngombe Stream, if she so permitted. She nodded rather indifferently as the wind covered us in spray. But we had made contact and an appointment to meet.

The definition 'arrogant and elusive' was perhaps not far wrong, but our meeting next day dispelled our misgivings and everyone fell in love with her. Soft-spoken, hospitable and interested, she invited us into her wilderness dwelling, a stone, bunker-like structure with a long wooden verandah roofed with palm fronds and completely wired with mesh, looking like a cage. 'It's to keep the monkeys out,' she explained. 'Otherwise we would have nothing left in here.' There was not much anyway, just the bare minimum for survival – a wooden table, three chairs, some boxes piled on each other served as shelves for tins of basic foods: canned milk, margarine, vegetables and meat, some biscuits, tea, sugar, flour and cooking oil and some packets of Knorr soups. There were two hurricane lamps and a kerosene burner on the floor beside a carton of tin pots and pans, a kettle and some crockery and cutlery. That was about all. On the wall some fantastic blow-ups of chimps in touchingly human poses and expressions, and a large map of Tanzania yellowed with age and humidity. This place had once been her home, but she had abandoned it when she moved to Dar-es-Salaam and now only used it as a shelter on her annual visits to Ngombe.

It was rather dark and uninviting inside, a bit like the interior of a store room with its wooden slatted floor, windows with wire mesh, contents spread in disarray, but Jane moved about in it like a Renaissance figurine, lending a certain professional solemnity to everything. This was the abode of a scientist who for twenty-five years had been observing chimp behaviour and whose findings were incorporated into the annals of wildlife and human studies. She had had the foresight and endurance to study the extraordinary lifestyle of the nearest primate relative to man because, she told us, when she left school she recognized a strong desire to observe and write about wildlife, a vocation she fully consummated. We walked with her in the forest and along the beach; we sat together for hours observing with her the different members of her chimp family; and she told us about her life, her findings and her methods. The chimps and baboons wandered through our conversations, illustrating the points she was making. Her loyal, dedicated and efficient African team had been well trained by her and relieved her of the time-consuming work of monitoring.

In Mahali, approximately two days south of Ngombe Stream, we had encountered our first wild chimps living in the forest undisturbed by humans. We had felt a strange empathy with them, one we had never experienced with other animals. It was almost as if they were more like humans; there seemed to be a recognizable link between them and us. Jane explained that chimps are, of course, our nearest living relatives, biologically speaking; they are all distinct individuals just as we are, each one is quite different from every other. Chimps live approximately fifty years and a baby is born every five or six years after the mother is thirteen years of age.

One of Jane's central interests is to try and define how childhood experiences affect the adult – hence the need for a long-term study. 'It is terribly important in this study,' she said, 'to know who is related to whom; that, for instance, there are strong supportive bonds between brothers and sisters which don't exist with outside members; a brother will help his brother, a grandmother will care for her grandchild. There exists a strong relationship between a mother and her adult daughters and sons; the children leave her between the ages of eight and eleven, for short periods to begin with, but when they return the strong supportive relationship persists right through life. It makes a tremendous difference to a young male as to

Jane Goodall has been studying and monitoring chimp behaviour at Ngombe Stream for over twenty-five years.

Chimps are our nearest living relatives, biologically speaking.

164

whether or not he has a brother, because two males working together in this close, supportive way have a much better chance of rising up through the male-dominated hierarchy than a male on his own; he knows he can always rely on his brother, who will never turn against him. I am only beginning to understand the intricacies of chimp behaviour as it is related to their own blood relationships, their own kinship network. Like humans, a grandmother, for instance, will play very much more with her grandchild than she ever did with her own child; she's got no responsibilities and she can just have fun with it. I am becoming increasingly involved with human child psychologists and psychiatrists because I find that chimps are very much like us as they are very complex, but they are not bound by culture, not to the extent that humans are, so they are not worried about what people think of them. If, for instance, a chimp has a bad experience in its early life, it is very much easier to see that scar in operation than it would be in humans. Humans learn to hide what they think or feel, they don't like to be belittled or laughed at, and so unless they are seriously mentally disturbed they learn to control their behaviour, which is not so in the case of a chimp. Now that the first twenty-five years of my study is completed I have a feeling that the next twenty-five years that stretch ahead of me are going to be even more fascinating, now that we have identified these family relationships.'

We asked Jane if she had devised any method of communicating with her chimps, if, for instance, she 'spoke chimpanzee'. She laughed. 'Well, I can understand it, but I don't speak it to the chimps because in fact chimps have very complicated communications. Part of it is posture and gesture, and this is so like ours, for instance reaching out, touching, greeting, embracing, kissing, holding hands, patting one another on the shoulder. We can understand that intuitively even if we have never seen a chimp before. Then they have this repertoire of calls, which I had to learn to understand. They have, for instance, the distance call, which they use to communicate between scattered groups. This is the "pant-hoot"; there are at least five different types of pant-hoots that mean different things. There is, for instance, "Here I am, where are you and who are you?" – each pant-hoot is individually distinct. There's "Here's some real nice food, I'm having a wonderful time." There's "I'm a little bit unhappy because I've lost my mother, but I'm a big boy, so I've got to make a big noise and feel better." And then there is the kind of sound they make in their nests or beds at night after a good day and they have a nice full belly and there are stars in the sky. It simply means "God is in his heaven, all's well with the world." It's a pant-hoot that has a singing quality; I can't do it very well, but it's high pitched and it sounds a bit like this.' Jane gave us an imitation of the pant-hoot that was so perfectly pitched and realistic that the chimps in the trees behind us responded and we were witness to an extraordinary and moving exchange between the two species.

She also amused us by showing us how she had devised a method to monitor the weight-growth of her chimps by tying a rope to a scale attached to a branch on which a tin containing a banana was fastened. When the chimp went after the banana he had to climb the rope and the scale registered his weight – an ingenious and effective method.

Our camp on the beach near Jane's compound was the focus for daily baboon raids, and we had to keep a close vigil to protect our food, soap, toothpaste and shoes. Their fearless familiarity with man culminated one evening as we watched a fisherman, carrying a bunch of bananas on his head, being assaulted and the cheeky invaders making off with the loot as the terrified man charged down the beach, to the general hilarity of our camp. Then it was the turn of our inflatables, where a forgotten bunch of bananas was ransacked and carried off down the beach in their mouths, in their hands, tucked in their armpits, as they fled like guilty robbers from the shouting and stick-waving of the expedition members. One old male attempted to retrieve some of the bananas from an irate female with a tiny baby clinging to her back. The violent combat that ensued was so hilariously human, as she screamed and slapped him in the face, that the two were instantly baptized Lorenzo and Mirella. We learned a lot about human behaviour during our week at Ngombe Stream with the primates and much light was shed on our own interactions on the expedition.

Baboons are more biologically distant from man than chimpanzees; they are monkeys whereas chimpanzees and gorillas are apes. The human line probably split from the apes anywhere between five and ten million years ago; it split from monkeys earlier than that. What makes apes seem different can be observed in the faces of the animals. The faces of gorillas and chimpanzees are much more like ours: they are more expressive, and the signals they send are signals that we can read better than those seen on a baboon's face.

Baboons, especially the males, have long muzzles because of their impressive canines. For those canines to grow they need that dog-like shape to the face. The communication and the behaviour of baboons in many respects is similar to humans. In fact in the 1950s and 1960s baboons were used as the model for human evolution. What is unique about baboons in relation to other primates is that they also live on the savannah and in semi-arid areas, not only in the forest. Only humans and baboons are able to live in open savannah.

— Overleaf above left —
During our week with the primates at Ngombe Stream we learned much about human behaviour and compared their interactions to our own on the expedition.

— Overleaf below left —
Communication and behaviour between baboons are in many respects similar to those of humans. They were so intrigued by their reflection in the lens of Bruno's camera that we had some hilarious moments together.

— Overleaf main picture —
The violent combat which ensued was so hilariously human that these two baboons were instantly christened Lorenzo and Mirella.

167

Families in baboon society are very strongly and very tightly knit. A female keeps all of her offspring, and usually the next generation and sometimes the next again, in her family group. The troop is composed of many different families. They help each other out in time of trouble and they like being together; they feed together, rest together, sleep together, and in this way the bond between mothers and babies – the basic closeness of the family – is very similar to that of chimps and also that of humans (although sometimes baboon families are nicer to each other than human families).

Shirley Strum, an American anthropologist from the University of San Diego, California, has studied baboon behaviour for fifteen years. We met her at her home in Kenya and she told us how one of the most impressive similarities between humans and baboons is politics – they actually have a kind of sophisticated social manoeuvring that can compare not to national politics but to local politics. A male, for instance, although he has got all that aggressive potential, great strength, long hair, superb teeth, doesn't fight very often and, when he does, he finds that there are all sorts of social alliances that come into play which prevent him from getting what he wants. So instead of using aggression, if he is going to succeed he has to form alliances. For example, baboons fight with each other for a receptive female, but the female does not necessarily have to cooperate; a male can get her, but he can't rape her, and in order for him to succeed in getting what he wants, which is to mate with her, she has to cooperate with him and she cooperates only with her male friends, not males who try to dominate her. So at an early stage the male has first to establish a friendship and do nice things to her and then later on he can call in his dues and a reciprocal relationship can be established.

The same sort of thing happens with their babies. Very often when two males come together in a fight the male who is losing will grab a baby and put it on his belly and then present himself to the other male instead of fighting. That turns off the aggression of the other male, but it only works if the baby cooperates; if the baby screams then the whole troop attacks and he really is in trouble: their relationships and interpersonal politics are based on reciprocity.

If baboons live in a very rich environment, such as at Ngombe Stream, for instance, they have babies every thirteen or fourteen months. If, on the other hand, the environment is more harsh, it could be every two to two-and-a-half years. An interesting observation – and this is the case with many animals – is that the age of the female determines her fertility. Young females, for instance, have more difficulty getting pregnant, while middle-aged females are at the peak of their fertility. As the female gets old her fertility drops off and probably, if baboons lived long enough, as they do in captivity, they would undergo menopause just like humans.

It is known that chimps and gorillas have bigger brains than baboons, but it is difficult to establish a comparative IQ between them because normally IQ is measured by human standards and in primates it has to be measured within the framework of each particular animal. One has to know a great deal about the animal to devise the test. Earlier on it was thought that gorillas were stupid, but in fact the problem with gorillas was one of motivation, not intelligence. They didn't want to do the test. But it was later established that in fact gorillas and chimps have about the same IQ. Chimps and gorillas have certain areas in their brains that baboons lack: those areas are related to performing certain things, so on that basis they are probably smarter than baboons, but on the other hand there are many things that a baboon can do that a chimp can't possibly do in its natural setting, and vice versa.

Tea had been served on a silver tray, placed by the house servant on a flat stone beside where we sat talking to Shirley. The deep and splendid Masai gorge with its tall yellow fever trees growing in its bed ran beneath her beautiful new home. We did not notice an old baboon male and his mate, carrying their baby on her back, creep up behind us, until a sudden clatter of crockery made us turn. The biscuits had gone and the tea things lay upset on the tray as the little baboon family scampered away from us across the lawn, chewing the biscuits stuffed into their cheek pockets.

CHAPTER NINE

RUZINA JOINS THE EXPEDITION

ARY ANNE FITZGERALD, THE AFRICAN STRINGER FOR the *International Herald Tribune*, joined us at Ujiji. She had been sent to meet Lorenzo by the same paper that had dispatched Stanley to find Livingstone. She came with us to Ngombe Stream; after a week we organized for her a farewell canoe regatta among the nearby villagers. Everyone had so much fun she almost missed the lake steamer back to Kigoma. When it was time for us to leave, the villagers begged us to remain a while longer, but we had to push on, and left them laughing and waving on the beach. The arrival of the weekly boat that calls at the larger villages along Lake Tanganyika is always a festive occasion; the villagers gather on the beach dressed in their best clothes. This modern vessel, plying a route which dates back to colonial times, has greatly increased the traffic between the villages, gradually modifying the lives of the inhabitants; it has spread a great desire for consumer goods, and has facilitated travel from the villages to the towns of Bujumbura in Burundi and Kigoma in Tanzania. Many young people are now leaving their families, their village and their traditions for the illusory promises of a European lifestyle few of them can afford, and shanty towns in the cities are expanding as work becomes scarcer. The weekly boat has also contributed to an increased migration towards the more prosperous villages, where the population growth is alarming and the afflictions of modern Africa are already apparent.

Bujumbura, at the northern end of Lake Tanganyika, was the first big city we had called at since leaving Dar-es-Salaam. Capital of Burundi, which until ten years ago was under Belgian administration, it has maintained its distinct European flavour. The tree-lined avenues and large classical administration buildings, the sidewalk cafés and *boulangeries* selling *chocolat chaud*, *croissants* and *baguettes*, and the Greek-run *supermarché* filled with European delicacies, catapulted us incongruously back into a world we had momentarily forgotten.

We pulled up late one evening on the beach of l'Hôtel du Lac, after an uncomfortably choppy ride on the lake. Monsieur Leopold, the distinguished manager of the hotel, generously offered us a two-room cottage with bathroom and hot water after hearing of our exploits, a luxury we blissfully accepted. Refined and well educated, Leopold spoke impeccable French with a soft rolling Burundi accent, and welcomed us with typical continental charm and enthusiasm, introducing us proudly to his friends at the bar and inviting us to *diner* and *déjeuner* with him. After so much rough living a bit of indulgence felt like bathing in asses' milk after weeks on salty seas. To sleep again in cool, ironed sheets, soak in a hot tub and sit at a table for meals assumed an immeasurably sophisticated importance. Lorenzo offered me a modest birthday dinner beneath the trees with bottles of red wine, camembert cheese and French *baguettes*, and Leopold brought me a cake with icing sugar and candles and a bottle of Moët et Chandon, which were all so ravenously consumed it was embarrassing.

There was a small zoo in the garden of the hotel which Leopold had set up for the entertainment of his guests, a disconsolate and pitiable affair that distressed us greatly. Among the captive birds and animals, a tiny chimp was confined with two frantic baby baboons to a small wire bird-cage. The baboons, who jumped all over the chimp in their frenzied attempt to break loose, had worn a bald spot on the top of its head. It sat clinging poignantly to the wire, looking at the outside world with vacant liquid eyes filled with despair. Each time we passed the cage it stretched out its hand beseechingly to us, pressing its little furry body against the wire. We fed it bananas and carrots, and gave it water and milk to drink in a teaspoon, speaking futile words of consolation that could not change its plight. Our daughter Amina, who had arrived with Mary Anne to join us, sat with it for hours stroking its hand through the cage bars and watching it respond to her attentions and her words of solace, until one day she could bear it no longer. 'We must do something about that chimp,' she said to me. 'If we don't, I'll always feel guilty about it.' So I bought it from Leopold next day and gave it to her.

We named her Ruzina, after the Ruzizi river up which we were due to travel on our way to Lake Kivu. Ruzina joined the expedition and from that moment on she clutched at our heartstrings and never let go. Clasped in Amina's arms, she went for walks along the beach, and at night she slept wrapped in a *kikoi* in a basket by her bed. Slowly she shook off the aggressive fear her captive life had engendered and we were able to handle her without getting bitten; it was touching to watch her gradually respond to our care and attentions, drawing reassurance from bodily contact. Biologically equivalent to a child of three, the emotional tie she needed to survive had been severed when her mother was shot by poachers and she was imprisoned in the bird-cage with her two hysterical cell-mates; but now, with Amina, she began regaining trust and comfort, and repaid us with her dependency, her funny human antics, her mischief and her tantrums. Each time she looked at us with those big soulful eyes, we felt a surge of such tenderness and devotion that we became her willing slaves around the clock, awakening in us all, regardless of age,

sex or colour, the primal parental instincts present in all living creatures. Ruzina added a whole new dimension to our expedition and we were all delighted to have taken her on board.

Burundi is the homeland of the elegant Watusi (Tutsi) tribe, famous throughout Africa for their height – few are shorter than six foot. They are known as the aristocrats of the black continent. Of obvious Nilotic descent, they share their country with the short and stocky Bantu Hutus from neighbouring Rwanda. The two countries were once annexed during the Belgian colonization, but divided again after independence, when bitter clashes between the two tribes broke out and it was said the Hutus chopped off the legs of their haughty adversaries so as to bring them down to their level. When peace was at last restored, after a ghastly massacre, Rwanda-Urundi became Rwanda and Burundi, and in an attempt to eliminate further conflict a Hutu and a Tutsi president were respectively elected for each country; the people are now referred to by their country's name and

Ruzina joined the expedition and from that moment on clutched at our heartstrings (as well as to Amina) and never let go.

never by their tribal one. They are still very touchy about the tribal issue, as we quickly discovered, and foreigners are advised to be careful about referring to them by their tribal names.

Perhaps because of their Nilotic origins, the Watusi have evolved more rapidly than the Hutu, whom in Burundi they dominate and employ as servants and labourers. Together with the Bugandas in Uganda, the Watusi have attempted to maintain their superiority and leadership; but independence brought change and upheavals. The Kabaka, King of Buganda, was deposed and had to flee his country with his family to an exile in England, where he later died; in Rwanda and Burundi the savage slaughter has barely been curtailed by a difficult and now broken truce with horrifying reports of internecine massacres.

In Burundi, where the Tutsi minority still predominates, the Government controls education and guides the Watusi towards more advanced schooling and European scholarships, relegating Hutu students to elementary studies so as to avoid any risk of rivalry and a repetition of past rebellion. The handsome elegance, indolent gait and exquisite manners of the Watusi enhance their natural air of pre-eminence, still very evident everywhere.

On market days, the beautifully kept tarmac roads are alive with statuesque women in long, vivid, flowing robes with huge baskets on their heads, who look much like costumed extras on the stage of some lavish Italian opera. The social character of an African market is obvious. Market day for many Africans, who are basically peasant folk, is an emotional release, a social occasion, and they go to market with the spirit of people who spend much time in isolated places, flavouring it with festive gaiety. In Burundi the graceful nature of the Watusi adds an almost lyrical aspect to the occasion.

When our vehicles caught up with us, we drove into the interior and visited the markets, which spilled across the lush mountain-sides like a vivid carpet in the misty mornings. We watched the Watusi-Intore dance in their bright ethnic costumes, modified alas to modern times, and listened to *Les Tambouriniers du Roi* (the royal drummers) jumping and cavorting to the savage rhythms of their great ancient drums. Because there is no longer a king, the royal drummers are now peasant farmers and fishermen who keep alive the old traditions that date back to the sixteenth century. They gather together regularly to pass on from father to son the customs of a medieval Africa still very much alive in the spirit of the people. The dance, they explained to us, is a prayer spread by the drummers over the fields, encouraging the workers to work well. The circle of drums is a song to God, the Intore dancers are the expression of His strength and clemency. The head-dresses personify the lion's mane and symbolize its strength. They now dance for themselves, they said, because the movements of the dance and the sound of the drums are as indispensable to them as air and water and fire. *Les Tambouriniers du Roi* have performed several times on tour in Europe, where they have understandably attracted great attention and applause.

—Overleaf—
We went to see Les Tambouriniers du Roi (the royal drummers) jumping and cavorting to the rhythm of their ancient drums.

The Watusi Intore
dancers gave us a regal
welcome.

The Ruzizi River descends from Lake Kivu, at 4,500 feet, to Lake Tanganyika and empties tons of mud into its blue waters.

Leopold accompanied us to the mouth of the Ruzizi river on the day of our departure and as he bade us farewell he said, clutching us firmly by the hand, 'Please be careful, remember that in Rwanda and Zaire the people are not like other Africans,' emphasizing an underlying fear of savagery born from past events. Only a few months earlier, the unfortunate French team who had attempted to shoot the Inga rapids, and had perished in Zaire, were rumoured to have been shot by snipers lurking in the trees and eaten by Zairian cannibals. They had been guests of Leopold at the Hôtel du Lac. Echoes of the horrific incident had in fact reached us in Mbeya and had created among our team a certain resistance to continuing.

The Ruzizi river links Lake Kivu at an altitude of 4,500 feet with Lake Tanganyika and empties tons of mud into its blue waters. (One hundred years ago Livingstone and Stanley, believing the Ruzizi to be the Nile, discovered, much to their disappointment, that the waters flowed into, instead of from, Lake Tanganyika.) Flocks of waterfowl, egrets and herons took flight in front of us, crocodiles slithered from exposed sandbanks into the muddy water and hippos plunged around us as we entered the delta. Ruzina, perched unperturbed astern our inflatable, took in the pageant with the aplomb of the weathered seaman, climbing all over everything and clutching at the steering wheel. Here we were back in primitive Africa, just a few miles north of the modern city of Bujumbura, bracing ourselves for cannibals . . .

The river is navigable for only three quarters of its length. We began hitting rocks just before the Rwanda border, and navigation became hazardous and difficult. The current was strong and we were often forced against the river banks and had to pull the boats through sticky patches by hand, standing in water that reached to our armpits. Hugo and Adam did us proud, keeping cool and concentrated under pressure and at times outsmarting Lorenzo with quick decisions and foresight that sometimes led to salty verbal exchanges. We damaged six propellors that day. Ruzina clutched the ropes, her eyes fixed on the churning waters. How quickly she had adapted to her new life with us, free from the awful harassment of her baboon

A hundred years ago Stanley and Livingstone, believing the Ruzizi to be the Nile, discovered to their disappointment that the waters flowed into — instead of from — Lake Tanganyika.

*Lorenzo and Hugo
plotting the day's route
on Lake Kivu.*

*— Opposite —
Our vehicles and our
team of Africans met us
at Makaro, where we
left the river and
continued into Rwanda
by road.*

cell-mates. She still clung to us a lot, but each day she ventured off more frequently on her own, rewarding us with moments of fearless independence.

Our vehicles, Charlie and our team of three Africans met us again at Makaro, where we left the river and continued into Rwanda by road, arriving at the border one Sunday afternoon at about four, intending to reach Cyangugu on Lake Kivu in Rwanda before nightfall. The customs officials were drunk and began questioning our permits, our film equipment and the enormous contents of our tightly packed lorry. Ruzina, who was travelling clandestinely without papers or permit, was tucked away at the bottom of our bedrolls in a special wooden box Hugo had built for her. Had she been discovered she would surely have been confiscated. After an hour of patient haggling with the drunk officials, assuring them that we had no guns, drugs or illegal merchandise and that the unloading of the vehicle at this late hour was not only a total waste of time but really quite unnecessary, they just looked at us with hooded, glazed eyes and slowly announced that it was not possible to proceed until permission from their superiors in Kigali – a hundred miles away – was obtained. It was Sunday evening and this was virtually impossible. Lorenzo tried to remain cool when the man insisted that he unload the vehicle before continuing, calling on every ruse in his repertoire to humour him, but to no avail. This was exactly the sort of situation we had dreaded and had so fortunately avoided when crossing the Tanzanian border at Lunga Lunga. Things began looking bleak as night crept in. Lorenzo pulled out the fake gold Rolex watch he had brought along for just such an eventuality, took the customs officer to one side and offered it to him as 'a little souvenir from our expedition'.

'*Mais, monsieur*, are you trying to bribe me?' he asked indignantly. 'I cannot accept this gift. It is against the law, don't you know?'

Taken aback by this unexpected reaction, Lorenzo turned away confused and embarrassed, hissing to us, 'The bloody man turned down my gold Rolex.'

It was getting cold and soon it would be dark; everyone was beginning to lose their carefully contained patience.

Arriving in an unknown town with no hotels and uncertain camping grounds at night was a problem we had not reckoned with, and we were making no headway. The outlook seemed grim.

When, after three hours, there seemed nothing more we could say or do, Lorenzo finally lost his temper. He began shouting at the customs officers, who gaped at him open-mouthed. He threatened to report them to the authorities in Kigali for being drunk on duty and obstructing his expedition, holding them responsible for time lost and consequent damages incurred. That did it. The arrogant authoritarian attitude collapsed and was instantly replaced by smiling servility.

'All right, all right, *monsieur*, don't get angry, we shall let you pass,' they laughed. 'You may go now, *bon voyage*,' they blurted as the barrier was lifted and we were ushered through.

No different from petty officials all over the world, in the borrowed authority of their uniform, they were pulling rank, but at the slightest show of strength they backed down. Their usual African joviality soon replaced any aggravation and there was much merriment as they waved goodbye and bade us '*bon voyage*', again imploring us to return to visit them. It was nine o'clock at night and we had been there, stuck, since four. We were now entering Hutu country, home of the Bantu tribe that had so savaged their aristocratic Watusi neighbours at independence; fearing for our safety, we began thinking of rescheduling our route to get out of Rwanda as fast as possible.

It was midnight when we finally entered Cyangugu. The winding road into the highlands had been heavy with mist and we had to proceed slowly round the hairpin bends, dodging downcoming traffic travelling fast with headlights full on. The delay at the border had drained us all and having now to search for a campsite in the dark put our resistance to test. We ended up in 'Rue de la Paix', the driveway of a Belgian Jesuit convent, to where a kindly soul at a bar directed us. A young Belgian padre, after hearing our story, invited us to pitch our tents for the night on the lawn of the convent, and we finally collapsed exhausted on our bedrolls after a long and enervating day. Ruzina snuggled up between Amina and me, and her little warm furry body and funny face helped erase the day's aggravation and rekindle a sense of humour.

We heard next day that there had been a volcanic eruption forty-eight hours earlier in the Virunga mountain chain to the north of Lake Kivu and that it was accessible on foot from Goma in Zaire. It was anyone's guess how long the eruption would continue and, because we didn't want to miss it, Lorenzo, Amina and I caught the shuttle plane from Bukavu, Cyangugu's sister town on the Zairian side of the border, and landed an hour later in Goma, leaving the rest of our team behind to rest or potter around the town.

In Goma one of our contacts lent us a vehicle which took us to the Park entrance from where, accompanied by a string of porters carrying our camping and camera equipment, we set out on one of the most gruelling treks I had yet had to cope with.

Initially the ascent was a gentle walk through a beautiful mountain forest with many extraordinary tropical trees of different varieties and mosses hanging from their branches. It was cool and encouraging beneath them and the footpath was soft, with only a gentle rise. We emerged from the forest two hours later and entered the lava zone, where an earlier flow had solidified into a carpet of jagged, porous stones that played havoc with our feet and ankles. The incline here was steep and the going began to slow down. Great cone-shaped mountains clad in trees rose to our left, where earlier eruptions had spewed out the molten innards of the earth and tufts of long grasses, cacti and flowering bushes had pushed through the black lava bed, clothing it with soft, faded colours. For three hours we snaked upwards in single file, stopping every half hour to catch our breath and rest our throbbing feet. The tough going had silenced us and all energy was now conserved for walking. No one was complaining yet, but the strain was beginning to show on our faces. The hardy, barefoot porters with the heavy loads on their heads, unaffected by the conditions, kept up a constant chatter, fuelling their rhythmic gait with endless stories, but when the day began fading and we realized that the four hours that still lay ahead of

A string of porters carried our camping and camera equipment on one of the most gruelling treks we had so far undertaken.

185

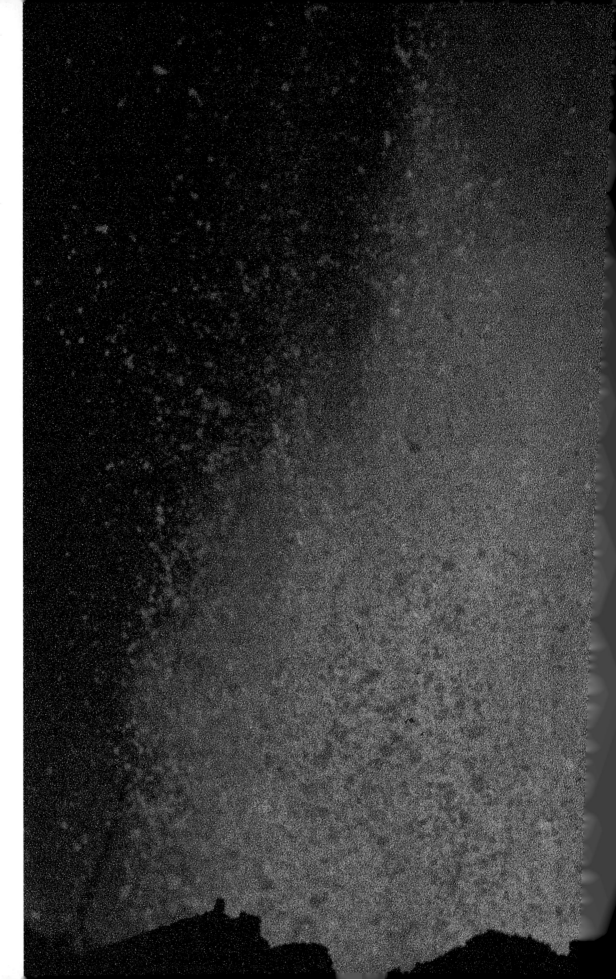

*And then we saw it —
enormous fountains of
fiery magma shooting
hundreds of feet into the
jet black sky at regular
intervals, followed by
fiendish exhalations as
the earth contracted and
vomited.*

us would have to be negotiated in the dark with torches, we understood that we had started out too late. 'A relatively easy walk will get you to the crater before dark,' we had been told in Goma.

As night fell, there was still no sign that we were getting near our goal other than a distant column of smoke ahead of us. The moon rose and then the first stars appeared in the clear sky, as the punishing, jagged lava slowly gave way to a porous gravel and outcroppings of petrified tree stumps that stood around us like pre-historic stone sculptures, strange devilish shapes, frozen and stilled long ago. An hour later, as we came over a rise, we saw the sky ahead of us aglow with firelight. 'Not far now,' the porters reassured us, injecting fresh vigour into our legs. We kept our eyes on the flow, trying to visualize the spectacle we were heading towards, imagining that with every step it was growing closer. On we went, step after step in silence, sweating and panting, with only our thoughts for company. But like a mirage it seemed always to be slipping back as we advanced. We were in fact drawing closer, but the dimensions we were dealing with dwarfed our footsteps and created a misleading optical illusion.

Then vision turned to sound and all around us the silent night began growling with bursts of distant thunder and the ghoulish swoosh of a giant evacuation. We were indeed getting close, but still all we could see was the glow in the sky. Moving like robots through the dark, stumbling over roots and fallen tree trunks, we entered another forest, and wove our way towards the light that was drawing us forward like a magnet. The air smelled of sulphur and the dark trees stood out rimmed in red. We were able to distinguish again the silhouettes of our companions, dark, ghostly figures moving through the trees, but by now we were so depleted we no longer felt our bodies; each step we took seemed to weigh a ton. On we went regardless of fatigue, drawing strength from anticipation, strangely exhilarated by the demonic sounds of Nature regurgitating, growing louder as the glow intensified. The air was getting warm and tiny particles of ash and charred pumice stone rained through the trees and settled over us; the ground crunched beneath our feet as step after step we moved closer to the giant cauldron.

Amina was in tears by now, imploring us to stop. 'Come on, we're nearly there,' I encouraged her, trying to pull her back on her feet. 'You can't stop now, just when we have almost arrived, we've come such a long way, get up.' And she forced herself to stand up again and put one foot in front of the other.

And then we saw it. Great fountains of fiery magma shooting hundreds of feet up into the jet-black sky at regular intervals, followed by fiendish exhalations as the earth contracted and vomited. We collapsed on to the bed of warm pumice gravel and sat in comatose silence propped against the charred trees, transfixed by the spectacle ahead of us. The rim of the crater, silhouetted like a cardboard cut-out against the curtain of shimmering, liquid fire, was hardly thirty yards from us. No one moved or spoke. My pulse was throbbing in my legs and hands. I looked at my watch; it was an hour before midnight. We had walked for nine hours to get here. Unaccustomed to such strenuous exercise, every muscle in our bodies screamed in pain as they began to stiffen, making any further movement difficult. But curiosity got the better of us; we pulled ourselves painfully back on to our feet and clambered up over the hot rocks to the edge of the crater. Below us the boiling cauldron of molten magma rose and fell in thick, sluggish waves as the earth heaved, and great sludgy bubbles swelled and burst, exuding sulphurous-smelling gas. Approximately every five seconds the liquid rock was ejected and rained back to earth in a shower of incinerated sparks that died and solidified again, slowly forming the cone-shaped mountains we had met along the way.

The rim of the crater was so hot that the soles of our shoes began to melt and we were forced to move back to the charred trees, where we looked for a suitable place to lay down our bedrolls for the night. The moon was now high in the sky and looked like a Christmas-tree decoration through the tinsel glitter of the fiery shower. Our porters had built a campfire and were brewing tea. We sat with them for a while and talked of God and Nature and the spirits of the Earth and listened to their mythic tales of dragons and ghosts, until one by one we keeled over and fell asleep among the roots of the trees beneath a soft rain of ash, rocked by the rumbling volcanic lullaby.

When we awoke next morning we were completely covered in a blanket of ash; the sleeping bodies lay in grey mounds amid the blackened tree skeletons rising naked and dead in the early-morning smoke haze. The volcano, still trembling and cracking with terrifying violence, was taking no rest. The phantasmagorical scene of the night before was now cold and menacing in the early-morning light. The fountain of fire had turned to billowing grey smoke through which the flames and incandescent rocks danced a last dance of death before falling forever to lifeless stone. Hypnotized by the intensity of this volcanic breathing we feared that the eruption might calm down, because it was more beautiful as it was: on the other hand we were aware that if it increased we could be incinerated in a few seconds.

It seemed as if we were in direct communication with the earth, but when later we met the volcanologist Maurice Kraft in Goma, he explained to us that this awesome sight was in fact only a small scratch on the earth's skin that was now bleeding. One assumes that the fiery magma comes from the centre of the earth, but

the fountains of lava rising one or two hundred yards into the air at a heat of 1,200 degrees Celsius are really only superficial. What we saw coming out of the volcano was superficial matter exiting under pressure from a depth of nine miles. The centre of the earth is at 3,750 miles. During the eruption which was just ending, the lava flow had travelled twelve miles in three days, which is considered a lot for this type of volcano. Here, where the excess energy of the Virunga mountain chain accumulates, eruptions occur every three or four years: the most impressive have been those of the Nyamuragira and the Nyragongo volcanoes. On 10 January 1977 the Nyragongo, which had a permanent lake of lava in its crater, emptied itself like a bath tub 1,200 yards above the town of Goma. All the lava came out of the side of the volcano and, travelling downhill at fifty miles per hour, the fastest flow Kraft had ever seen, killed about a hundred people and destroyed hundreds of acres of land.

Africa, Kraft explained, is a continent that is cracking. It has about three or four thousand volcanoes, several of which are still erupting, especially in the eastern region, better known as the Rift Valley, and in the central region where we now were. These cracks can reach eighteen or twenty miles in depth, allowing the molten rock, known as magma, to surface, and each eruption forms a cone-like volcano. This explains the existence of the Virunga chain surrounding Lake Kivu, considered one of the most beautiful volcanic areas of the world. Volcanoes produce small earthquakes, known as shakings, but real earthquakes, those of tectonic origins, are not attributable to volcanoes even though they take place in the same zones of the earth's crust. Earthquakes kill an average of 15,000 people per year and serve absolutely no purpose, while volcanoes provide a livelihood for millions of human beings, because volcanic earth is very fertile and contains calcium, potassium and many of the necessary substances for life. Volcanic ash in a hot and humid climate is fertilizer that falls from the sky, and this volcanic fertility provides life for three hundred million people in the world, three hundred million people who exist thanks to the volcanoes.

The return journey back down the mountain next day reduced us to pulp. We had not slept much the night before and the ascent had taxed us sorely. What was left of our energy was barely sufficient to get us back to base. Although the ground we were now covering was familiar, the journey seemed endless, and it was with indescribable relief that we stumbled back into the little compound.

When the manager of the hotel in Goma where we spent the night informed us on arrival that there was no hot water I almost wept. 'How could there be no hot water?' I sobbed to Amina. 'An expensive three-star hotel, even in Zaire, should have hot water, dammit.'

—Opposite—
Hypnotized by the intense beauty of the 'breathing' volcano, we feared that the eruption might calm down, yet we were also aware that, if it increased, we could be incinerated in a few seconds.

191

CHAPTER TEN

NEVER STAND UP TO A GORILLA

A WEEK LATER WE CROSSED THE BORDER INTO ZAIRE, AND in Bukavu made arrangements to visit the mountain gorillas of the Kahuzi Biega National Park, about twelve miles from the Rwanda border. Due to paranoid Zairian bureaucracy we had had to leave our vehicles and the African team behind in Rwanda. We set up a small 'fly' camp on the edge of the park; movement was confined to our feet and the occasional park vehicle.

Citoyen Mushenzi, the Zairian park warden who had replaced the founder of the park, Adrian de Shriver, who, with Dian Fossey, had brought the plight of the endangered great apes to the attention of the world, received us with courtesy and grace, especially so after reading an introductory letter from the Minister of Wildlife in Kinshasa, whom we had met by chance on the slopes of the volcano – a fortunate coincidence, like many others that had facilitated our expedition; 'We have divine guidance,' Lorenzo would often chuckle to me on such occasions. Mushenzi, a soft-spoken, educated Zairois, personally took us into the forest to introduce us to his apes and provided a rare insight into the possible relationship between man and beast once confidence and respect is established.

The Kahuzi Biega National Park was created in 1973; since then it has changed greatly, growing from 150,000 to 1,500,000 acres. Although the exact number of the total population is not yet known, at present only 250 gorillas living in the park are protected by the rangers. The two families of Maeshe and Mushamuka which

Citoyen Mushenzi and his team are monitoring consist of twenty-seven and eighteen members respectively, and are relatively easily approached by visitors.

As with the volcano, the encounter with the gorillas was as primal and fundamental as the setting. To get to them we trudged again for several hours through undergrowth so thick it had to be cut away by trackers to allow for our passage. The heat and humidity trapped in the vegetation was intense and debilitating and the tall trees shut out the daylight, emphasizing once again the inflexible nature of the wilderness, where survival is a ceaseless battle and stamina the immutable law; where only the strong survive. It was our first encounter with gorillas and we were not quite sure what to expect. The prelude was filled with mystery, and the knowledge that they were lurking somewhere behind the leaves, like prehistoric shadows, provoked a certain apprehension.

At the Kahuzi Biega National Park, the day begins with the hoisting of the Zairian flag, an attempt at military discipline. The duty of the guards here is to protect the mountain gorillas who live in the forest designated to the park, and the day we arrived they had pulled in four poachers, who now stood manacled to each other as the flag went up and the bugle sounded. Poachers do not kill gorillas only for food: they now fashion severed hands into ashtrays and skulls into grotesque lamps which they sell to passing tourists. In the camp we found an old colonial litter used a century ago by the Belgian King Leopold. Comfortably travelling on the shoulders of porters in this way, many colonial civil servants wrote home, describing their travels in Africa as 'exhausting'. We were asked not to sit in the chair, perhaps in order to avoid unpleasant recollections, and we couldn't help wondering what sentiments the people here still felt towards their colonial past.

Citoyen Mushenzi gave us a little talk before we started on our trek through the forest. 'Never stand up to a gorilla when charged, never mimic his gestures; never eat or smoke in his presence. Although partially habituated to the presence of humans, gorillas are wild animals to be respected, and any misinterpretations of the basic jungle laws can be hazardous. Gorilla families are protected by a dominant male called a silver back, because of the silvery-white fur that grows like a saddle on his back. He demands total submission and wields absolute power; when this is challenged his castigation can be alarming and sometimes fatal. Alarm or displeasure must be met with meekness and respect, never challenged. Mock charges are initial warnings, and should a male gorilla stand erect, prostration is one's only defence.' One of Mushenzi's visitors had once stood up to a silver back's ire and in a flash had had his shoulder dislocated and was flung sprawling to his knees in the bushes.

With Mushenzi's words still ringing in our ears, we moved forward with caution, senses on full alert, as there was no saying how soon we would meet up with our quarry. Gorillas are browsers; their daily movements are determined by food availability. Their range in the park is anything from half an hour's to five hours' trek through the forest. Mushenzi and his team kept tabs on the two families of Maeshe and Mushamuka, monitoring them and habituating them to man. Although he knew more or less in what direction to lead us, it was not until signs began appearing in the undergrowth that we knew we were approaching our quarry. Stripped bark, discarded overnight nests, and fresh faeces traced a definite trail for us to follow, and our anticipation grew as the evidence became more apparent. Now and again a great crashing of branches or a chilling scream would make us freeze in our steps and look up at the silent wall of green around us; but the buzz of invisible insects or the flight of an unseen bird was the only message emanating from the silent green tapestry.

Then we came upon him, suddenly, without further warning, sitting like a silent black Buddha among the leaves; my heart immediately began to beat faster. There we were, hardly ten feet from him. 'It's Mushamuka,' Mushenzi whispered quietly. 'His family must be close by.' The great face with its squashed 'plastic' snout and gaping nostrils remained immobile; the deepset jet eyes pinned us like lasers to the greenery. Mushenzi talked to him with soothing tones, quietly interspersing his words with a deep throaty growl, a sign, he later explained, that we had come in peace. Mushamuka answered him with an identical growl; a greeting was exchanged. He momentarily relaxed his gaze and began looking around for edible leaves. Then he put out a long hairy arm and grabbed hold of a vine above his head. He yanked it towards him and slowly drew it through the great yellow fangs from one side of his mouth to the other, disdainfully discarding the stripped stem and masticating the leaves that remained in his mouth. He was calm and it was clear he did not resent our presence. Then he turned from us and ambled heavily into the undergrowth like a haughty, bored monarch, momentarily showing us his great haunches and powerful silver back. He left us standing there, as the vegetation closed over him and he disappeared from sight. We followed him, keeping a respectful distance, until we came upon his family.

In a clearing, three females were searching in the undergrowth for edible leaves and berries, while several youngsters gambolled around them on the carpet of dry forest leaves. Mushamuka sauntered up to them through the trees, bearing down on his knuckles, his muscular body rippling through his fur. He was an impressive beast; his sheer size and corpulence commanded respect and subordination.

The structure of a gorilla family varies little. There is always a dominant silverback male who controls every activity from the feeding grounds to the nesting and reproduction. The male mates from the age of fifteen and the female from the age of eight, when she becomes fertile. There are several females in each family and they produce one infant at a time after a gestation period of nine months. As long as the dominant male remains head of the family no other male may couple with them.

Gorillas are not territorial, so the families do not defend the areas in which they live, cohabiting peacefully in the same environment without frontiers or conflicts. In the volcanic mountain regions of Kahuzi Biega, at an altitude of 3,500 to 10,000 feet, live less than a thousand gorillas. The steady growth of the local human population is rapidly eroding their territories and in Rwanda, where this growth has reached a density of 1,500 people per square mile, the highest in all Africa, the gorillas are now on the endangered-species list. Despite the laudable efforts of conservationists around the world, gorillas are still being hunted both in Rwanda and in Zaire, and are being driven further into the centre of the great forests, their existence threatened by the advancing masses, who cut down the forests and destroy their natural habitat to make room for plantations.

Gorillas eat medicinal plants; the only cases of premature death are caused by broncho-pulmonary diseases, as gorillas are vulnerable during seasonal changes of climate. The young especially do not know how to protect themselves from the cold and rain and they know no remedies for these sicknesses, but by eating certain herbs, which they recognize in the forest, they can rid themselves of diarrhoea and other minor illnesses.

We stayed with Mushamuka and his family for approximately one hour before they moved away from us through the trees. 'It's time to go,' Mushenzi told us. 'We must not overstay our welcome; I think they have had enough for today.' But we persuaded him to let us stay a little longer. Mushamuka threw furtive glances at us over his shoulder as he herded his family in front of him. Aware of these nervous signals, Mushenzi kept between him and us, cajoling him with soothing words and grunts. We were too engrossed to notice his subtle change in mood, when suddenly Mushamuka stopped and faced us and in a flash came at us, hurtling like an express train through the undergrowth, baring his great yellow fangs and growling like an angry lion. Lorenzo remained poised behind his camera as he felt there was nothing else he could do, but we others froze and dropped to our knees, our eyes glued to the ground in front of us. About a yard from us, Mushamuka skidded to a halt and remained menacingly immobile, piercing us with his irate eyes, defying us to take another step. There was no question who was the dominant figure at this point. '*Du calme, mon vieux, du calme!*' (Keep calm, old boy, keep calm), Mushenzi reassured

—*Overleaf left*—
Citoyen Mushenzi, the Zairian park warden who replaced Adrian de Shriver, talked to Mushamuka in soothing tones, interspersing his words with a deep, throaty growl.

—*Overleaf right*—
We came across Mushamuka suddenly, without warning, sitting like a silent black Buddha among the leaves.

195

him, grunting loudly. Mushamuka held his ground until he was satisfied we had understood and then turned slowly and merged with the forest. 'I think we'd better go now,' Mushenzi said politely. 'It is a warning we must not ignore.' No one protested, and we obediently turned and started our homeward trek.

That night around the camp fire Mushenzi talked to us about his life with the gorillas and introduced us to Romain Baertson, a Belgian, who had spent many years filming the gorillas. Next day we again went into the forest, this time with Romain, and sat with him observing Maeshe and his family; a young female detached herself from the group and moved over to him. Romain did not stir as she climbed on to his lap, put an arm around his neck and remained locked for a moment in a tender embrace. Then she turned and faced him, straddling him, a leg on either side, and began gently pounding him on the shoulders with her cupped hands, in a gesture of such familiarity and trust he could have been her mate. We remained transfixed, gawking at them in disbelief, astonished at Romain's cool head. This was, after all, a wild gorilla; we were not in a circus. Then she got bored and climbed off, pulling him over behind her by the neck as she left him. Romain rolled on to the ground and remained quite still as her jealous partner admonished her in no uncertain terms. A furious skirmish ensued in which she defended herself valiantly, indicating clearly the existence of a sexual rivalry similar to our own.

Approximately sixty miles west of Kahuzi Biega, on the severed road between Bukavu and Kisangani, we transferred our equipment across the Irangi river by means of an ingenious vine bridge, one of those original masterpieces Africa sometimes surprises one with. Constructed entirely with offshoots from the forest, the bridge hangs about thirty feet above the rocky river bed, spanning it in a great 200-yard swoop, suspended by thick, ropy vines that vibrated like the strings of a great jungle harp as we passed, and fastened to overhanging branches. Made entirely of bamboo, lashed and fastened together by slimmer vines, 'le pont des lianes' is a masterly creation of jungle engineering. On the other side of the river the abandoned hunting lodge of Leopold II, King of the Belgians, hung disconsolately over the rushing waters, empty and useless now, a lonely landmark to a contemptible colonial reign in what Joseph Conrad referred to as the 'vilest race towards destruction in the history of mankind'.

We spread out our bedrolls on the slatted wooden verandah and prepared to spend the night in the royal hunting lodge. The gamekeeper was still there, only just alive, perhaps 90 or 100 years old – hard to tell with Africans. Wizened, bent and white-haired he resembled one of those wooden statuettes sold to passing tourists on the roads of Africa. The years had gnawed at his body, but his mind and memory were still sharp and his beady black eyes full of the inextinguishable laughter of Africa. His name was Alfonse. He shuffled over and greeted us in the endearing manner of the colonial epoch, when blacks were subservient to whites; he addressed us as *Bwana* and *Memsahib*, a label now unfamiliar to our ears, but which still struck a chord somewhere deep inside. His welcome was suffused with the jubilation once extended to a returning master, and we were all deeply moved. We told him briefly of our expedition, and asked permission to stay the night. 'Of course, of course, but the house is quite empty, there are only two wooden beds, and no mattresses,' he said almost apologetically as he led us down the little path to the lodge.

A grand and regal quality still permeated the site, sheltered on all sides by the majestic primal forest and the sparkling water, dancing and rumbling over the stony river bed. The simple wooden construction hung over it, and little log bridges with vine banisters led to the quiet interior, where the wood of the floor was swept clean and was still surprisingly bright, almost polished. There were some old colonial armchairs and a round drinks table on the covered verandah, and in the centre of the room stood a long refectory table with benches on either side. The place had once belonged to a king and, as such, its ancient keeper watched over it with veneration. It was astonishing still to meet such deeply implanted devotion after the atrocities once perpetrated by the colonial overlords, particularly in view of the manner in which the country was ravaged at independence, when all the savagery of Africa was unleashed in one of the most diabolical dances of death and destruction the continent has known. The gentleness and laughter of black people, their lack of rancour and their welcome were all embodied in this shrivelled old man, who himself contributed a natural sense of ancestral dignity to the place.

But an unhappy incident that evening cast a pall across the timeless scene. At our candle-lit dinner around the refectory table, Hugo said he had an announcement to make: he and the rest of the team had decided to withdraw from the expedition. The words rang like bullet fire in the quiet night. Aware of their gravity, Hugo's delivery was nervous, his face flushed; one could almost feel his heart beating beneath his light cotton shirt. He stumbled on, searching for appropriate words, while the others sat stony-faced around him, watching our reactions, like a bunch of rebellious students confronting their tutors; an incongruous situation, I thought, for such an unreal setting. Outside the river rushed on and the nightjars ululated in the trees.

Lorenzo waited for Hugo to stop. He let the silence hang for a while and then

— Overleaf left —
We transported our equipment over the Irangi river, sixty miles west of Kahuzi Biega, by means of this ingenious bridge.

— Overleaf right —
Made entirely of bamboo lashed together with vines, le pont des lianes is a masterly creation of jungle engineering.

199

Each night, beside the campfire, Lorenzo would brief the team on his plan for the next day.

203

slowly rose from his seat, keeping his blue headlight eyes fixed on Hugo. Then he exploded. He banged the table hard with the palm of his right hand and shouted, 'Traitors, you are a bunch of traitors! Now that we are entering Zaire and you have had the fun, you're walking out on me, just when I need you most . . . cowards, get out of here, all of you, tomorrow, take your things and go, find your own ways back to Kenya, you make me sick . . . I'm going to bed.' He marched off into the dark, towards the room with the two wooden beds. It was an impressive exit if nothing else, even though I didn't entirely approve of the delivery.

All eyes turned to me, expecting some conciliatory reaction. I was momentarily speechless. The four young faces with their intense, worried expressions and tousled, sun-streaked hair lit by the candlelight demanded a response from me. I took my time, trying to remain collected as I searched for the right words and arguments to reopen a dialogue, rummaging in my mind through the past month for tell-tale signs of discontent.

As each one unloaded his or her feelings, a pattern not dissimilar to the malaise of our 'pilgrims' earlier in the trip began to take shape, and many of the same symptoms surfaced, symptoms which have always plagued all expeditions: the lack, among the ordinary members of the expedition, of a sense of purpose. This was essentially Lorenzo's dream and, no matter how committed and enthusiastic our teams might have been, their motivations could not in any way be as strong as ours. It is a subtle nuance which in an expedition is very significant because of the diversity of objectives; a gnawing sense of inadequacy begins to undermine the goal until a point is reached at which everything is tainted by it. The explorers of Africa all referred to the same symptoms in their memoirs. Although this second team was head and shoulders above the first, the basic human elements we were dealing with were the same: those of the leader and the led. Lorenzo's temper is easily roused and he refused to allow any negative input to undermine the expedition, regardless of its nature. His single-minded determination to move forward at all costs could understandably have sometimes seemed ruthless and unacceptable and have given rise to tensions, misinterpretations and insecurities which, if not dispersed, could be very disruptive. I heard them out one by one. I sympathized at times with their arguments; they were a good bunch, but mental fatigue was beginning to set in. There was no malice or devilry in what they said; they were understandably in need of a booster and I sensed an unspoken reticence to enter Zaire. They had been frightened by the stories we had heard. I interjected my own feelings and comments and tried to explain Lorenzo and his reaction, leaving it to them to decide whether they wished to continue or not. When we had exhausted the subject we simply stopped. There was nothing left to say and we all felt better for it.

The candles on the table had burned down and had spread in a little wax flow around each flame.

'OK, let's call it a day and go to bed,' I said. 'We'll sort something out tomorrow.'

One by one they got up and came over to me. They put their arms around me and kissed me. 'Thanks for listening,' they said, a bit bashfully.

'That's what I'm here for,' I said, tweaking a muscular buttock, feeling much like an old mama.

We parted in good spirits and headed for our respective bedrolls. I blew out the candles on the table and tiptoed in the dark to the room where Lorenzo was fast asleep, spread-eagled on one of the wooden beds. I crawled in beside him and he awoke.

He held out his arms and said, 'This has got to be the most fantastic night of my life, listen to the river and the wind in the trees, the sounds of Africa are so clear and mysterious, how lucky we are!'

I burst out laughing. 'You really are a strange bird. Have you been listening to the conversation on the other side of this partition?' I asked a little bemused.

'Bits of it,' he mumbled. 'Let them go, we'll get another team together, this time it will be all black; no one is indispensable, you know.'

My mind veered back to the month I spent in Nairobi single-handedly getting this team together and the difficulties and complexities of making the right match. The idea of starting again in mid-flight was not enticing at the moment. 'We'll talk about that in the morning,' I yawned, trying to draw down the shutter of my brain. It was two o'clock; I was feeling the strain. I lay awake for a while in the silence and the dark, listening to the night sounds of the jungle, sorting out a multitude of conflicting sensations, and finally fell asleep.

Next morning everyone was feeling better. I persuaded Lorenzo to apologize for his outburst and another exchange took place, in which differences were aired and cleared over percolating coffee and dunking bread. Lorenzo's choleric outbursts are instantaneous but thankfully shortlived, and he bears no rancour. He has a ready handshake, is quick to apologize if he has wronged someone, and he can usually offer a witty comment that can turn the tables, leaving the aggrieved party off balance, confused and, in this particular case, reconciled. That is the diabolical side of his nature. He had forced them to talk. We moved on, reinforced, towards a common goal in a new spirit of kinship and dependency, propelled by Lorenzo's enthusiasm, his good humour and ready wit.

CHAPTER ELEVEN

SLAVES, CANNIBALS AND SHARPSHOOTERS

BACK IN BUKAVU ONCE MORE, WE PREPARED FOR ANOTHER important overland portage, this time by air, there being no other recourse. We decided to hire Adrian de Shriver and his aircraft, a strange antediluvian-looking machine, the like of which still operate in remote regions like Zaire, as the only other way to reach the Ulindi river in Zaire was a ten-day march on foot. Man and machine shared a certain no-nonsense sullenness that had to do with the nature of their work, transport flying to the remoter regions of the country, inaccessible to any other conveyance, which in Zaire meant touching down and lifting off on makeshift strips that only a seasoned flier like Adrian could negotiate. For a thousand dollars he flew us and our expedition 200 miles west to Shabunda, deep in the heart of Zaire, where we planned to relaunch our boats on the Ulindi river, the nearest fluvial junction on our westward route.

For four hours we flew over an unending expanse of matted green jungle that undulated in a leafy symphony to the horizon. Above us the hazy sky looked ominous, with great banks of storm clouds spiralling into the blue yonder. An aura of foreboding permeated the scene outside. Inside the aircraft we all sat subdued and silent among our equipment, piled haphazardly on the floor. Brooding thoughts of the ugly tales we had heard came creeping back to mind; we were entering the heart of darkness, and no one knew what lay beneath the thick green mantle below us. This was the land of the cannibals and sharpshooters whom we had been warned about earlier on in Kenya, and then again by Leopold when he bade us goodbye in Bujumbura, and we would be on our own once the aircraft had deposited us and flown off. Now and again the vegetation parted and we sighted great bends of brown river snaking through the trees; thatched huts set out in clearings on the river banks indicated the presence of humans – the cannibals, no doubt – then the green mantle closed and the secret world vanished. We were left with an intensifying sense of mystery.

Without warning the aircraft dipped and dropped through one of the openings in the clouds, and within minutes we were circling the airstrip of Shabunda. A lonely, partially ripped windsock, the only familiar beacon in this alien setting, guided us to touchdown, and we bumped and vibrated along the grassy strip as the great trees on either side shot past. The place looked desolate enough, just thick vegetation and long, pale green grass, no sign of life; but as the aircraft swung around at the end of the runway a mass of people, perhaps 500 or 1,000 strong, had already emerged from the trees and had gathered in a tightly packed cluster, moving like a coloured oil slick on to the strip – a vivid tableau against the lush green backdrop.

The airblast from the propellors made their bright clothes flap about their legs, and made them squint and grimace. When the engines were turned off and the door flung open, a momentary hush hung in the steaming air, a feeling of excited expectancy, as the plane prepared to disgorge its load.

When Lorenzo appeared at the door with his white beard and straw hat a wave of 'aaahs' rolled towards the plane and then exploded in a cacophony of animated chatter and much laughter, which surged as each one of us appeared and the outboard engines, boats, bags and boxes were unloaded.

'Well, here we are in Shabunda,' Lorenzo said cheerfully. 'These must be the cannibals!'

Half a dozen men detached themselves from the crowd and came forward to greet Adrian, shaking him by the hand, clearly happy to see him. Adrian, in his dark blue flying slacks, spotless white cotton shirt and golden shoulder pips, his close-shaved, no-nonsense face and tightly cropped hair, stood out among them much like ET arriving on earth. A roar went up when Ruzina appeared in Amina's arms; the crowd went wild and rushed the plane with so much enthusiasm they had to be beaten off with long whips.

A couple of sinister-looking fellows in camouflage combat fatigues and mirror sunglasses holding Kalashnikovs pushed through the crowd and sauntered arrogantly over to us, greeting us churlishly in French. '*Donne-moi tes cigarettes,*' one of them barked at Adam as he was lighting up. I felt Adam's spine contract as he swung around to face him. Without a murmur he handed him the pack, distinctly intimidated by the aggressiveness.

'What did you do that for?' I hissed at him. 'There was no need to give him the whole pack, they'll strip you naked if you let them get away with it.' Adam looked disconcerted and a bit crestfallen. '*Tu me donnes une cigarette?*' I asked them as they began lighting up, and watched for a reaction.

'*Mais bien sûr, madame,*' they retorted, offering me the pack.

'*Merci,*' I said, withdrawing one and gently taking the pack from them. 'I'll give them back to my friend. They are his last pack, you know.'

Adam looked at me agog.

'You've got to know how to play the game,' I said to him. 'We must test the temperature and establish exactly who is who.'

The two men laughed. Zairians, I knew, were great comedians and used any ruse to obtain what they wanted. Military uniforms and guns were an excellent ploy in their little mind-games.

Adrian bade us farewell and wished us luck; he swung the props, climbed back into his white space-machine and was soon airborne, leaving us behind on the ground with our new entourage and only our legs for transport. Beyond the airstrip the secret world awaited us.

Lorenzo and Hugo left us to mind the equipment while they set off to explore. As they turned to leave, a white man appeared through the maze of black faces and moved towards us. He introduced himself in a thick German accent.

'Klaus Klass is my name, I live here, can I be of help?' His manner was friendly and reassuringly warm. 'I have a small truck, maybe you would like to load your equipment on it and leave it in my compound for the time being.'

If this was not divine guidance I don't know what is. Lorenzo winked at me and then introduced us one at a time. How many times had situations like this arisen all along our expedition, to help us solve impending dilemmas.

Klaus was prospecting for gold, he told us later as we swilled bottles of ice-cold Heineken beer beneath a thatched straw gazebo in his compound. He had been in Shabunda for three years and only twice touched base in Bukavu, where he kept a Zairian wife. He had not been back to the *Vaterland* for twenty years, and had no desire to return. He was making good money here in Zaire, buying gold from the Zairian miners who excavated it from deep inside the jungle, about 150 miles from Shabunda.

Klaus was one of those white men one encounters only in Africa, one of a breed of solitary fortune-hunters who pit their brains against the devilish elements of Nature and, if they do not die, usually come away with the booty and retire from the race. Guts, patience and perseverance and a certain dose of luck are the essential elements required to resist the monotony and solitude of such a strange and bizarre existence, but it has its challenges, he assured us, and for some men can be understandably alluring. What drives a man like Klaus into the heart of Zaire to look for gold, I wondered. His neat appearance, sandalled feet, tightly cropped hair, and the gold neck chain didn't fit the preconceived idea of this type of man. Refined and well read, he spoke perfect French and English and Lingala, a Zairian dialect, and what he did not know about Zaire was not worth knowing.

He was obviously pleased at our arrival and laughed when we told him of our fears and the rumours of savagery.

'The Zairians', he told us, 'are among the most hospitable, friendly and intelligent people in this part of Africa. I am in business with at least a dozen of them and have never yet had reason to complain. I travel around the country on my own or with them, sometimes with considerable amounts of gold in my vehicles; there has never been an incident. If you treat them right they respect you, but if you try to trick or outsmart them they can become very vicious. These are the incidents one hears about. Zairians still have a great respect for white people, perhaps because of the colonial period. The Belgians were tough, exacting masters who exploited them to the bone, but who also cared for them. Since the Belgian exodus they have had to revert back to living by their wits, and the living conditions have naturally deteriorated considerably. Very few white people come to Zaire these days, and when they do the Zairois try to exploit them whenever possible, but they never lose respect: nasty incidents are rare.'

I watched the expressions on the faces of our team reveal a mixture of relief and still a certain disbelief as they listened to Klaus's reassuring words. The farewell message of Leopold in Bujumbura returned to mind: 'Be careful of the Zairois, they are not like other Africans . . .' We were off to a good start, and were suddenly much elated by the prospects ahead. The Zairian leg we always felt was going to be the most complex but also the most intriguing and stimulating. And now that the element of menace had been removed, the anticipation was reinforced. Meeting Klaus had done a lot to boost morale and put us on the right course.

We set up camp within his compound and that night were hit by one of the heaviest rainstorms of the expedition. The fat tropical raindrops began to fall soon after we had retired to our tents and were snugly tucked away inside our sleeping bags. We listened to the drops explode on the canvas of our tents, thankful for the relative shelter Klaus had offered us inside the compound, but as the night wore on the rain increased and soon the ground was so saturated that water began seeping up through the groundsheet; before long we were floating as if we were lying on waterbeds. Through the little opening in the flap of the tent I watched my sandals float away and could see the hurricane lamp I had left outside now half-immersed in water. I quickly realized this was to be the end of our peaceful night. One by one we crawled out of our little dome tents and, disregarding the rain, broke camp in the dark, transferring bedrolls, goods and chattels into Klaus's store room, which had a rainproof roof. A few hours before daybreak, soaked and muddied inside Klaus's shed, we crawled back into our sodden sleeping bags. What was extraordinary was that we all actually went back to sleep in our waterlogged predicament and awoke next morning, stiff and grouchy, to a brilliant sunny day, and began to dry out.

The elders of the village dropped by to pay their respects. They brought us freshly baked *petit pain* from the local *boulangerie* and we shared our *café au lait* with them. They were intrigued by our expedition route and wanted news from the world outside. Shabunda had once been one of the provincial administrative centres of the Belgians, but since they had left all manner of communication with the outside world had been interrupted, and Adrian's plane was now the only purveyor of news and goods, such as Klaus's Heineken beer. Our little group of new friends all spoke French and through them we were able slowly to penetrate the mood of the country we were about to cross. The forecasts were encouraging and reassuring, a significant element in our long journey to the Atlantic, for here in Zaire we would be almost entirely dependent on the goodwill of the people. Points of contact and communications were few and far between and one had to learn to use the jungle network; it was important to connect with the people.

Outside the compound gates the village of Shabunda was still drenched in rain mist. The palm trees on either side of the main earth avenue rose dark and ghostlike through the vapour haze, steeped in morning stillness. People moved about like dark shadows wandering in a dream. The hot, harsh colours of the day before on the airstrip were now soft and subdued, as if the rain had mellowed the vigour of this forceful country, concealing the harshness of its dire struggle to survive. Mist, on hot rainy days, gives Africa a Nordic aspect to which one is not accustomed, especially here in the midst of the tropics. Here in Shabunda people had learned to survive with little. The market-place was pathetically devoid of produce. Women sat with legs stretched out in front of them hawking pitiable mounds of beans and manioc, a few sticks of sugar cane, three or four sweet potatoes, a few sun-dried river fish, some green bananas, all carefully laid out beside them on fibre mats.

The abandoned Belgian administration buildings were soiled and flaking and in need of repair. The tin shacks and mud huts strung out in a row around the market-place were primitive; some served as shops selling printed Zairian cloth, never more than a dozen pieces, or bread baked each morning when flour was available and *terminé* an hour later. It was a hand-to-mouth existence which seemed shocking at first glance, but somehow the people appeared to cope and now, in the misty morning, as the sun seeped through the palm fronds, the reality of this vast, dramatic country seemed chastened, and the eternal, redeeming smile of Africa came through. I gave some flour and yeast from our provision box to the fat Zairian Mama who kept the bakery and asked her if she would bake some bread for our journey. She was happy to oblige, of course, if we could also give her some wood or charcoal for her oven; she smiled at me and in that smile I read a millennium of struggle and resignation, but there was also the courage and defiance which kept the nation and indeed the whole continent from foundering.

Klaus drove us in his pickup to the edge of the Ulindi river about five miles outside the village, where we launched one of the inflatables for an initial reconnaissance trip. We had heard conflicting reports about its navigability and Lorenzo proposed an exploratory spin. We had planned to reach Kindu on the Laulaba river by boat from Shabunda, but some impassable rapids a few miles downstream soon put an end to the day's exploration.

Back in Klaus's compound that night we rerouted our westerly journey to Kalima, which we would now have to reach by road. Mme Thérèse, an energetic black lady of about forty, was called in and we negotiated to hire her ten-ton M.A.N. lorry for the next day's journey through the jungle.

Mme Thérèse lived next door to Klaus's compound. Her husband, she told us, had been Minister of Transport and, when he died a few years back in a road accident, he left her the lorry and the compound with the two tin-roofed brick houses she now lived in with her family. Two married daughters and a brood of grandchildren sat around her on wooden chairs when we stopped by to inspect the vehicle. Mme Thérèse made an adequate living with her transport business. She was not rich, but she was comfortable and she had educated all her children, several of them at a Belgian university, she told us proudly.

All transactions were payable in advance and for cash, of course; she made no distinctions between her clients and credit was not accepted. Thérèse was a respected figure in Shabunda. She carried on her business with aplomb, counting payments personally on her lap and stashing the money in great elastic-bound wads in a locked box beneath her bed.

The palm trees down the main avenue of Shabunda rose dark and ghostlike through the mist, steeped in morning stillness.

Her driver, Louis, was a seasoned road warrior, strong, thickset, about fifty, with a large beer belly and prominent biceps accentuated by the tight T-shirt he wore beneath his blue denim jacket; he had the aspect of a man on the move; little things about him, his cap, his shoes, the signet ring on his finger, were obvious city merchandise. Louis had worked for Mme Thérèse and her husband for many years and was as much part of the set-up as the massive vehicle he drove. Like Adrian de Shriver and his aircraft, man and vehicle resembled one another. They were tough. Louis was a friendly, jovial fellow and nothing was ever a problem for him. If the road was passable and the bridges intact after the last rainstorm, he would get us to Kalima before nightfall of the day of departure, but of course much depended on the conditions of travel, which he could not vouch for.

'Don't worry, you are in good hands,' Mme Thérèse assured us, patting Louis on the shoulder as she received the wads of grubby 'Zaires' Klaus handed her in exchange for the crisp dollar travellers' cheques Lorenzo had given him.

Money here in Shabunda held the same power as anywhere else, even if there was precious little to spend it on. Because we were well accustomed to the hazards of

Before leaving Shabunda, Klaus snapped a souvenir picture of his new friends.

overloading in Africa, we paid a little more to have Louis and the truck exclusively for ourselves.

'Ça va, the truck is yours all the way to Kalima,' Mme Thérèse confirmed; but when next day it appeared ready for loading in front of the gates of Klaus's compound, a long line of people had already collected along the palm avenue with their belongings in great baskets on their heads or in bags strapped to their backs. News of an imminent departure had leaked and these were evidently hopeful passengers, just what we had expected and wanted to avoid by paying extra.

'Don't worry,' Louis said again, 'the lorry is yours today, I will not let anyone board.'

But once our expedition equipment was loaded and we were ready to depart, the line of patient, waiting people broke ranks and began throwing their belongings on board, scrambling after them like refugees on a last departing vessel, passing their babies, their chickens and their goats to those already embarked. Louis made some feeble attempts to stop them and then moved over and stood next to Mme Thérèse on the side of the road and looked on helplessly without saying anything. We exchanged glances and they just shrugged their shoulders and grinned at me.

'I thought we had hired your lorry just for ourselves,' I shouted down at them.

'What can we do, these people have been waiting for transport for two weeks,' she laughed back passively.

Any further comment was pointless. This was part of the jungle network and we had to go along with it.

All our equipment, the engines, the rubber boats, the hurricane lamps, the bedrolls were now submerged beneath bags of smelly manioc and charcoal, chickens, bananas and goats. Seventy-five people climbed on board.

'Alors, on y va,' Louis shouted, honking the horn as he climbed into his seat and fired the great diesel engine with a roar.

Everyone shouted and waved and Klaus blew kisses at us. He seemed sad to see us go. We had become friends over the past three days and he had put himself entirely at our disposal. It was part of the solidarity of bush people.

Perched on top of the cabin roof and squeezed in among the load of freight, shoulder to shoulder with our new travelling companions, hugging their babies, we took off down the majestic palm avenue to a roar of joyfulness. The whole village came to see us off, and were now shouting 'Bon voyage, revenez vite nous voir, on vous aime' (Have a good trip, come back and see us, we love you). Klaus was wearing the African Rainbow T-shirt and slacks we had given him as a souvenir; slowly we left Shabunda, and a little piece of our hearts, behind.

Hugo, Adrian, Charlie and Juliette enjoyed the expedition more than our first team from Europe.

The 500-mile journey from Shabunda to Kalima was memorable. The road was rough and deeply furrowed and still very wet, but Louis was a veteran driver and he guided his vehicle forward with great expertise, keeping the engine revs constant and the tyres level whenever possible. Perched high on top, it felt much as if we were riding on a camel, and we had to maintain a steady grip in order to avoid ejection. From our elevated vantage-point the spectacle of the rain forest we had flown over a few days before was formidable. The great trees rose hundreds of feet in a massive wall of green to either side of the ochre road. Beneath them it was dark and dank and the shafts of sunlight filtered down through them as in a holy picture, picking out the profusion of shades and shapes and outlining the long dark tree trunks, the pillars of the great green cathedral.

The daunting force of this primal jungle was incontestable and emphasized once again our own insignificance. Living in such close proximity with Nature, we were kept acutely aware of the planet which man today is slowly destroying as he ventures to dominate it. This unequal relationship between man and Nature in Africa is similar to his relationship with a masterpiece he disregards. In Africa Nature has unwittingly erected the greatest of all monuments to herself, and man, whether through greed or necessity, is systematically dismantling it. The journey from Shabunda to Kalima gave us a revealing insight into Nature's ecosystems when man and his environment are in balance. In most parts of Zaire the inhabitants have been forced to maintain a particular affinity with their surroundings; because progress here has been halted, the rhythm of Nature has been mercifully preserved, and, just as in Joseph Conrad's days, in the great forest 'the vegetation still riots and the tall trees are kings'; whereas in Rwanda and all round the shores of Lake Kivu, where the devastation is almost total, the situation is alarming, acting like a regenerating cancerous cell multiplying and spreading through the trees, which are slowly converted into charcoal, firewood and planks for sale in the towns or exported to neighbouring countries, and the land lies barren.

We halted every fifty miles or so to load and unload our passengers; each time the exchange took on a ritualistic flavour. Time here had no meaning and the passage of a vehicle, especially one as large as ours, brought forth a revelry that reached way beyond the confines of a simple halt, resembling that of a returning schooner in the olden days. The sheer joy of reunion, barter and exchange of news was sufficient reason for merriment and transformed each pause into a celebration.

What was significant, however, was the total absence of wildlife of any sort. We never saw a bird, a monkey or a deer unless it was strung up by its tail to a weapon or disfigured and charred up for sale. In Zaire, where protein is at a premium, everything that moves is eaten, and the hapless wildlife has little chance of survival.

Louis had friends and family everywhere and was in great demand at each stop. He would be dragged off by clusters of children or laughing girls and would disappear behind some rusty tin door or palm-frond enclosure, to emerge sometimes an hour later. Once he invited us to follow him to his mother's house for tea and when we protested because of time, he just laughed saying that tea with his family was more important than time, and marched off, beckoning us to follow him. His was a wholly different mentality, and there was of course a lot to be said for this happy-go-lucky approach to life . . . it was just part of the old jungle network.

Shortly before dusk, as we were entering Kalima, we encountered a group of women, fifty, perhaps seventy-five of them, walking down the road towards us, carrying large bundles of firewood stacked on their backs, held in place by a leather strap across the forehead. Ahead of them marched a young man in slacks and an open shirt, bare-handed except for a walking stick, followed by a small white dog. At our request, Louis pulled over to the side of the road and stopped. They were on their way to a circumcision ceremony being held in a village a few miles up the road, they told us. The wood, they explained, was for a fire for the witchdoctors, who

would expel evil spirits from the young men's bodies.

When we asked if we could attend they laughed, putting their hands to their mouths. 'No, no, no: white people can't be present at these ceremonies otherwise the powers of the witchdoctor do not work.'

'Not even if we give him some money,' Lorenzo said mischievously.

'Oh,' they said, taken aback, 'that would be different.'

But then Louis intervened and said he would not be able to stop here overnight because he had to return next day to Shabunda.

That put an end to our conversation and we moved a mile further on where, in a clearing in the trees, we came across the young novices gathered together, preparing for the initiation ceremony. There must have been five hundred of them, completely naked, their heads and eyebrows shaved, standing in a tight group so that their smooth round heads looked like a mass of brown eggs stashed beside each other. They faced us in stony silence against the brilliant green backdrop, a pristine tableau that reached back to the realms of antiquity. When I lifted my camera to my eye they went wild and started shouting at us to stop. '*Pas de photos, nous ne sommes pas des animaux*' (No photos, we are not animals), as some picked up stones to throw at us.

'Put away your camera,' Louis hissed at me as I ducked behind the protective wall of my fellow-travellers. Without a word Louis shoved the vehicle into first gear and we lurched forward before any retaliation could develop.

When incidents like this occur, I become painfully aware of the disrespectful intrusion of an image-hunter and I feel a deep aversion for my work. I am very conscious of my violation of the individual, almost as if my camera turns into a weapon, but then the hunter instinct takes over and I am blinded by the chase; there is no time for hesitation or courtesy. I have learned to move fast and sometimes recklessly, taking split-second decisions, aware of the fleeting, unrecurring instants, and all sense of dignity and respect is overruled. Most times I get away with it, but sometimes – as in this case – when I encounter hostility or aggression, my empathy and disappointment leave me feeling frustrated and the only outlet is retreat. Hunters learn to accept defeat but are never discouraged by it.

Our fellow-passengers had all disembarked by now and we reached Kalima just before nightfall. Louis deposited us and our equipment a few miles out of town on the banks of the Elila river, where we set up a fly-camp for the night. Next day we reassembled our inflatables with the help of the usual bunch of curious bystanders who always emerged from anywhere we stopped, making us feel that wherever we went, invisible eyes, hidden behind the wall of green, were watching us.

—Opposite—
Louis invited us to his mother's house for tea with the family.

CHAPTER TWELVE

THEN THE PARROTS BEGAN TO SING

A S WE PENETRATED FURTHER INTO THE CORE OF THIS immense country its very essence began to emerge. It was subtle and indefinable but very present everywhere, an impression of timeless authenticity, much like that encountered by the early explorers and the colonizers; little seemed to have changed and, although the inhabitants now wore western clothes, they retained a simple purity in their faces and attitudes. The ageless setting still held an archaic grandeur which time, colonization and every manner of abuse and attempt at conversion had failed to disfigure. It was as if all the energy of Africa had accumulated here in Zaire and any attempts at constriction or subordination had been simply shrugged off. How many times we were to encounter this during our descent towards the Atlantic.

Above us the long suspension bridge that spanned the river provided an excellent vantage-point for the passers-by; intrigued and fascinated by what was going on below them, they stopped and slowly gathered into an interested – and interesting – audience, offering a revealing insight into the indigenous life of the interior. An old man with one eye, sheltered from the sun beneath a ragged black umbrella he held open above his head, stood beside a fat, squat granny walking a pair of identical two-year-old twins whom she clutched by the hand; then came a youth with his hunting dog, a wooden bell tied around its neck lest it should go astray; another on a bicycle with a dozen dead giant rats he was taking home to roast strapped to the carrier; then came a husband and wife walking to Kalima with their teenage son; the wife was laden down by a heavy basket she carried on her back fastened to her forehead with a leather thong, the son had a home-made shotgun slung across his shoulder and the husband, as always, was empty-handed, looking dapper in a bright yellow nylon sports jacket, black slacks and a black beret set to one side of his head; a smooth black wooden baton with a rounded knob was tucked under his arm. Three pretty girls dressed in colourful Zairian cloth and frilly blouses hugging long, slender bodies, with exposed soft, brown, rounded shoulders, glided sexily by, throwing furtive glances at us; then came a sturdy, bare-chested fellow in a pair of long army shorts with, on his head, a large bunch of bright orange palm oil kernels, suggestive of an exotic Carmen Miranda hat, and yet another cyclist with two chickens in flat wicker baskets strapped on either side of the back wheel.

Whatever they were doing or wherever they were going, they stopped and gazed transfixed at the goings-on in the river beneath the bridge. They were a friendly, jovial lot, eager for conversation and avid for news and information about our origins, our travels and our destination. They remained with us until we were ready to depart, helping us gather up our bits and pieces and load the boats. We left them with that now familiar sensation of affinity that seemed to constitute the very fabric of the jungle network. These simple, unassuming people epitomized the timeless essence of Zaire; there's little doubt that had we called on them for support or assistance they would not have hesitated to lend a helping hand. There was a guileless candour in their manner which I have always found to be characteristic of all indigenous people whose lives have not been violated by the white man; the deeper we penetrated into this wild and untamed land, the more we found this to be so.

We had been on land for almost a month and it felt good to be back on the river, to feel the warm breeze on our faces and hear again the now familiar purr of our outboard engines as we glided smoothly over the brown water. The Elila river, wide and deep and unencumbered, enabled us to plane at considerable speeds downstream. Our friends on the bridge waved and shouted gleefully as we sped grandly away beneath them in a white wake. They were still waving as we went out of sight and they turned into little silhouettes against the black iron rails of the bridge. The mighty trees and vegetation, which had now become so much part of our journey, towered on either side of us; the river was low, adding an extra dimension to the awesome scenery, making us feel small and unimportant, like flies skimming over a huge sheet of water. There was a magnetic quality to this great green wall that kept us mesmerized and eliminated all feeling of monotony. Here again that indefinable element of mystery was present, that strange enigma that had

221

to do with pre-history perhaps, with powers beyond our comprehension, with witchcraft, with the origins of man; we had not felt this elsewhere. Was this perhaps the very element that had earned Zaire its reputation and has so intimidated its neighbours?

We travelled until dusk, rarely sighting possible campsites. The trees and vines grew right to the water's edge, making any landing impossible, and it was only as night was falling that an open space, a kind of muddy platform, presented itself.

'The trees kept shedding their dew upon us like rain in great round drops, every leaf seemed to be weeping,' Stanley wrote of this same place in one of his diaries in 1874;

Down the holes and branches, creepers and vegetable cords, the moisture trickled and fell on us – overhead the wide, spreading branches, in many interlaced strata, absolutely shut out the daylight – we knew not whether it was a sunshiny day or a dull foggy day, for we marched in a feeble, solemn twilight; to our right and left to the height of about 20 feet towered the undergrowth, the lower world of vegetation. The tempest might roar without the leafy world, but in its deep bosom there is absolute stillness . . . The atmosphere was stifling, the steam from the hot earth could be seen ascending upwards and settling in a grey cloud above our heads; this country was not made for travel, it was made for vile pagans, monkeys and wild beasts . . .

We fastened our ropes to a desiccated fallen tree lying half submerged in the river; a few feet above us stood an abandoned shack with two home-made wooden stools in front of it, indicating that somewhere sometime there was human habitation in the area. Until then we had seen no sign of any kind of life, it was just us and the forest. As we pitched our tents, got the fire started and began settling down for the night, three long, slender canoes appeared slipping silently over the river surface, gently poled by dark silhouettes standing two in each boat, a man and a boy. The drops of water dripping from the punting poles fell in a luminous shower into the sunlit silvery wake behind each craft. We watched them approach, moving fast and gracefully towards us in this silent, almost mystical setting.

A sudden hush fell over us; everything was calm and peaceful and soft; then the parrots in the trees began to sing. One at a time they called to each other across the river, and soon the most astonishing bird concert we had ever heard filled the air in a repetitive medley of trills and ululations that could have been easily orchestrated. Lorenzo recorded it on tape and when we got back to Rome we incorporated it, unaltered, into the sound track of our films. It was one of those fleeting moments of magic Africa sometimes offers to the intrepid traveller who dares to venture into its secret realm.

As night fell the parrots became silent and winged across the river to their nesting trees, giving us a fleeting glimpse of the vermilion inner lining of their wings. The three canoes reached the shore and the men inside threw fibre ropes to us; in so doing they extended the great jungle network to our remote camping site and, from the place Joseph Conrad referred to as the 'Heart of Darkness', there flowed more light than in most places I have been to, that inner light of human contact that joins all men regardless of colour and is becoming so dim in the world we come from. Did we need anything, some firewood, some fresh water or some fish perhaps, they asked us gently, as they alighted from their wooden craft, eyeing our fat twentieth-century inflatables and outboard engines as if they belonged to James Bond. We bought two long, whiskered catfish from them and accepted their offer to show us a spring of clear mountain water flowing from a rock on the other bank. They sat with us into the night sipping cups of sweet ginger tea, a treat they had almost forgotten, and we exchanged bits of information. Then they left us quietly, as quietly as they had come, and were quickly absorbed into the darkness, taking with them our promise to visit them and their families next day, a hundred yards back upriver on the left.

It was full moon that night and as we sat around the fire savouring the dark, the wall of trees opposite us, obliterated by the night, very slowly reappeared, as out of a dusky dream, as the moon rose in the east. The quiet scene was bathed in moonlight and we were able to distinguish again each tree and leaf and the cascades of vines sweeping downwards to the water's edge. The river began to shimmer like a milky mirror and, as the sky grew lighter, the tallest trees stood out against it, silent sentinels of a secret world. Then a slender canoe glided by, a shadow in the night, floating, it seemed, in space, for moonlight has a special ethereal quality that transforms ordinary things into fantasy.

Next day our friends of the previous evening returned to guide us to their family compound. The families were waiting for us at the water's edge, standing ankle-deep on a mud ledge. A steep path cut in the vegetation led from the water to the compound about twenty feet above. In a clearing in the forest some huts with palm-frond thatch surrounded a patch of earth that had been swept and pounded hard. About ten members of the family followed us back from the river and invited us to sit with them. After some moments of 'eye rinsing', during which time every detail on both sides was scrutinized and the relevant comments made, everyone settled down to their domestic chores, stoking fires, cooking food in soot-blackened earthen pots, breast-feeding babies, sharpening spearheads, whacking the dog, chasing off chickens picking at the midday meal or just sitting around on wooden

—Overleaf—
With the intense heat the humidity hanging over the massive forests turns to rain and feeds the Zaire river, which pours hundreds of thousands of cubic feet of water every second into the Atlantic.

223

stools commenting on everything. It reminded me of a stage on which some rural play was about to begin, enclosed on three sides with panels of green vegetation.

We sat with the family exchanging banalities as I took my pictures.

'Will you send us some photos?' the father asked me in French.

'Of course,' I lied to him, 'but where do I send them? You live so far away on the river.'

'I'll give you my address,' he answered simply.

What address could he possibly have given me on the Elila river? I imagined my letter being delivered by canoe in a forked stick, if it ever reached him at all.

He carefully wrote his name and address on the back of my note pad – 'Jean Baptiste Wagogo, chez Mme Walla, B.P. 153, Kalima, Zaire.' His writing was childlike, but clear, and he told us that each month he went to Kalima, about 250 miles away, to collect his pension, and any mail would be given to him. Jean Baptiste told us he had worked for the Belgians on a road-construction team during the colonial days, and at independence had been shot in the lungs by a Simba rebel sniper bullet. He was now a *grand blessé de guerre* (a war invalid), and each month drew a meagre invalidity pension from the government. He talked of the Belgians with melancholy in his voice and admitted he much regretted their absence.

'Life in Zaire has gone down, down, down,' he told us, 'since the Belgians left. Now our President Mobutu is milking the country dry and we are all suffering; only those around him and those of his tribe get fat, the rest of us are starving and we have to fend for ourselves as best we can. Here on the Elila river we are completely forgotten; if it were not for the Belgian aid, what would I do, and my family?' There was anger and bitterness and frustration in his voice. He put his head in his hands and spat on the ground between his feet.

'Let's go,' Lorenzo said. 'It's getting late.'

As we left our new friends they brought us gifts of coconuts and papaya and some green bananas for our journey, and we gave them some tea and biscuits and sugar in exchange.

'Thank you for stopping by. Very few white people come this way. We enjoyed your visit.'

They accompanied us to our boats, we started the engines and turned away in a spray of foam, on towards the Atlantic, leaving them behind on the muddy ledge surrounded by the towering forest, a drop of colour in the immense green canvas.

We spent one last, memorable night on the Elila river before sailing next day into the Lualaba river just north of Kindu, the Zairian river port where one of the most infamous incidents – the kind that earned Zaire her reputation – took place. In 1961, shortly before independence, an Italian UN plane crash-landed there. Caught in the fever of independence, the rebel soldiers, mistaking the thirteen Air Force men for the hated colonial oppressors they were overthrowing, stormed the aircraft, dragged out the occupants, imprisoned them, beat them to death and then, it was discovered later, ate them. The Kindu massacre went down in the annals of Zairian history together with the other acts of demoniacal savagery. A memorial to the murdered Italian aviators now stands outside Fiumicino airport on the outskirts of Rome, and Zaire has confirmed its reputation for cannibalism.

Entering the great Lualaba river, down which Henry Morton Stanley first sailed in 1874 and from which both Livingstone and his fellow explorer Lovett Cameron turned away during their various searches for the headwaters of the Nile, was much like embarking on a highway after travelling in a country lane. Why had Cameron and Livingstone turned away from the Lualaba, Stanley wanted to find out. As I read aloud to the others from Peter Forbath's book *The River Congo* some of the reasons began to emerge:

Cameron and members of his caravan had heard fresh horror stories of what lay ahead on the river. The natives were very fierce and warlike and used poisoned arrows, from which a mere scratch proved fatal in four or five minutes, unless an antidote known only to the natives was immediately applied . . . and there were cannibals more cruel and treacherous than any with whom we had met, consequently stragglers would most certainly be cut off, killed and probably eaten. So forbidding was the prospect that even the Arab caravans, despite their greed for slaves and ivory and despite their armies of riflemen, did not dare venture into those regions. So within a few weeks Cameron's resolve to go down the Lualaba eroded and he seized the first opportunity to turn away from the terrible challenge of the river . . . and Livingstone, after 15,000 miles of travel and a lifetime of experience among Africans, would not have yielded the brave struggle without reason.

To illustrate these points a young Arab was brought before Stanley to tell of his adventures with one of the few caravans that had ever attempted to penetrate these regions. It was, the youth related, a forest land where there is nothing but woods and woods and woods for days and weeks and months. There was no end to the woods. He went on to tell of cannibal warriors, of monstrous boa constrictors and gorillas 'that run up to you and seize your hands and bite the fingers off one by one; if one tries to go by river there are falls and falls which carry the people over and drown them'.

At times the banks were so far apart it was impossible to discern the features of the land and the going became less interesting; we left behind us the wonderful pristine quality of the interior and cruised rather grandly down the grey highway, feeling a bit exposed and vulnerable in so much space. The surface was so still we

Stanley wanted to find out why both Cameron and Livingstone, after a 15,000-mile journey and a lifetime of experience among Africans, had turned away from the Lualaba.

were reflected in a mirror image, and in the noonday heat-haze we seemed to be floating somewhere in between water and sky. It was in these moments that we lay back and drifted into another space, where fantasy and reality merge and all perspective is lost, a sort of no man's land of the mind where perceptions are enhanced and there is time for reflection.

'We saw before us a black curving wall of forest,' Stanley wrote in his diaries upon entering the Lualaba,

which beginning from the river bank extended south-east until hills and distance made it undistinguishable ... downwards it flows into the unknown, to the night's black clouds of mystery and fable ... something strange must surely be in the vast space occupied by total blankness on our maps ... here lies a broad watery avenue cleaving the unknown to some sea like a path of light.

Suddenly from the crest of a low ridge we saw the majestic Lualaba. It is about 1,400 yards wide, a broad river of pale grey colour winding slowly from south to east. We hailed its appearance with shouts of joy and rested on the spot to enjoy the view. A secret rapture filled my soul as I gazed upon the majestic stream. The mystery that for all these centuries nature had kept hidden away from the world of science was waiting to be solved. My task was to follow it to the ocean. This great stream must be one of the headwaters of the Congo, for where else could that giant

The cannibals gathered along the banks, rattling bows and poisoned arrows, a mere scratch from which proved fatal in four or five minutes unless an antidote known only to the natives was immediately applied.

among rivers, second only to the Amazon in its volume, obtain the two million cubic feet of water which unceasingly pours each second into the Atlantic?

'Stanley launched the *Lady Alice* on the river,' I read to Lorenzo at this point, 'and although the travelling was slightly eased, the expedition now began to encounter the other great terror of the forest, its inhabitants.' Ochre-coloured villages carved out of the green embankments began to appear now, and every few miles the inhabitants rushed out to wave at us and beckon us to stop. 'At first the villages were deserted,' Stanley wrote one hundred years before,

the tribesmen fleeing into the dark forests at the news of the advance of the strange caravan; there wasn't any question about what sort of people live in them. Row upon row of human skulls lined the palisades around the villages and bones from every part of the human anatomy could be seen scattered around the cooking sites. From time to time a solitary grotesquely painted savage would be caught sight of peering out from the thick undergrowth, and throughout the day and night we heard the drums beating, telling of their progress; eerie cries calling warriors to assemble in the gloom of the woods and the blare of ivory war horns sounding from another world . . . and then we saw eight large canoes coming up river along the island in midstream and six along the left bank. The cannibals gathered along the banks rattling bows and arrows and shrieking 'bo-bo-bo-bo' (meat,

—Overleaf left—
Hugo and Charlie were not only good looking but also identified completely with the expedition.

—Overleaf right—
Ochre-coloured villages carved out of green embankments began to appear. The inhabitants rushed out to wave and beckoned us to stop.

We came across the wreck of a half-submerged river vessel bearing the name of the man who, sixty years earlier, had invited my family to Africa – Le Baron Empain.

meat, we shall have plenty of meat). Painted half red and half white, with broad black stripes streaked across them, they came out into the river in their giant war canoes; one which was captured measured 85 feet long, with a bas-relief of a crocodile adorning its sides.

Our own encounters, fortunately, were less threatening. We met our first river steamer on the second day, a sort of antiquated two-storied barge crammed solid with people travelling between Ubundu, towards which we were heading, and Kindu behind us. A solitary young white man with pale blue eyes, an adventurous soul like us no doubt, stood among the black faces looking like an albino, and an instant rush of recognition and solidarity flowed between us as we drew up alongside the moving vessel and exchanged a few short sentences before casting off and slipping away in the opposite direction.

It took us five days to reach Ubundu from Kindu, and for the first time on the expedition we feared our fuel supply would run out; we contemplated the possibility of drifting downstream on the current. Travelling with the current would have meant a considerable reduction of speed, which would have drawn us into the timeless rhythm of the river. Despite the many months on the expedition we still had not adjusted completely to the pace of Africa; such an eventuality still seemed difficult to comprehend. Several times we passed log rafts gliding downstream on the current, transporting passengers and merchandise on journeys that lasted weeks and sometimes months. The travellers on board had settled down to a daily routine of minimum activity until it was time to disembark. They cooked and slept and talked and washed their clothes oblivious of the passage of time. Time was simply not a factor to be reckoned with. This difference between our western ways and theirs was one of the most significant and constant we had to deal with.

One of these rafts was transporting bright yellow crates of Primus beer. The accompanying crew, swilling beer all day long to break the boredom, were so 'high' that, when we passed them, they waved the bottles at us, beckoning us to draw close, and with much merriment gave us each one for our onward journey. A black goat tethered to the rear munched at some sweet potato leaves; seen in context the tableau seemed quite natural.

We spent one night on a spit of white sand rising just above the level of the water and when we awoke next morning we were enveloped in a shroud of mist so thick we could barely see the river. As the sun rose the mist began to lift and, floating through it as in a dream, we saw three rafts fastened to each other, laden with people. They passed for a brief moment in front of us and then disappeared from sight as the mist closed in, leaving us with the eerie sensation of a river spectre, straight from a scene in a Fellini movie.

Approximately fifty miles outside Ubundu we cut the engines of one inflatable and attached it with a tow line to the other so as to save on fuel. This did slow us down considerably, but we were still moving faster than the current and reducing the risk of running dry, a possibility we wanted to avoid at all costs. Fortunately the weather was cool and balmy and the river had narrowed slightly; the banks were now fringed with immense bamboos that added a whole new dimension to the scenery. Long, supple stems bent over by the weight of thousands of pale-green, slender leaves like giant plumes grew over a hundred feet upwards from the ground. For miles the river banks on both sides were cloaked with this light feathered mantle, lightening the ominous – sometimes menacing – impact of the heavy jungle we had encountered until now.

We spent one last night on the Lualaba beneath a great bamboo cathedral created from three massive clumps meeting a hundred feet above us; the circular clearing beneath them was thick and springy with dry fallen leaves, providing a soft mattress for us to unroll our sleeping bags on; but that night another thunderstorm descended upon us with cataclysmic force. The bamboo mesh above considerably lessened the impact of the rain, and gave us time to hastily erect some shelter, but we still got soaked; when we finally reached Ubundu next day we were ready for a bit of *terra firma* again.

Further downstream we came across the wrecks of two river vessels, half submerged beneath the water. One lay in the mud and vegetation like a decaying carcass of some dinosaur, abandoned and sinking slowly back into the river, being re-absorbed by Africa. From the funnel, cracked and corroded by rust, a vine with delicate mauve flowers cascaded full of life over the eroded metal skeleton; its name, *Le Baron Empain*, in raised bronze letters on the front recalled the man who sixty years ago had invited my family to Africa. My mother had talked to me often about him when she told us of her own adventures in the Congo in 1929. As the majority shareholder of the Katanga copper mines to the south, Empain was then an important personality in the Belgian Congo. The other vessel was completely submerged in the river except for the faded pink flying deck still protruding above the surface. It seemed at first to be some kind of aquatic refuge on stilts but, as we approached, it had that same dejected air of lost abandon. Birds had nested beneath the roof and in the still water below an eerie creaking conveyed an uncanny sensation of life; the wake from our boats disturbed some giant catfish inside; they scuttled through the portholes sending bubbles to the surface and all around us it was very still beneath the great green forest curtain.

CHAPTER THIRTEEN

THE CONGO THROWS OFF HER SHACKLES

UBUNDU, PREVIOUSLY CALLED PONTIERVILLE, WAS ONCE an important river port, for it is here, at the Stanley Falls, that the Lualaba becomes the great Zaire river, marking the end of its navigable portion. The Stanley Falls impede any passage for about half a mile, and then for eighty miles between Ubundu and Kisangani (once known as Stanleyville) seven more sets of rapids make river travel impossible. Another portage, this time by train, was necessary to get us to Kisangani. From Peter Forbath's book *The River Congo* we learned that

it took Stanley just over three weeks to descend the falls; wherever there was a stretch of relatively calm water he would make use of it, and retained the Lady Alice *and his fleet of canoes; then the horrendous labour of portage would begin again. A path of fifteen feet wide had to be hacked through the jungle sometimes two, three and four miles long while the other half of the expedition dragged the boats after them, and throughout it all they had to fight the relentless, terrifying attacks of the cannibals.*

Many long wooden canoes were tethered together beside the cement pier leading up from the water to the railway siding. They fanned out into the river and rocked against each other in our wake. The arrival in Ubundu was a landmark on our journey; we felt elated and even a bit surprised at the smooth trip, especially after all we had heard and read. We unloaded and dismantled the boats and carried everything to an ideal campsite about fifty yards up the slope, where a bright green lawn spread invitingly beneath tall shade trees. We had a 180-degree view over the river. Like most places built and then abandoned by the Belgians, Ubundu had an air of dilapidated decline, although the setting still retained a certain grandeur and one could still detect the significance this inland port must once have had. But now it was just another bruise in the country, a memento to colonial interference and to the violence that followed it, for here in Ubundu, we found out later, the Simba rebels had created such savage havoc that people still talk about it today, almost twenty-five years later.

'I would like at this point,' Lorenzo said to us one night around the fireplace, 'to read you some passages from Peter Forbath's book concerning the turbulent events in Zaire's history relevant to our journey.'

More than fifty years were to pass after the establishing of the Belgian Congo, before the final story in the narrative of the river's discovery, exploration and exploitation began to unfold. Although these were relatively tranquil years, certainly in comparison to Leopold's reign of terror, they were the years in which the dragon seeds of the Congo's final tragedy were sown, for unarguably that tragedy was the direct and inevitable consequence of Belgium's half-century of colonial rule. For all that the Belgians unquestionably did in and for the Congo, there was one thing that they crucially failed to do: take into consideration and prepare for the possibility, if not to say the necessity, of their colony's eventual independence; and by that failure they condemned the Congo to chaos.

Lorenzo threw a log on to the fire and went on.

'*The object of our presence in the Dark Continent*' – as defined by Leopold II in 1909 – '*is to open these backward countries to European civilization, to call their people to emancipation, liberty and progress after having saved them from slavery, disease and poverty.*' *When, many years later, Leopold's nephew King Baudouin of the Belgians, in a broadcast to the nation, declared that 'In continuance of our noble aims, our firm resolve today is to lead, without fatal evasion but without imprudent haste, the Congolese people to independence in prosperity and in peace' it was already too late; the Congolese nationalists' blood was up and they were in no mood to settle for anything less than total and immediate independence.*

When in his formal address at the independence celebrations in 1960, King Baudouin dwelt again on Leopold's 'beneficence', Patrice Lumumba, now Prime Minister, responded angrily, recalling the atrocities of the Congo Free State and the indignities of Belgian colonial rule. He turned to Baudouin and shouted, 'We are no longer your monkeys.' In the course of the next few days the mood of the Congolese turned ugly, there were sporadic outbursts of rioting, attacks on whites and clashes with the Forces Publiques *(the police); then disaster struck when the* Forces Publiques *mutinied; what had started as a mutiny turned into a savage, mindless rampage which* no reason or moderation was able to control. One by one virtually all the army and police garrisons throughout the country exploded in an orgy of rampage, rioting and murder. This triggered a wave of terrible violence by Congolese civilians as well. Europeans were humiliated, stripped naked, people spat in their faces, they were beaten and ridiculed. The natives also attacked women, including those obviously pregnant or ill and those who had recently given birth to children. To achieve their aim the natives used physical violence and the menace of their weapons; in innumerable cases they threatened to kill the children if the mothers did not yield. The result of these outrages, not surprisingly, was a panic-stricken flight of whites; with their sudden departure, the functioning of the administration and the economy abruptly broke down.

Finally, with the army wildly out of control, a cable was sent to Dag Hammerskjöld appealing for U.N. assistance. White mercenary soldiers were recruited by the new Prime Minister, Tshombe, to replace the Belgians in his army; this led to a full-scale, bloody civil war. The requested secession of the Katanga copper province was over but the Congo's troubles were not.

A follower of Lumumba recruited a rebel army from the once cannibal tribesmen of the Lualaba, doped them up on MIRA (a local marijuana-type drug), sprinkled them with magic water to make them invulnerable to bullets and sent them on a rampage through the rain forest of the Upper Congo. The 'Simbas' (Swahili for lions) proved more than a match for the regular Congolese army and in a year and a half managed to overrun more than half the Congo. Tshombe then provided a perfect solution for the Simba menace. In turn he recruited an army more frightening than the cannibal warriors and hired more white mercenaries, whom he threw into the fray. They were a deadly, savage force; armed with the most modern weapons, motivated by a sadistic blood-lust and a hatred for the blacks, rewarded by all the loot they could lay their hands on, free to commit the most awful atrocities, clearly unafraid of the 'ju-ju' men and unimpressed by magic, they easily drove the Simbas back through the forest into the north-eastern corner of the Congo basin until the only major city they still held was Stanleyville, now renamed Kisangani.

There were some 1,300 Europeans in Stanleyville at the time that Tshombe's mercenary army reached the city. Gbenye, who had launched the Simbas into battle, immediately had them seized as hostages and he sent a message to the United Nations warning that they would be killed and 'we will wear their hearts around our necks like fetishes and dress ourselves in their flayed skins if Tshombe's forces attempt to take Stanleyville'. The mercenary army's advance was halted and negotiations were entered into, in the hope of saving the hostages' lives. While the talks were going on the hostages' situation became increasingly dangerous. With the mercenaries besieging Stanleyville, the city's supplies ran perilously low and its essential services broke down, and so the outside world decided to act.

On November 24th, 1964, 600 Belgian paratroopers, flown in U.S. airforce transport planes, jumped on Stanleyville. At the same time, on the ground, the mercenary army attacked; the fighting lasted less than a day. The Simbas made a brief stand and then fled in disorder into the surrounding

—Opposite—
The white mercenaries were a deadly, savage force armed with the most modern weapons and motivated by a sadistic blood-lust combined with hatred of the blacks.

238

rain forest, but before they ran, they managed to do their savage work. Nearly a hundred white hostages were killed and the corpses of hundreds, perhaps thousands of blacks whom Gbenye had condemned as enemies of the revolution were found strewn in the city streets and floating in the river. The Congo was in a tragic state. Since independence more than 200,000 Congolese had been killed, the economy had collapsed entirely, shortages and unemployment were rife and there were tens of thousands of refugees. The situation was so bad there was every reason to anticipate that the relentless violence, despite the destruction of the Simbas, would go on forever.

But then Joseph Mobutu, an NCO in the Forces Publiques *who was named by Lumumba as the new commander of the* Forces Publiques *after the dismissal of the commanding Belgian general, once again intervened. His second regime marked the Congo's final passage — for better or for worse — from the mysterious mythological darkness of its savage past into the rather banal light of the modern age . . . he introduced his 'authenticité' campaign to change not only all the European place-names but all the river people's Christian names as well (Mobutu changed his own name from Joseph to Sese Seko). It is, in short, the struggle by which the Congo was, in fact as well as in name, transformed into Zaire . . .*

'We should look on colonization as a collective act of charity which, in some circumstances, highly developed nations have to extend to the less fortunate races,' the Belgian Cardinal Mercier wrote in a pastoral letter in 1909. This was followed by Joseph Conrad's bitter lines: 'It is an extraordinary thing that the conscience of Europe, which seventy years ago put down the slave trade on humanitarian grounds, tolerates the Congo State today.'

From 1965 onwards, the story of Zaire belongs less to the history of its discovery, exploration and exploitation by Europe than to the politics of modern independent Africa. These politics are characterized by the struggle going on all over the continent — with some admirable successes and many dismal failures but always with much agony and hope — to recover the virtues and values that prevailed in Africa before the white man came, to combine them with the inarguable advantages of the civilization that the white man brought, and out of that combination forge a new but genuine African identity and society.

The dramatic images conjured up by the words we had just heard silenced us all. Lorenzo shut the book. No one spoke. We just sat and looked into the fire nursing our thoughts; wondering, perhaps, what devilry exists in man to provoke such savagery.

The train for Kisangani had left on the morning of our arrival, and the stationmaster informed us the next one would not leave for three days. On one of our peregrinations through the crumbling town, we came across Padre Gianni, an Italian missionary who was attached to the Catholic Mission Centre in Kisangani, and who had been sent to Ubundu for a six-week sabbatical to assess the situation of the Church. It was a fortunate encounter: Padre Gianni was the only other white in Ubundu and eager for companionship. His African counterpart, Père Gabriel Mokoto, was a survivor of the Simba rampage in Ubundu and later, with his wife Amarante, gave us a first-hand account of the atrocities.

Padre Gianni was working in his vegetable garden when we approached down the earth road that led to the mission. He was sweating copiously and his T-shirt, his face and his hands were stained with red dust. It was the middle of the day and the debilitating heat had sapped our energy, so that his immediate invitation to come in and share some refreshments with him was much welcomed.

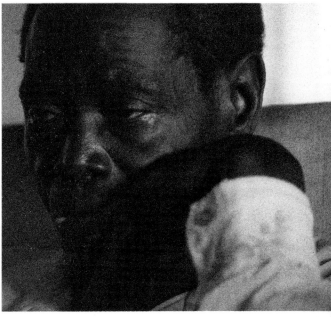

Father Gabriel Mokoto was one of the few survivors of the Simba rampage in Ubundu. He was caught between two conflicting beliefs – that of the Church he now represented and that of the essence of Africa to which he had been born.

The interior of his simple stone dwelling was cool and sparse, with just the bare essentials: some wooden furniture, cotton curtains, and a crucifix on the bare white wall beside a statuette of the Madonna and child in a niche. A tray with some bottles of liquor and some glasses on the table added a touch of worldliness to the otherwise austere surroundings. Amarante came in with a bottle of ice-cold water from the refrigerator and Padre Gianni poured us some Pernod from one of the bottles.

Padre Gianni was a warm and friendly person, and somewhat emancipated in his religious beliefs. He told us of his twenty years in Zaire, the problems and the satisfactions of his missionary work and his conflicts within the missionary framework. He no longer approved of the Papal doctrines and felt strongly that if the Church does not modify its perspectives in today's Africa, its teachings could be more detrimental than beneficial to the people, because, he said, the problems facing Africa today reach far beyond religion. Overpopulation, unemployment and Aids are factors over which the Church has little control: its continued opposition towards birth control can only exacerbate the problem. Père Gabriel sat beside us with his fingers crossed in front of his face, staring ahead of him and saying nothing. He was a man caught between two conflicting beliefs, that of the Church he now represented and that of the reality of Africa he was born to.

When we left Padre Gianni to return to camp, Père Gabriel and his wife Amarante came with us. On the way we passed what had once been the Church of

241

St Joseph's stood
engulfed by vegetation.

Jungle trees and bushes
had grown up through
the armature of what
had once been the roof of
St Joseph's Church.

St Joseph, now engulfed in vegetation. Only the stone front still stood unimpaired, with the statue of St Joseph and the Christ-child standing in an alcove above the Gothic architrave. Behind, the walls no longer existed and the trees and bushes of the jungle had pushed up through the armature of what had once been the roof. It had a strange, wraithlike quality much like that of the sunken wrecks in the river, giving the undeniable sensation that, until man dominates Nature the way he has in Europe, the hidden force of Africa will somehow always erase his traces.

Further down the road we stopped at the old mission station; a long, red-brick classical building with a red-tiled roof; the windows were paneless and there was no door. Everything except the stone had been demolished. Shattered glass still lay strewn on the floor of the inner portico and the flaking white walls were smeared with faded, rust-coloured smudges and streaked with black fire soot.

'This is where all the nuns and padres took refuge when the Simbas erupted in Ubundu,' Amarante began quietly. 'The rebels broke down the door and smashed all the windows with their guns; they came in like crazed animals high on Mira; my husband tried to reason with them; they jumped on him and beat him so hard they left him for dead on the ground. The nuns and padres were pulled out of the rooms and herded here where we are standing; they were slaughtered like pigs; then they set fire to the furniture and the wooden beams in the roof began to burn. There are still traces of blood on the wall here and you can see the sky through the roof.'

As she looked up the sunlight caught her round black face framed in a bright cotton kerchief; infinite sadness and resignation were etched all over it as she spoke, but then instantly disappeared when she smiled, which she did often. Her husband stood beside her and let her speak; he looked frail and beaten as if he had given up trying to understand. Sunlight through the roof threw a dappled pattern over them.

'What did they do with the bodies of the people they murdered?' I asked.

'They sent them to Kisangani with some of the survivors, who were then later murdered there; they were buried in the cemetery in Kisangani along with the other Europeans who were murdered. The Zairians were thrown in the river or reclaimed by their families and buried in the cemetery here,' Amarante said disconsolately. 'It was a very bad period for Zaire after the Belgians left, but now things have calmed down and Mobutu has managed to keep the peace for twenty years, and we have gone back to living almost as we did before the Belgians came. There is, of course, no longer any work for anyone, and if it were not for the Catholic mission, even my husband and I would have no way of earning money.'

'Would you like it if the whites returned?' I asked.

'But of course, we were much better off when they were here. We had hospitals and medicine and roads and the trains and steamers ran frequently and there was work for everyone, even if we did not earn too much money and we knew that they were exploiting us. But at least they looked after us. But now, look around, there is so much poverty everywhere and the people just seem to accept their lot. They just live from day to day. Slowly we shall go back to living the way we always did.'

We wandered on through the native village, where those who had not managed to secure themselves a hold in the brick houses abandoned by the Belgians lived in huts beneath palm and mango trees. It was significant to note the contrast in mood between the homogeneous indigenous villages, neatly constructed and laid out, swept clean, with wild flowering shrubs or trees growing everywhere, and the ill-cared-for ex-European homes and administration buildings where dirt, decay and detritus proclaimed a sense of almost vindictive retaliation towards anything European, as if the animosity of those who lived in them had forced them into an alien lifestyle in which they felt uncomfortable, allowing it to slowly deteriorate, not having the means, the desire or the know-how to maintain it. I encountered this same attitude in most of my travels in Africa. It has helped my understanding of how the African mind works. The desire to adopt a European lifestyle which they have not yet learned to adapt to their standards is largely responsible for the overall malaise one finds everywhere in Africa where the whites have been.

In a little palm-frond-covered shelter a group of young people sitting on benches were rehearsing some hymns they were to sing at the next Sunday Mass. We sat with them for a while and listened to the simple words and pure voices; the earnestness on the young, shining faces and the seeming commitment they had towards their faith was touching and revealing after the horror stories we had just listened to. To try and preserve what they had been taught by their peers, they clung to their faith; they seemed happy at our interest and welcomed us to sit with them.

We spent each evening with Padre Gianni at the mission, sharing our plates of spaghetti and many soul-searching conversations with him. The hours spent with him, and the many hot showers he offered us, helped greatly to pass the time.

On the morning of the third day we were told to start loading our truck by 10 am for a two o'clock train departure. At midday, when everything was on board, the stationmaster informed us that the train had been cancelled. There was to be no departure until further notice, by order of HQ in Kisangani. We squealed our protests vehemently, but there was nothing he could do, and it was clear that anything we said was pointless. We had become accustomed by now to the African sense of time; there was no alternative but to unload the equipment, stash it in the station storeroom and return to Padre Gianni for the night.

Next morning at seven, as we were sipping our morning tea, a messenger came panting up the pathway to the mission with a communiqué from the stationmaster. 'The train is leaving in an hour, you better hurry down if you wish to catch it.'

We gulped down our tea, pulled on our clothes, and arrived quickly on the station platform half expecting to see the train pulling out. Our equipment was hastily reloaded and we climbed on board with the usual huge crowd of fellow-travellers. The train was packed to bursting; not only was every seat occupied but every inch in the aisles and corridors was taken up. We hung out of the window last-minute-talking with Padre Gianni, who had brought us down in his Landrover. Père Gabriel and Amarante and a gaggle of friends had come to see us off. Eight o'clock passed, then nine, then ten. The train didn't move. People kept coming and going, the locomotive let out bursts of steam, the whistle sounded but the train didn't move. It was becoming stifling inside. People began disembarking on to the platform and milling around.

Suddenly, without warning, the train moved forward. Everyone scrambled back on board in a great heave of laughter and shouting, and before we could say anything more, we were chugging out of the station to the wild cheering and waving of those left behind on the platform. Padre Gianni stood among the black faces, a solitary figure waving a white handkerchief in a sea of colour.

We were off at last – midday of the fourth day. Ten hours lay ahead of us if all went well, otherwise two, three, or four days; one could never tell in Zaire. Juliette had begun a fever the day before and was feeling very low. We fixed a temporary bed for her across the seats and gave her as much air as possible. Impossible to tell what was the matter with her; perhaps malaria, but the symptoms were not sufficiently evident yet to begin treatment. We fed her Disprin every four hours and plenty of liquid, and waited. Through the jungle we charged, shaking and swaying at alarming speeds. The vegetation whipped at the sides of the train and from the open windows we could see it rioting around us: vast ferns, palms, papayas and abandoned coffee growing wild, tall as trees; and other magnificent trees with fingerlike leaves in the shape of an open hand hanging downwards, suspended in great clusters at the end of branches like exotic lanterns.

The train stopped at every village and, as with our bus journey, each stop brought out all the inhabitants of the area. Edibles of unknown composition were offered to the passengers on large trays balanced on top of heads. There were also some recognizably African fried doughnuts, bananas, avocado, sliced pineapple, cashew nuts, and boiled manioc paste wrapped and tied in little banana-leaf parcels, basins of tadpoles or baby eels squirming around in water, roasted white ants and

245

The train was packed to
bursting: not only was
every seat occupied but
also every inch in the
aisles and corridors.

boiled fat yellow tree-grubs that live in the trunks of palms. And then there were the monkeys, smoked and barbecued, ready for consumption, tied together by the neck in groups of three and offered up to us with grotesquely human grinning teeth exposed, eyes wide open, glazed and frozen in a final death-stare.

The stifling, overcrowded, claustrophobic interior of the carriage finally got the better of us and we climbed on to the roof of the engine-driver's cabin. From then on our journey turned into a sort of aeronautical experience, with the wind blowing in our faces and tangling our hair. Perched high above the ground, we were in direct contact with our wild and magnificent surroundings; when we hurtled over the narrow bridges without railings that spanned the deep ravines and were only wide enough to accommodate the railway tracks, with the land falling away hundreds of feet to either side of us, it felt as if we were flying through space.

We pulled into Kisangani after dark, drained, dishevelled and relieved. The passengers poured away from the train and very quickly there was only us left in the darkness on the empty platform with our equipment piled around us. Juliette had grown worse during the journey and we decided to leave the boys to bed down for the night on the platform, while Lorenzo, Amina, Juliette and I went in search of some accommodation, hopefully at the mission, where I knew the Bishop of old.

After all these weeks in the wilderness the lights of Kisangani on the other side of the Zaire river looked like Staten Island to us. We picked our way in the dark from the station to the water's edge, where some large dugouts with 5 h.p. engines ferried us, along with a cluster of Zairians, into the night across the inky river.

The Bishop of Kisangani took us into his mission headquarters on the night we arrived.

The Bishop of Kisangani was sitting with some of his clergy in the open patio of the Procure, the Catholic mission's headquarters in Kisangani, taking in the cool of the evening. It was ten o'clock at night when Lorenzo and I walked in on them, looking and feeling like a day spent on a Zairian train. The Bishop greeted us benevolently. He listened graciously to a telescoped version of our African expedition, at the end of which he kindly agreed to allow us to spend the night at the mission and gave orders for a car and driver to pick up Juliette and Amina, whom we had left with our bags and bedrolls at the river edge. A hot shower, cool sheets, a sprung mattress and a mosquito net restored our energy level and, revitalized by a good night's sleep in the high-ceilinged monastery room, we were ready to face the next day.

The mission doctor came to see Juliette, but was non-committal; he did not think it was malaria. She seemed a little better, but still not well. I was loath to treat her for malaria without a blood test. This was arranged as soon as we settled in at a nearby priory on the outskirts of town, kept by some lay priests and nuns attached to the mission, where we were invited to camp by a kindly Belgian churchman whom Lorenzo had got talking to in the courtyard of the Procure. Next day Hugo, Charlie and Adam came across on a small tugboat from the other side, where we had left them the night before with the equipment, and were ferried to the priory by a mission vehicle.

The weather had been changing, getting hotter and more overcast with each day, and here in Kisangani the rains broke all over us once again. The rainy seasons in Zaire are particularly heavy, virtually paralyzing all movement, and in view of the likelihood of several months of such wet weather, Lorenzo decided to call a halt, and bring to a close the second leg of the expedition. Once again he had the names and addresses of all the right people to contact in Kisangani (an uncanny knack he has), and we were invited to store our boats, engines and equipment at the Sotexki Cotton Mills, where they would remain in safe-keeping until the rains subsided and we resumed the third and last leg of our journey.

Juliette's malaria blood test was negative, but her condition worsened. Bad pains in her joints, her legs, her neck and her back left her virtually immobile, so we moved her from the tent to the nunnery, where she lay in semi-torpor for three days, but in more comfortable, dry conditions. Meanwhile we sorted out and packed up the expedition in the rain, and made arrangements to fly back to Goma, where we had left the vehicles and the African team when we flew out with Adrian to Shabunda. Still unable to assess Juliette's ailment, I opted for the water cure, eliminating all food, giving her only water in an attempt to dilute and eliminate any noxious toxins she was reacting to and Disprin to ease the pains when they became too severe. In the absence of a precise diagnosis I have found this method to be the safest; with total rest it allows the body to fight back on its own. Within three days her pains had mercifully almost disappeared; we never found out what had hit her.

We flew by Air Zaire from Kisangani back to Goma, where our African team had been without news for over a month and were overjoyed to see us. I caught a plane to Nairobi with Hugo, while Lorenzo and the rest of the team brought back the vehicles and remaining equipment by road in constant rains through Rwanda and Uganda. Back in Nairobi, the team dispersed and Lorenzo and I dug in to wait for the weather to clear while we developed our films and sifted hundreds of photographs, reliving the whole adventure again through the frames on the light-table.

PART
THREE

CHAPTER FOURTEEN

IN THE GRIP
OF THE RIVER

WE RETURNED TO KISANGANI ON 3 DECEMBER, THREE
months later, with a new crew, batteries recharged and braced for the
last stretch to the Atlantic. With us this time we had Mario, an Italian
cameraman, Brian Larkey, a crack American white-water rafting expert, and three
Italian friends of Lorenzo's. I was now the only woman in the team.

We camped above the Wagenia Falls, the last of the seven cataracts on the 100-
mile stretch of river between Ubundu and Kisangani, where the river rushes
unchecked over a series of rocky steps as the river bed drops ten feet. Here the
Wagenia fishermen have devised an ingenious method of fishing with large wicker
traps that hang in the raging waters from pole structures inserted into the rockbed.
The fish swept downriver by the current get caught in the traps and, unable to
escape, are retrieved every few hours by the fishermen, perched precariously on the
wooden structures twenty or thirty feet above the water. The baskets are pulled up,
the fish extracted, and the traps are returned back into the water. This assured a daily
supply of fresh fish for the expedition and provided some beautiful sequences for
Mario's cameras.

With Brian's white-water expertise we felt more secure and, accompanied by a
dozen Wagenia fishermen in an outsize wooden canoe, we went out into the centre
of the river just above the rapids to scout for a minimum-hazard course on which to
shoot the rapids. The water was flowing fast and, at full throttle, we were having
difficulty controlling the inflatable; suddenly we got sucked forward by the force of
the water and, totally unprepared, found ourselves bouncing across the rapids,
waves breaking and splashing over the sides and on to us. We mustered up whatever
courage we had and tried to remain calm. Brian, the old pro, in perfect control, kept

the inflatable straight with an oar. The engines were well balanced and we rode the churning water with exceptional buoyancy. The Wagenia rowers, on the other hand, realizing that they had ventured out too far with us, lunged forward and grabbed one of our ropes, but we were in the grip of the river and even with both engines at full throttle there was no turning back.

As we entered the rapids, the canoe capsized and the men were swept away from us. The twelve men went under and disappeared, swept forward by the convulsive current, their heavy wooden craft, upside down, crashing along behind us like a piece of driftwood. We could but look back helplessly at them thrashing about in the foam.

It was the end of the day and light was fading; as we entered calmer waters, there was no longer any sign of fishermen or craft behind us. 'They have all drowned,' I thought to myself in panic, aware of the terrible consequences that would ensue, for in Zaire today Europeans responsible for the death or injury of blacks are severely punished with lengthy prison sentences, if they are not stoned or lynched beforehand. The villagers who had been watching us on the opposite bank beside our camp were now shouting and gesticulating in an angry mood. If any of their people had drowned, they would hold us responsible and a Zairian jail is as bad as it sounds. As we returned to shore below the rapids, many of the villagers were waiting for us. Angry words and comments commanded us to set up a search party. It was almost dark by now.

We set out with our torches back into the blackness of the river, towards the opposite bank, where we calculated the flow of the current would have washed the fishermen. For almost two hours we chugged up and down the water's edge, sweeping the reeds with our torch beams and interrogating anyone we saw. Lorenzo remained calm and said nothing. With no sign of the missing men my anxiety grew. We were about to give up when two figures entered our beam, waving and shouting at us. We cut the engines and threw out an anchor, and in the lapping of the wavelets heard them tell us the dugout had been washed up and retrieved and all the men were out of the water and safely back on the other side. I felt the muscles in my body relax. 'Well, thank God for that,' Lorenzo breathed out in a prolonged sigh, betraying his tension.

Back on the other side we abandoned the inflatable and returned to camp on foot. We trudged up a little path among the river reeds to the top of the embankment and then through a coconut grove to the Wagenia village, now almost deserted, all its residents presumably gathered at our campsite. It was ten o'clock at night. We walked silently in single file along the soft, sandy path towards

— Top —

Our engines were well balanced and we rode the churning water with exceptional buoyancy.

— Above —

Fish swept downriver by the current are caught in traps and retrieved every few hours by the fishermen.

— Right —

The Wagenia fishermen have devised an ingenious method of fishing with large wooden baskets which hang in the raging water from pole structures fixed into the rockbed.

254

Accompanied by a dozen Wagenia fishermen in an outsize wooden canoe, we went out into the centre of the river just above the rapids.

256

the village compound. A half-moon hung in the sky; visible through the palm fronds, it bathed the scene in its milky light. The compound, empty but for a few old people sitting in front of their huts beside cooking fires, was still and peaceful. A thin mantle of smoke mingled with the warm breeze that caressed our skins and rustled the palm-tree fronds. After the events earlier on, I knew that ahead the villagers, in ferment, awaited us. I prayed as I walked that the rowers would be with them. A dog rushed out and barked at our shadows passing in the night.

As we emerged from among the reeds once more, we identified the large dugout fastened to a stump at the water's edge. Relief. Our intrepid rowers sat in silence beside each other on the bottom of it, bareheaded, barechested and barefoot, looking dejected and humbled by the experience, like a bunch of captured slaves with only the shackles missing. All the loud-mouthed bravado of the afternoon had vanished now; the experience had made them mute.

'*Mungu Iko* (God is here),' I said to them joyfully in Swahili as we pulled up.

They looked up and shook their heads, '*Mungu Iko Kweli* (God is indeed here),' they murmured sullenly in unison, and I had a distinct feeling they were trying to make the most of the incident in the hope of extracting money from us. The families had seeped down from the embankment and stood around in silence.

'*Mungu Iko*,' I said to them as we moved towards them.

'*Kweli Mungu Iko*,' they cheered, coming forward to grab us by the hand. '*Asante Sana, Asante Sana* (Thank you, thank you),' they sang out. The ugly mood had subsided and we marched back together, singing in the dark, towards the campsite. The incident ended in jubilation and dancing.

When we reached the camp, Lelio Picciotto, the managing director of the Sotexki Cotton Mills, whom we had seen several times and who had by now become our friend, was waiting for us. We were inordinately glad to see him.

'If you want my advice, I suggest you pack up and get out of here as soon as possible and come and stay with us, you'll be better off there, you know what I mean?' he said with a wink.

Lelio was Italian, born in Egypt, and had been in Zaire for twenty years, five of them in Kisangani. His invitation was part of the white man's solidarity in a black country. We took up Lelio's invitation, packed up and moved into town next day, to the Sotexki Yacht Club, a little corner of Europe on the banks of the river, fenced off from the rest of Zaire. Strictly private, only members and their guests were permitted beyond the confines of the high, wrought-iron gates, which were guarded day and night by a watchman in a blue uniform and cap. Behind it among the trees lay the cemetery.

The French petrol firm Total, who had provided the expedition with fuel and had never let us down, had once again lived up to their promises: we found three barrels of fuel awaiting us at their Kisangani depot. Logistics of an expedition like this tend to be overlooked in a narrative where the essence of the story flows on the current of rivers, but logistics were an essential element in the expedition, and fuel availability was paramount. Finding fuel in remote regions, where rationing can bring transport to a halt, smacked at times of the miraculous. Despite communication difficulties, everywhere we went Total had managed to make supplies available to us; the expedition would have ground to a halt long ago without their substantial support and powers of organization. We refilled our empty tanks in Kisangani, and hoped that in Bandaka, 500 miles downriver, we would refuel again for the last stretch to Kinshasa.

There was a strange and ominous aura in Kisangani. Perhaps because of its history, the events we had read and heard about, its position on the great muddy river, or perhaps because both Joseph Conrad and V. S. Naipaul had, in their books *Heart of Darkness* and *A Bend in the River*, immortalized it in literature, this sprawling, ungainly river town, carved out of the jungle, made me feel uneasy. It could have been my imagination, born from too much hearsay, but everywhere I felt a sense of menace among the people in the streets. Traces of past violence were still very evident and the somewhat hostile presence of the army, with their sullen arrogance, their camouflage uniforms, heavy black boots and sten guns, the suspicious customs officials and the police force, gave one the feeling that a false move or word could unleash the restrained aggression I felt hanging in the air, as if a sort of uncontested ancient jungle force still lay beyond the confines of the town; almost as if all the anger and vengeance the people felt towards their colonial oppressors had accumulated here: the very whiteness of our skins made us feel conspicuous and uneasy, a bit like a red flag to a bull.

Photography in town is prohibited, unless a special permit is obtained from the Ministry of Tourism. Hapless tourists are always being dragged away to the police station by toughs in army clothing toting sten guns, and sometimes end up in remand. Lorenzo had, of course, obtained the necessary letters and permits from the various ministries in Kinshasa that enabled us to film and photograph almost anywhere. However, one day in Kisangani we were filming a sequence on the ivory street carvers when two pugnacious individuals came up and tried to stop us.

'We want to see your permits,' they demanded belligerently.

Of course, as luck would have it, we had left our permits in camp and could not produce them.

'Come with us to the police station. You may not continue filming, it is against the law,' they growled, revelling in their position of advantage. No manner of persuasion convinced them and when they began getting tough I lost my temper.

'OK, get into the car with us and we'll take you to our camp and show you the permits,' I told them, irritated almost beyond control. 'Come on, get into the car, before we go to the police station.'

They hesitated, obviously taken aback by my firm stand, but finally got into the car. The drive was several miles out of town, and I told them they would have to find their own way back, which meant walking. Suddenly the aggression subsided, and they said, 'OK, just give us something so that we can have a beer and we'll get out.' The situation felt a bit like a game of chess – I looked at Lorenzo and winked.

'Give it to them and push them out, for God's sake,' Lorenzo hissed, losing patience. He gave them a few Zaires, about 50p, and they left, smiling and bowing, as is often the case in these situations, and we returned to our filming. But if one is unaware of the little games they play, it can be very scary.

The cement monument in the town centre commemorating the Simba massacres of 1962, with the letters MPR (*Mouvement Populaire de la Révolution*) beneath a clenched fist holding a burning flame, was itself a reminder of the strong arm of the man who had quelled the violence and the bloodshed and was now the highest power in the land.

The once elegant Hôtel des Chutes on the Avenue du Port, now run down and slovenly, served Zairian 'Primus' beer in bottles without glasses to customers who sat around in plastic chairs on the cheerless cement terrace, or in the semi-darkness of the denuded interior, where a frayed receptionist behind a dark wood counter struggled with the role of a changing Africa. The only shops worth visiting carried outrageously expensive imported stock and belonged to Greeks with Zairian passports, with God knows what compromises attached. All the other stores were half empty; they catered to basic Zairian needs and to threadbare pockets. They now occupied the premises that once accommodated Belgian businesses; for Stanleyville during the Belgian era was a European showplace town with pretty shops, cinemas, theatres, restaurants and cafés, street and traffic lights and white-uniformed gendarmes directing traffic. The streets, now badly potholed, had once all been tarmacked.

The crumbling homes of the Belgian civil servants beneath the sprawling trees, once pretty and surrounded by well-tended tropical gardens, still gave an air of gracious prosperity to the town. The élite had at one time lived in mansions along the river, and the busy port had been run by skilled officials on European lines.

Africans dance not only for pleasure but also as an expression of communal spirit.

It was from here, and from other such towns, that the Belgians had fled when the savagery was unleashed, taking with them only what they could carry; what was left behind was plundered and dismantled; those who remained are buried in the cemetery. Now, twenty years later, despite the opulent tropical vegetation and flowering trees, the scars are still evident everywhere, silent reminders of the nature of the land. In the cemetery behind the Yacht Club, the graves are abandoned, though some are still marginally tended, with plastic flowers in bottles and photographs of the deceased, both black and white, with loving *in memoriam* messages to the French, Belgian, Greek, Italian and Zairian names inscribed on the tombstones. Some, covered in moss, date back a century and some, divided by a little gravel path, have chains around them to keep the spirits, I was told, from escaping or entering. Huge old trees throw a filigree of leaves above them. On the outer edge lies the collective grave of the slaughtered priests and nuns from Ubundu, their names carved in the marble slab beneath a simple cross and blood-red flowers like a crimson collar grow around the stark white stone.

I stayed a while in the cemetery among the dead, recalling the dramatic history of the country. It was cool and very quiet in there, and the bent old caretaker with his long broom came and sat beside me and we had a chat about past events. He

261

Dance is part of
everyday life for
Africans and it
influences their most
mundane gestures and
movements. These street
performers reminded us
of Fellini's film La
Strada.

263

asked me for some money – he was hungry, he said – and I was happy to give him what I had on me.

On my way back to the Yacht Club over the road I met three old women pushing a large wooden cart, pulled by a strapping youth. The cart was piled high with bunches of bananas they were transporting to market. The youth seemed to be yoked to the cart like an ox, a leather strap across his forehead. He was bent in half as he strained with the load, reminding me of a donkey I had once seen in Cairo in a similar situation. How far had they come like that, how far had they still to go? It did not seem to have any importance, since there was no alternative.

A bunch of laughing kids kicking a stone came scuttling towards me and greeted me in French, grabbing hold of my hands. The eldest could not have been more than seven or eight – Zairian street urchins – lovely kids with bright faces of different shades, some with charcoal eyes, some with curly blond hair and blue eyes, others with straight black hair and light green eyes; children of foreign men who had spawned them and then left them behind with their Zairian mothers in the care of Africa. They did not seem any the worse for it; they had not known any other way of life.

The crumbling homes of Belgian civil servants who fled when the savagery was unleashed were sad reminders of more prosperous times.

About five miles out of town, the Sotexki Cotton Mills (Société Textile de Kinshasa) belongs to a Swiss company; further down the river the Bralima Breweries are run by the Dutch. Lelio has some fifty Europeans working under him and up to five hundred Zairians. The production, from the crude cotton bales to the finished fabrics, is handled entirely from within the compound, run by Belgians with Swiss precision. The million yards of cloth produced each month is exclusively for local consumption and, since Mobutu's programme of 'authenticité', every woman in Zaire is wrapped in Sotexki cloth. One of the few profitable European industries in Zaire, Sotexki gives work to a large number of Zairians, who keep their families in money, and it provides a constant outlet to the cotton growers of the country. Well organized, it is run as smoothly as one might expect and in exchange no one interferes at any level, and the old, pre-independence lifestyle and opulence are maintained. President Mobutu, an 'honorary' shareholder, has been trying over the past decade to encourage more European firms to return and branch out into Zaire, but the once-bitten-twice-shy syndrome is still very much present: few are prepared to invest in a country whose stability hangs on the whims of one 'strong man' who holds all the reins of the country in his fist.

In these two compounds, measuring approximately one mile by a half, and surrounded by a high stone wall, the European 'expats' live and work. They rarely go out, unless to dine and dance at the exclusive Yacht Club. Inside the walls another piece of Europe has been transposed to the edge of the river: pretty modern cottages containing every mod. con., with flowered verandahs and luxuriant gardens set out in closely clipped lawns, are joined together by tarmacked driveways on which expensive Range Rovers and Landcruisers are parked. The luxurious interiors are tastefully decorated and each house has three servants. Here life goes on more or less as it does in Europe, with cocktails, tennis and video evenings, to which few, if any, Zairians are invited. We were graciously entertained, with lavish meals exquisitely prepared and washed down with excellent imported wines. Across the river the dense jungle rises in a dark, mysterious wall from which plumes of wispy smoke drift skywards and little black figures trot down to the water on well-trodden paths, while slender canoes loaded with jungle produce, hay, bamboo, bananas and thatch, glide silently by. We waved at them from the lawn on the other side as we sipped champagne from fluted glasses, our two worlds divided by a strip of water.

CHAPTER FIFTEEN

A GIANT
AMONG RIVERS

BEFORE LEAVING NAIROBI WE RECEIVED A MESSAGE FROM
my brother's daughter Fiametta, a financial journalist in the City of
London; she wanted to write some articles on the expedition for international
publication. We were happy at the prospect of her joining us, not only because she
would have added her feminine presence to mine on the last leg of our journey but,
because she was part of the family, the idea seemed particularly appealing. The
question of synchronizing dates posed an immediate problem, for her arrival date in
Kisangani, where we were to meet up, was crucial. Lorenzo insisted on 6 December,
for after that date he could not guarantee our whereabouts. The day-to-day
movements of the expedition were totally unpredictable, and he could not alter or
delay departures because of expected arrivals. His emphasis on the date had a ring of
urgency which only he understood at the time.

No news of Fiametta had reached us by the time we were ready to leave
Kisangani; so we informed Lelio of her expected arrival and he promised to keep in
touch with daily flight arrivals and look after her until she left on one of the Sotexki
river boats, which was sailing a few days after us and planned to meet up with us in
Mbandaka, 750 miles downriver. Reassured that all was well, we cast off on
7 December without her. I was disappointed and concerned, but heartened at this
convenient arrangement with Lelio. Travelling on the Sotexki steamer with its nice
Portuguese captain would be the next best introduction to our adventure and after
London would have given her a few days to acclimatize to the equatorial heat.

The 750-mile stretch between Kisangani and Mbandaka embodies all the
romance and the mystery of the Zaire river. It was to Kisangani, to the Stanley Falls
station, that Joseph Conrad came in 1890 in search of the dying government agent

Kurtz, whom he later immortalized in *Heart of Darkness* and Naipaul described as 'the ivory agent degraded from idealism to savagery, taken back to the earliest ages of man, by wilderness, solitude and power, his home surrounded by impaled human heads'. It is to this very bend in the river that Salim comes when he accepts the offer of a small business in V. S. Naipaul's classic *A Bend in the River*, and it is this same stretch of the Zaire river that inspired both authors to unleash 'the unbound power of eloquence, of words, of burning noble words', just as it had inspired Kurtz to declare that 'the whites must necessarily appear to them [the savages] in the nature of supernatural beings – we approach them with the might as of a deity.'

Conrad's well-known description of the river came to mind as we began our descent from Kisangani. Since his day certain aspects had changed superficially, but the core was still there, and travelling past this same vegetation, these same trees, emphasized life's eternal rondo and the insignificance of man's passage on earth. What had all man's noise and turmoil, his self-assertion, his quest for power, his dissemination, destruction and despair finally led to here, other than guiding the hand of some writers of genius to preserve it for posterity?

Africa's dialogue with humans varies with each individual. People who are sensitive to Africa rarely completely acclimatize to other cultures. They share a cohesion of spirit. This is referred to as 'African Fever', a somewhat undervalued condition, that leads to a deep understanding of Nature's life-force. For us whites born in Africa there is no real allegiance to any one country or flag; we are destined to a sort of perpetual exile, but we do all identify with Nature, which in Africa knows no bounds. Nature seems to be the real link between us.

Of all the rivers we travelled on, the Zaire is without doubt the most mysterious. We were now crossing the Zaire basin, the liquid belly of Africa that stretches from Kisangani to the Atlantic. One could imagine that all the water that falls in the north, absorbed by the arid sponge of the Sahara, re-emerges here in Zaire and then slips wastefully into the Atlantic Ocean. If the Nile evokes the ancient Pharaonic civilization, the Zaire river evokes primeval Africa, the virgin forests of the dawn of creation. It also evokes a more painful modern Africa, that of Joseph Conrad, who understood, a hundred years ago, that the problems confronting contemporary Africa had their roots in the colonial invasion, perpetrated by the Europeans and defined by him as 'the vilest plunder in human history'. The 'darkness' Conrad referred to was not that invented by popular imagination, a country barbarous and inhabited by hostile and pagan savages. It is the darkness that envelops our civilization, a darkness of the soul and of the mind, maintained and imposed by the rich nations to the detriment of the poorer ones, a civilization itself turning to

—Overleaf—
We were now crossing the Zaire basin, the liquid belly of Africa which stretches from Kisangani to the Atlantic.

barbarism, eroded by its own machinations.

Commercial navigation on the river was introduced by the Belgians and as such has remained a beneficial legacy left by the colonial oppressors. Today it still provides a regular means of transport for the jungle-dwellers along the 1,250-mile route from Kisangani to Zaire's capital, Kinshasa. This river transport is in fact a floating village, consisting of barges, rafts, pontoons and canoes, propelled forward by a large motorized tug known as *le grand pousseur* (the big pusher). If the inhabitants cannot get to the village, the village travels to them along the cataract-free stretch of river between Kisangani and Kinshasa.

The people in canoes await the tug's arrival in midstream, and the river surface, at such times, is streaked with long, slender dugouts, moving fast and gracefully through the water, propelled by the rhythmic motion of those whose very survival depends on the excellence of their art and craft. Steering their canoes is as much part of their lives as walking; the agility and delicacy of the manoeuvres are impressive. The steamer calls only at the larger trading ports; elsewhere it just slows down, and precise calculation alone allows for contact with the mother-ship. Misjudgement can cost goods, trade and sometimes life. To get attached to the floating mass moving forward on the river is a risky and dangerous business. Desperate hands have only a few moments to gain a precarious grip on the moving vessel; failure to do so can sometimes separate families for days and annihilate weeks of hard work, and two or three weeks may elapse before another occasion presents itself. The journeys of these steamers are real odysseys on the rivers of this vast country.

As the trading dugouts are skilfully poled in, activity on board is whipped up as by a sudden gust of wind. The excitement generated is intense and often violent, and many an encounter erupts in a free-for-all fist-fight. The impact is felt throughout the vessel. A wave of what sounds like jungle hoots envelops the point of contact, as half-crazed black bodies shout and gesticulate with angry, excited voices, out-stretched arms and clenched fists, as if their very existence depended on the exchange of their goods. Hanging from the railings with one arm, they stretch out over the water towards the advancing pirogues in an effort to be the first to grab hold of the merchandise. Often several hands grab hold of the goods together and a savage tug-of-war ensues. The scuffle then ends abruptly with one man's victory, and can begin again immediately with a fresh arrival. Trading is always intense and brisk, regardless of day or night. These vigorous scenes reminded me of a Stock Exchange floor or of wild beasts on a kill.

As the journey progresses the produce from the jungle piles up on the decks – hundreds of kilos of fish (fresh, sun-dried and smoked), slender antelopes, wicker

Baby monkeys and chimps from the forest are transported to Kinshasa, where they are sold to tourists.

Trading is always intense and brisk regardless of whether it is day or night.

Steering their canoes is as much a part of their lives as walking; the agility and delicacy of the manoeuvres are impressive.

People in canoes await the tug's arrival in midstream.

Desperate hands have only a few moments to gain a precarious grip on the moving vessel. Misjudgement can cost goods, trade and sometimes lives.

—Overleaf—
In the first light of dawn we caught sight of a floating village advancing through the mist.

Early morning activities had already started on board – people washing, cooking, cleaning dishes.

Lorenzo and Brian Larkey with the four members of our third team.

The steamer carries cartridges to the hunters and returns with the smoked carcasses of monkeys and other animals.

chairs, pestles and mortars carved from tree trunks, enamel basins filled with pineapple, papaya and avocado pears, eels, tadpoles and baby fish alive in water, bags of manioc and bunches of bananas, and monkeys alive or dead and smoked into grotesque shapes.

A few days after leaving Kisangani, we encountered *Le Colonel Ebea*, one of the ONATRA fleet of six steamers that plough up and down the river. We had stopped the night at Bumba, where some Catholic nuns stationed there opened their ascetic, fenced-off mission compound to us. We camped on the lawn which lay between the river and the simple stone building, and that night were once again dowsed by a heavy storm which chased us out of our tents to the shelter of the covered verandah.

In the first light of dawn we caught sight of the floating village advancing through the mist, a strange and awesome apparition, like a great water beast from another world. We went out to meet it in the inflatables and travelled beside it for a while, through the eerie morning light in the twilight zone that precedes the rising sun. Hundreds of canoes, tethered one to the other, were attached to either side of the barges like clams to the belly of a tanker. Early-morning activities had already begun on board: people washing, cooking, waking up. Loud music blared from speakers, with a garish gaiety that enveloped and somehow suited the phantas-

magorical spectacle: '*Félicité, tu es l'enfant du bonheur*' (Happiness, you are the child of joy) bounced in heavily accented words off the still waters and echoed through the trees, capturing all the uncrushable joyfulness of Africa in its catchy rhythm and simple phrases.

We were wanderers on prehistoric earth, on an earth that wore the aspect of an unknown planet. We could have fancied ourselves the first of men taking possession of an accursed inheritance, to be subdued at the cost of profound anguish and of excessive toil. But suddenly, as we struggled round a bend, there would be a glimpse of rush walls, of peaked grass roofs, a burst of yells, a whirl of black limbs, a mass of hands clapping, of feet stamping, of bodies swaying, of eyes rolling, under the droop of heavy motionless foliage... We were cut off from the comprehension of our surroundings; we glided past like phantoms, wondering and secretly appalled, as sane men would before an enthusiastic outbreak in a madhouse. We could not understand because we were travelling in the night of first ages, of those ages that are gone, leaving hardly a sign – no memories ... the earth seemed unearthly. We are accustomed to look upon the shackled form of a conquered monster, but there, there you could look at a thing monstrous and free. It was unearthly and the men were – no, they were not inhuman, well, you know, that was the worst of it, this suspicion of their not being inhuman.

Harsh words these of Joseph Conrad's, ironic but true. A hundred years later, the spirit of our encounter remained unchanged and the heart-beat of Africa was still pounding with the same force.

Approximately a hundred miles south of Kisangani, the Aruvimi river enters the Zaire and, at the confluence of the two rivers, the Zaire widens considerably, its course scattered with sandbanks and small wooded islands, some of which are inhabited, resembling floating rafts waiting to be dragged away by tugs. Here some large canoes converged towards us, curious for a look at the *wasungu* (whites) in their rubber boats. The sight of these powerful rowers approaching brought to mind the pages of Stanley's diary. In 1874, at approximately this point on the river, he had waged his twenty-fourth battle against 2,000 cannibals who had attacked him from fifty-four pirogues, ten of which had eighty men each on board. On his voyage from the Indian Ocean to the Atlantic, Stanley had to open his route with

— Above —
Lorenzo with Antoinette, the captain's girlfriend.

— Opposite —
The sight of these powerful rowers approaching brought to mind the pages of Stanley's diary.

— Overleaf —
We were forced to cross a dark lagoon dense with giant trees, the roots of which sank deep into the river.

279

— Previous page —
How can people live in a place like this, in this dim, watery wilderness of matted leaves, roots and branches, buzzing with mosquitoes and hung with cobwebs? Are they immune to malaria and what do they do when they fall ill? Do they get cerebral malaria and die the way we do?

gunfire. His men destroyed a hundred villages and fought thirty-two battles, all of them victorious, he tells us, extracting 50,000 dollars-worth of ivory from them.

We stopped now and again and went on land to visit the island families, descendants of these wild 'cannibals', who are quite autonomous and seem to have adapted perfectly to their surroundings, living simple, monotonous lives which appeared quite intolerable to us. We were always received with much friendliness and none of them ever asked to come away with us. Instead of attacking us, they offered us smoked river fish that looked like sculpted bronze.

Clumps of water hyacinth, detached from the shores, floated downstream with us on the current towards the Atlantic estuary 1,000 miles away. An inland canal without an outlet forced us to cross a dark lagoon, dense with giant trees whose roots sank deep into the river. Due to the heat and humidity the atmosphere was stifling, and the hot air smelled of moist leaves; it was like being enclosed in an immense greenhouse. Giant cobwebs in the form of Chinese lanterns hung from the branches, and the sunlight ricocheted in all directions through their delicate filaments, quivering on the drops of moisture, guiding us back to the river.

At the mouth of the canal strange little heads resembling giant toads appeared from the muddy water; they were small turtles. Only their cone-shaped noses and round beady eyes were visible, and they sank at our approach. Their silent presence was just part of the life-force throbbing around us; how many other aquatic creatures, we wondered, have their habitat in these murky waters?

We moved forward slowly in this green labyrinth of roots and submerged branches. Suddenly a group of black faces appeared among the leaves, people of the forest with smooth skins and wide eyes. They peered at us in silence and when we greeted them they ran away and hid, to reappear further down, overcome by curiosity; reassured that we would not harm them, they returned our greetings and eventually showed us the way to a tunnel-like opening into the open river beyond. The water around us, filtered through the roots and fallen leaves, was strangely transparent, but became clouded and rather menacing as our propellors stirred up the soft, gooey mud at the bottom.

How can people live in a place like this, in this dim, watery wilderness of matted leaves, roots and branches, buzzing with mosquitoes and hung with cobwebs? At least on the islands in midstream there is sunlight and no mosquitoes. Are they immune to malaria? What do they do when they become ill? Do they get cerebral malaria and die the way we do?

As we left this natural hothouse the air outside seemed suddenly thinner and it was easier to breathe. The water hyacinths, pushed together by the current, fringed the river with a border of lush green leaves – approximately three yards wide – which undulated indolently as we passed. Dozens of water locusts, a local variety of *Tettigonia viridissima*, hung like exotic jewels on the smooth, juicy leaves. To protect themselves from preying reptiles and birds, they hide in couples or alone beneath the hyacinth leaves. With their six-inch wing-span and their tiny heads dotted with bright red, yellow and green like beads inserted into plastic, they resemble medieval warriors, samurai of the river, waiting for battle. Fried or boiled, they are also delicious to eat, it seems.

Some voyages are remembered by colours, forms or objects, but the scenery of the Zaire river leaves one with a memory of silence and solitude, of immobility and emptiness. Sometimes our journey seemed to go on and on endlessly; at times a feeling of repetitious monotony enveloped us; but it was perhaps this very monotony which was its fascination: one moved forward, but one had the impression of immobility. The days went by, but it was always like the first day. The Zaire river is a moving lagoon, a running marsh, a bog that is never still. Its waters are a compact mass that slip in between bushy islands where the odd hut, often abandoned, recalls the presence of man. Strangely, in this aqueous expanse we never felt lost, because the river gave direction to everything; one just had to flow with the current and one was bound to arrive somewhere.

At this point of the river the water, through the millennia, has dug deep into the calcium cliffs; serrated by the rain into savage bas-reliefs and hung with delicate creepers, they could belong to some great stage set for a wilderness version of *A Midsummer Night's Dream*. Drifting downstream on the current in the silence of this blue-green highway, we sometimes wished it never to end, for it was as if we were travelling on a rolling carpet into eternity. The silence did, however, underline the total absence of wildlife of any sort: no birds or hippos or crocs; it was almost as if even we didn't exist. The further we drifted the wider the river became as we prepared to meet the Atlantic Ocean, and as we approached the Zaire delta the banks were ever more scattered with the ruins of abandoned Belgian buildings, constant reminders of the European colonization of Africa, ultimate monuments to that barbaric invasion and to the hypocrisy of our society. Now and again we encountered the pirogues which are so much part of the ever-changing *tableau vivant* of the river. Will we ever return to these regions other than in our memory?

One evening at dusk, gunshots suddenly disturbed the peace and put us on alert. As we drifted towards the sun, setting in a great red ball behind the dark trees, the thought of some demon using it as a target crossed our minds. Then we came across him: an innocent wilderness demon with his home-made gun, on the river bank.

—Overleaf—
Mist seems strangely to suit tropical scenery – the colours become bland, the greens pleasantly opaque.

A chimp, like any other animal, is merely a source of food, of survival.

—Previous page—
As we drifted towards the sun setting in a huge red ball behind the dark trees, the idea of some demon using it as a target crossed our minds.

'What are you shooting at?' we shouted at him.

'Chimpanzees,' he shouted back matter-of-factly.

The word came at us loud and clear: chimpanzees. Ruzina, fast asleep, snuggled up like a baby in the rough folds of the canvas tarpaulin, at least was safe: her breathing barely visible, the eyes closed, the little hands open and relaxed, tiny beads of perspiration hovering around her nostrils; safe and at peace with the world. These are the people who had killed her mother, who had orphaned her and landed her in the horrible cage in Bujumbura. You bastard, we all thought. How can you kill a chimp? But then when we talked to him we realized that for him a chimp is just like any other animal, a source of food, of protein, of survival. Here in Zaire there is no room for sentimentality.

'What is your name?'

'My name is Joseph.'

We introduced ourselves and a brief exchange in French established contact.

'So you shoot chimps with this gun?'

'Yes.'

'Are there many?'

'Yes, many.'

'Where did you get this gun?'

'I made it.'

Lorenzo took the gun from him and examined it. 'It's a bit rusty, your gun. I can see the cartridge in the barrel – be careful, it can be dangerous, you know.'

'I know,' came the simple reply.

'Shall I take out the cartridge?'

'No, no, leave it alone, it's OK.'

'But don't you have accidents with this weapon?'

'Yes, there are accidents, but it doesn't matter.'

'What d'you mean, it doesn't matter?'

'Because we make them ourselves.'

'But if the barrel explodes?' Lorenzo retorted with his white man's logic.

'No, no, no, it can't,' Joseph replied, laughing. 'It can't happen.'

'But why, because of *le bon Dieu*?'

'Yes, because of *le bon Dieu*...'

'Apart from chimps, what else do you kill in the forest?'

'Only monkeys; there are also some antelope, but these are more difficult. We catch them in a different way, with traps. It is a lot of hard work and I have a large family to feed, nine children, a wife and my old father and mother. I also have to buy clothes for them and there is not always much fish in the river; we have to hunt to live.'

Lorenzo was not convinced by Joseph's explanation and asked him if he could go with him next day on a chimp hunt. He would have prevented him from killing any in his presence, but he was curious to know the truth.

We spent that night beside Joseph's compound in a small clearing in the forest and met his family. Joseph became our friend, our guide, our informer; Joseph was part of the wilderness we were travelling through; he could speak about it. Until we met him we were like Conrad, 'wanderers on a prehistoric earth, on an earth that wore the aspect of an unknown planet'; now we were to become part of it, for Joseph, who belonged to it, had agreed to take us into it, to introduce us to it, to shoot its chimpanzees.

LORENZO: Joseph was barefoot; with his tobacco-coloured skin he was indeed a striking-looking individual. Not a trace of fat on his chest and arms; his waist was slim and his legs elastic, like those of an Olympic athlete. He walked fast. It was an effort to keep up with him and we were still only at the start of a long walk. The path was level and soft, crossed by huge, knotted roots that transformed our march into a kind of gymkhana, an obstacle race. Glimpses of the river were visible through the trees, low down to our right. We followed it for a mile or so across a seemingly endless manioc plantation.

'Here everything that moves is eaten.' Mirella had said, describing her impressions of her first voyage down the Zaire river. I was sure that Joseph hunted monkeys, squirrels, any animal worth the bullet. I was, however, not yet quite sure that, as he had told me a few hours before, we were really going to hunt chimps.

The energy I managed to muster to keep up with Joseph was purely because of my desire to prevent him killing any monkeys or chimps that appeared on our path. Joseph had caressed Ruzina and said she was '*très tendre*' (very tender). His sympathetic, open smile seemed to underline the absolute purity of his primitive soul. It was, however, impossible to convince him that chimps were not chickens or fish to be smoked and eaten.

It was hard to resist Joseph's indestructible good faith. Of course, if he pointed his gun at any animal, I would in some way prevent him from firing. I would lower his gun barrel and I would compensate him for his lost prey – and so thinking, I arrived at the end of the manioc plantation on the edge of the green forest wall.

Slowing down, Joseph turned and, always smiling, explained in his archaic French that from this moment onwards we would be communicating only with gestures. He ended by squeezing his lips between the thumb and index finger of his left hand. With his right hand he brandished his rifle as if it were a walking stick. Joseph had no respect for safety rules and as he spoke he pointed the barrel of his loaded gun at me. I jumped about from left to right in an attempt to keep out of his way. His locally-made gun could hardly be referred to as a weapon. It was, however, a lethal twelve-bore whose barrel had been scavenged from a car steering-wheel rod. The cartridges were of good European manufacture and were still visible once the gun was locked. I couldn't imagine firing such a weapon, so apparently ready to explode in the hands of the hunter.

From the moment we entered the forest Joseph changed pace. At first he was sprinting, then he seemed to be dancing on his toes in rhythm with his hearing, his sight and his smell. He moved, looking and listening around him, stopping now and again to sniff the air. I wondered with how much speed I would have been able to intervene had I wanted to prevent him firing. I made the most of his sudden halts to catch up with him. Now and again he left the beaten path and melted into the bushes in order to inspect the trees from the roots upwards. In these tense moments Joseph would look at me and point his index finger towards the forest as if to reassure me of the outcome of our hunt, to confirm the presence of the chimps. Then he continued.

It was pleasant beneath the green canopy of the forest. The air was fresher and the dim arboreal light reminded me of a medieval church where the air was impregnated by an opaque antique green, the damp colour of moss born from the patina of time. At times I felt I was at the bottom of the sea.

Without warning Joseph shouldered his gun and aimed. I threw myself at him, grabbed him by the shoulder and gave him a good shaking.

'What is it?' I asked him, pretending ignorance, in order to justify my strange gesture, conscious of having disturbed him.

Joseph turned his head and smiled. 'Squirrel,' he said.

'Squirrel or chimpanzee?' I repeated for reassurance.

'No, no' – Joseph used an African name – 'Small, but good to eat. To eat,' he repeated with the classical hand and joined fingertip gesture towards the mouth. 'To eat,' he repeated, explaining to me the only reason worth explaining.

I touched the barrel of his gun, and with a grimace whispered, 'You'd be better off using a bow and arrow.'

He replied with a terrible phrase, almost as if it were a proverb: 'With a bow and arrow you can bag one chimp every thirty days – with a gun you can bag thirty chimps in one day.'

The further we ventured the more aware I became of the intense silence of the forest. There was nothing here, no birds, no insects, not even any mosquitoes. There were only plants, and trees with invisible tops. There were no flowers or fruit. There must, however, be some animals somewhere. I found two empty twelve-bore cartridge cases lying among the roots of a tree trunk. I picked them up and showed them to Joseph.

'Chimpanzee,' he said immediately, sniffing them. He returned them to me. I sniffed them myself; the sweet smell of gunpowder still lingered. Those cartridges must have been fired about a week earlier – the red plastic cases had not yet begun to decay. They were identical to Joseph's ammunition. He told me they were made at Pointe Noire, and brought into Zaire illegally from the Congo, then brought into the interior by the boats that travel upstream from Kinshasa.

At four in the afternoon we decided to turn back. We couldn't proceed further: we had been on the go for three hours, and by seven it would be dark. Joseph beckoned me to sit beside him at the foot of a tree-trunk around which some roots were entwined in great spirals, transforming it into a mighty column seemingly sculpted by the hand of some great ebonist. Joseph shinned easily upwards, balancing himself against the branches of the tree. Four yards from the ground he stopped, turned his head, bent forward and listened.

He looked down at me, smiled and opened his left hand to signal that there was nothing – no chimpanzees or anything else.

Perhaps Joseph was lying to me, like an innocent child. I hoped so. Perhaps he took me on a wild-goose chase in order to give himself importance. It is not every day that white strangers appear in these areas and ask to go hunting. He descended the tree and began to explain that in order to hunt well one must sleep in the forest, remain two or three days in a row. But we had no water or food or blankets. It sounded like an excuse. Perhaps there were no longer any chimps in these green depths.

On our return I felt the fatigue of the walk biting at my legs. Joseph's fast pace remained unchanged. He suddenly halted and listened. In the distance we heard the echo of gunfire. Joseph's face lit up with a big ear-to-ear smile.

'Chimpanzee,' he said.

'Why not squirrel?' I replied.

'No, chimpanzee,' he assured me emphatically.

I couldn't quite understand the reason for this insistence on chimpanzees. Perhaps it was because they are the most sought-after prey, perhaps because he thought he was pleasing me. It was six o'clock; the green of the forest had become sombre. We could no longer see ten yards ahead of us. A fine mist was rising from the ground, much like that emanating from hot, wet asphalt. It was claustrophobic beneath the dense cupola of the tropical forest. I would not be able to remain here for long; this greenery suffocated me. I thought of the pygmies who dislike the light of the sun. I couldn't wait to see its rays again, those rays which at dusk rip through the vegetation like whiplashes of light, hitting me in the face as blinding as a searchlight, inebriating as a mouthful of pure oxygen after a long immersion. On the edge of the forest, almost suddenly, I found again the magic of the sun and its colours.

We returned to the manioc plantation. The river was sparkling through the trees. We were not far from the forest station where Mirella awaited us. The path followed the river bank about ten feet above it. On the river a pirogue approached. Two rowers propelled it forward on the edge of the current. A third character sat between them on the floor of the pirogue, motionless.

'Chimpanzee.' Joseph pointed at the pirogue with his gun and his voice froze my blood.

The third figure was indeed an adult chimpanzee, dead, wedged into the bottom of the vessel. Its upright position gave the impression of a passenger looking ahead, certainly not that of a corpse. As the pirogue passed beside us I noticed that buckshot had smashed into its skull above the right eye, leaving a gaping wound about three inches round.

'Chimpanzee,' Joseph repeated with a grin.

'Chimpanzee,' I said, shaking my head sadly, thinking of Ruzina. Now I was sure, now I knew that it was true. Chimp-hunting was indeed a sad reality. Joseph explained that as it was a large male they had to cut it in half to facilitate transport. They were taking it to the nearby village to await the steamer due to pass by that night. Because of the size they would get much money for it, and some more cartridges.

Mirella joined us. Her sadness echoed mine. Joseph asked us if we wished to buy the chimp in order to eat it. His gun was pointing towards my face. With my right hand I gently moved it.

The bright orange sun was setting behind a green sea of trees. As it disappeared we heard another shot. I turned to Joseph.

'Chimpanzee?'

'*Bien sûr* – yes, of course,' he replied, grinning.

At Pointe Noire on the Atlantic coast of the Democratic Republic of Congo, a cartridge factory has been built that enriches a few industrialists and contributes towards the destruction of the fauna of this part of the world. Joseph paid the equivalent of one dollar per cartridge, and for each smoked monkey or dead chimp he collected ten dollars. Simple arithmetic explained his occupation: business is business. The steamers carried cartridges to him and returned with carcasses of animals he killed with them. Joseph told us that, if he could no longer acquire cartridges, he would have to find some other way of surviving, but hunting is what he prefers; for the moment cartridges are available and are getting cheaper.

The third figure was indeed an adult chimp, but dead, wedged into the bottom of the canoe. Buckshot had smashed its skull above the right eye.

:MIRELLA

After the chimp hunt, Joseph led us to a forestry concession whose HQ lies a few miles from where Lorenzo and he had been hunting. The Siforzal concession (*Société Forestière Zairois-Allemand*) is cutting down the primeval forests of Zaire, which means that in a few years, here also, there will be the most vacant of empty spaces. The site was already heavily compromised, a dust bowl with giant tractors, lorries and bulldozers ploughing up and down in a thick, suffocating cloud of fine dust, underlining our feeling that man is like a crazed virus that infects its own

The Siforzal concession
is cutting down the
primeval forests of Zaire
and in a few years this
too will be the most
vacant of empty spaces.

surroundings in order to destroy it. If we as single individuals reacted to this situation, then why, we asked ourselves, cannot man react, and reason collectively for his own benefit? About a hundred yards inland from the river, the magnificent, imperilled forest, from which the remaining chimps and other animals had fled, stood silently awaiting execution.

A young French couple in charge of the concession invited us in for the night and the hopeless reality of the industrial destruction of the planet was rammed home to us; as with the ivory trade, so long as there is financial gain then trees, like elephants, will fall; our hosts, like Joseph, had a living to make and did not question the motives that provided them with their livelihood. Their forest home was entirely made of wood, tastefully built and designed and containing every comfort, which we, of course, much appreciated, together with the excellent wines, French cheeses, European fruits and *filet mignon*, all flown in from Europe and delivered weekly to this remote forest outpost by the company aircraft.

Our conversation with Cornelius, the loyal Zairian foreman who had been in charge of the compound for ten years, was horrifically revealing in its innocent pride.

'What do the numbers on these logs signify?' Lorenzo asked him, pointing to the mountain of tree trunks ready for the descent downstream to Kinshasa.

'They indicate the cutting areas.'

'How many trees are there in each area?'

'400, 500, sometimes 600.'

'And you cut them all?'

'Yes, we cut them all, all of them.'

'But you replant each tree you cut, don't you?'

'No, no, we don't replant anything.'

'How many acres are there in each concession?'

'This concession has 650,000 acres.'

'650,000 acres?' Lorenzo repeated, verifying that he had understood.

'Yes, 650,000 acres.'

'How many concessions of this size are there?'

'For the moment we have one, but soon we shall have another.'

'How many acres will that be?'

'Two and a half million acres,' Cornelius replied proudly.

'And you will cut all the trees there too?'

'Yes, we shall cut them all, the Sipos, the Tiama, the Cosi, the Dola, the Doveti, all the biggest trees, those that have reached at least a yard in diameter.' Cornelius's eyes were shining.

'When the tree falls you cut it with an electric saw?'

'Yes, the mechanical saw brings the tree down and then cuts it up.'

'When the tree falls, it damages all the smaller ones around it?'

'Of course. It is impossible to avoid that. When one tree falls, those around fall with it.'

'So nothing is left?'

'No, nothing is left. We just move on to the next spot. We have many trees in Zaire.'

'But, you know, don't you, that the oxygen of the world and the rainfall depend on the forests?'

'How's that?'

'You don't know that the trees provide oxygen and create rain?'

'No.'

'Well, they do.'

Cornelius was momentarily disconcerted and then, as if wanting to justify himself, continued, 'But we have no control over the situation. We are just employees and we do what we are told. It's the boss in Kinshasa who reaps the benefits. We don't. He gives the concessions to the Europeans and he reaps the benefits. For every tree that falls, he gets a percentage. We remain poor and helpless – he gets richer and fatter every day. If we say anything, we lose our jobs and we starve.'

Back on the river we encountered a shipment of logs floating downstream on the current. Strapped together by large steel cables, they formed a giant platform pushed by a Siforzal tug. The journey to Kinshasa or Matadi lasts two or three weeks, and temporary shelters are erected on the platform for those who accompany it. A warm, milky mist enveloped us, lending a surreal aspect to the scene. It seemed as if all of a sudden the climate was changing; the sun appeared to be getting closer to the earth, evaporating the waters of the planet; the heat within the mist was more intense. Once again the magic of the Zaire river was unleashed. Mist seems strangely to suit the tropical scenery: the colours become more bland, the greens pleasantly opaque.

A week after casting off in Kisangani we reached Mbandaka, the other major port on the Zaire, known during the Belgian colonial era as Coquilhatville. Like everywhere else in Zaire, Mbandaka had the now familiar air of dereliction. From the water level only the Catholic cathedral, standing grand and stolid among the

— Above —
A dust bowl with enormous tractors, lorries and bulldozers ploughing up and down in a suffocating cloud of fine dust underlined our feelings that man is like a crazed virus infecting its own surroundings in order to destroy it.

— Opposite —
People carry away smaller logs for firewood.

— Overleaf —
Cleared forest land is cultivated for a few years and then abandoned.

palm trees high on the bank, still presented a definite countenance of religious stoicism that time and events had not affected. The town still maintained a certain grandeur, with its large square stone buildings, now empty and useless, its magnificent tree-lined alleys in full brilliant flower, leading to Government House, where the regional Belgian Governor had once lived haughtily with his family and his bevy of servants. Now it is the HQ of the Zairian Governor. The magnificent setting, high on a headland with a sweeping view across the river, still retained its eminence, overlooking a pristine scene filled with mystery, through which the locals enveloped in the heat-haze wove simple patterns in slender black canoes.

I sat for a while on the carpet lawns beneath the ancient trees in the garden, where a bunch of weary gardeners half-heartedly swept up fallen leaves. Here in Mbandaka, unless you worked for the government there was no work – survival depended on the generosity of the land.

A wonderful stillness, broken only by the staccato calls of the hidden birds and the ugly black crows feeding on the rubbish rotting in the street gutters and shallow depressions in the ground, impregnated the hot air. A semblance of old grandeur was, however, being maintained in the gravelled driveway, the black wrought-iron gates and the uniformed sentinels, but it was only superficial, for beneath the thin

We imagined ourselves as the first men taking possession of an accursed inheritance.

veneer the naked, uncouth mien of Africa was very visible. One could imagine it becoming more so with the passage of time.

Mbandaka, however, was bursting with charm. There was something undeniably picturesque in its decay, the abandoned Belgian homes with long grasses growing through the windows and trees sprouting through the roofs, the fragile *favela* shacks dribbling down to the water's edge between the great stone buildings, the carcasses of the forsaken river steamers and barges parked beside each other in the mud, in a symphony of crumbling shapes and rust colours. From these old skeletons new life had sprung in a different form; people fished with nets and lines, clothes were washed and dried, children leapt into the muddy water and, all day, canoes crisscrossed in front of them. It seemed as if this parasitic life, mirrored in the still waters, was breathing new vitality into the debris of another age.

About a mile from the port, at the junction with the Ruki river, a village perched on poles driven deep into the mud spread for half a mile, three feet above the water. Here we were back on the Equator, which we had already crossed three times on our journey, for 20,000 miles of water routes wind through this immense Zaire basin, which is the size of Europe. No one is rich on the river, but no one is forced to beg. Simple structures house simple lives, and the usual gaiety and bustle of a Zairian day was in full swing as we pulled up, cut our engines and gently manoeuvred through the narrow, stilted passages. Our cameras, inflatables and engines caused the usual stir and everyone presented themselves, hanging above us out of doors and windows, wedged between poles or crammed on precarious perches. The smell of hot oil from frying fish and doughnuts wafted on the air; a school canoe-bus passed beside us, ferrying pupils to the elementary mission school in town.

We spent the night attached to one of the rusty ship skeletons, awaiting the Sotexki steamer which was due in the early hours of next day with Fiametta. But Fiametta never arrived. She was not on board. My heart sank. What had happened to her? The Portuguese captain had waited an extra twenty-four hours for her in Kisangani, but she had not arrived there either. My arrangements with Lelio had seemed so foolproof. Perhaps a change of plans had prevented her departure from London. We did not know what had happened to her until we returned to London two months later and found her letter.

As I read it out loud to Lorenzo the ghastly story unfolded. She had indeed arrived in Kisangani the day after we left. Lelio was not at the airport to meet her – she never met up with him – and my careful plan had been totally ineffective. She spent a horrible week alone in Kisangani waiting for a flight out. She flew to Mbandaka in the hope of catching up with us, but found no sign of our passage. In rage and despair she decided to return to London, but, as there was no plane out of Mbandaka to Kinshasa for several days, she climbed on to a lorry leaving that night with a bunch of Zairians. Perched on top of a pile of bags, she was ejected into a nearby marsh where she landed face down in the water when the lorry turned over an hour after departing, killing nine of the passengers. She regained consciousness in the Zairian hospital in Mbandaka with three crushed vertebrae. Three days later, strapped to a stretcher, she was loaded on to a British Airways plane in Kinshasa for London, after convincing the doctors in Mbandaka that she did not wish to undergo an operation in Zaire. Her dreadful tale showed the other side of our coin, revealing how easily a favourable situation can turn sour when careful planning goes unheeded and mistakes are made.

CHAPTER SIXTEEN

AT LAST THE ATLANTIC

THE ZAIRE RIVER BEGINS TO WIDEN CONSIDERABLY OUTSIDE Mbandaka. The forest starts to thin and the waters spread into an endless marsh which stretches to the horizon; one becomes increasingly aware of the two million cubic feet per second that rush towards the Atlantic all year round. At its widest point the Zaire measures ten miles across; it is then sucked back into the steep rock canyon beyond the Livingstone Falls at Kinshasa. 'The river gradually expands . . . which admitted us in view of a mighty breadth of river; sandy islands rose in front of us like a sea-beach, and on the right towered a long row of cliffs, white and glistening; the grassy table-land above the cliffs appeared as green as a lawn,' Stanley noted in his diary; and Frank Pocock, one of his faithful team members, looking across the mighty river below and surveying its strange and sudden expansion, said to him, 'Why, I declare, sir, this place is just like a pool, as broad as it is long. There are mountains all round it and it appears almost circular. Why not call it Stanley Pool?'

Stanley's description continued: 'We heard for the first time the low and sullen thunder of the first cataract. The furious river, rushing down a steep bed obstructed by reefs of lava, projected barriers of rock, lines of immense boulders, winding a crooked course through deep chasms and dropping down over terraces in a long series of falls and cataracts and rapids; it was a descent into a watery hell.'

Our last days on the river before reaching Kinshasa were monotonous and seemed endless, perhaps because we had by now reached saturation point and the glitter of novelty had begun to tarnish. The flatlands stretched either side of us as far as we could see. We entered the Stanley Pool and ahead of us the ugly harbour of

Kinshasa with its tall cement buildings rose against the skyline like mini-skyscrapers. We could have been arriving in any similar ugly European port – Marseilles, Genoa or La Spezia – and the knowledge that we were still on the great Zaire river seemed rather disconcerting. The prospect of our journey drawing to a close was strangely welcome: our arrival in Kinshasa was the first step back towards the world we had left almost eighteen months before.

The director of the Inter-Continental Hotel, another of Lorenzo's useful contacts, gave us two double rooms and, as we stepped through the revolving door into the great foyer, we had the distinct feeling that our adventure was coming to an end. Only 400 miles were left to the Atlantic, 200 of which were unnavigable because of the cataracts.

Kinshasa, like Nairobi, Bujumbura and Dar-es-Salaam, was designed by the Europeans and inherited by the Africans. Their needs, no better or worse than our own, are nevertheless different; these old colonial towns, never having taken colonial climate, culture and traditions into consideration, have suffered badly during the transition from one era to the other. The sprawling town spreads for miles above the cliffs and over the hills south of the river in a labyrinth of streets and roads, paths and alleyways, knitting together the shanty urban habitat of 5 million Zairians, whose roots have remained in the majestic jungles we had just traversed. The European quarter, with its beautiful homes and gardens, its mini-skyscrapers, restaurants and elegant shopping malls, covers only a small fraction of the rambling metropolis and has not been affected by the struggle for independence. Much has changed, of course, since the departure of the Belgians, but the might and muscle of the whites was soon re-established, even if in another form, and much of the old glamour and prestige has been maintained. Set apart from the native inhabitants in homes which spread high above the river, most of the whites now living in Kinshasa are either diplomats or 'two-year-wonders' attached to industries at the invitation of President Mobutu, the strong man who sits on Mont Galiema and controls 'the rain and the fair weather' of the country. The contrast between the two life-styles can be considered interesting, disgraceful or natural according to one's point of view. Wherever poverty and wealth cohabit the shock-waves are the same, but somehow in Kinshasa the *status quo* has been accepted and for the moment no one contests it, presumably because of the shadow of the strong arm that controls the nation, for here in Kinshasa, where the 'almighty' has his seat, no one dares lift his head and his name is spoken in hushed tones.

From Mont Galiema, where Stanley's statue once stood overlooking the Livingstone Falls below, one can look across the river to Brazzaville, capital of the

French Congo, on the other side. Behind, the royal compound spreads over acres of rolling green lawns beneath ancient mango trees where a rare variety of captive antelope graze and a solitary lion and a chimp sit and stare in stony silence at the world beyond the high-walled confines. Sentinels in frayed Navy uniforms and imitation leopard-skin *képis* stand guard, with Kalashnikovs, in front of the wrought-iron gate in an arrogant show of force.

The night of our arrival the Inter-Continental threw a massive cocktail party to which we were invited for the inauguration of a new wing. After weeks in jungle conditions, in close touch with the dire struggle for survival which is the daily lot of most Zairians, the lavish opulence of this cocktail party seemed an outrage. The 800 guests arrived in limousines, dressed to the nines in French couture, jewels and scent

— Above —
*Alfred Liyolo is the
leading sculptor of Zaire
and a protégé of
Mobutu, whose bronze
statue he created.*

— Right —
*The wife of President
Mobutu proudly
displays the spoils of his
office: jewellery signed
by the world's foremost
jewellers.*

with all the elegance and style of Paris. The beautiful Zairian ladies of Kinshasa society, escorted by their immaculate partners, mixed with graceful ease among the European diplomats, industrialists and representatives of the EEC, and looked quite at home amid the extravagant décor, the mirrored walls, the polished imported marble floors and the Venetian chandeliers. The massive quantity of food, flown expressly from Europe for the occasion and hardly touched, outrageously epitomized the very essence of refined European cuisine. Out-of-season grapes and peaches, apricots and pears, artichokes and endives and asparagus poured from a silver cornucopia on to white linen table cloths beside huge rounds of Brie and Camembert and Swiss Gruyère. A three-tiered cake dusted with icing sugar, the size of a ten-year-old child, rose like a snowy apparition amid a forest of Moët et Chandon bottles. Tall-hatted chefs, both black and white, in starched white uniforms and kitchen aprons, moved among the guests bearing silver trays with champagne glasses and cocktail delicacies – vol-au-vents, petit fours *à la crème, éclairs au chocolat*, stuffed olives and caviar on toast – they hadn't forgotten anything. The only word I could think of was 'outrageous'; but in a way it was just part of the extravagance of this country, where extreme conditions unashamedly walk hand in hand.

For the next three days we dismantled the expedition and sorted out the equipment, the remaining food, the bedding and the tents; sheets and clothes were laundered, bedrolls and mattresses laid out in the sun to dry out; then many luxurious hours were spent sleeping and generally recuperating in the cool, air-conditioned rooms, soaking off, in frothy pine-oil baths, the expedition grime which had accumulated in our hair and ears and beneath our toe- and finger-nails.

We visited the famous Kinshasa artists' market, where one of Africa's largest arrays of 'art' is displayed and hawked: creative manifestations of the country's artistic temperament ranging from the worst naive kitsch to some – not many – prestigious antiques worthy of any collection. This is also where all the ivory of Zaire accumulates in an extraordinary variety of sculpted creations, executed with outstanding dexterity and finesse and polished smooth as only ivory can be: chessboards, bracelets, miniature busts – every imaginable image. We talked, and bargained, with some of the carvers. Their responses were interesting and revealing. $2,000 for a carved tusk; we offered $500 and after ten minutes settled on $600. The next was $5,000 – 'to be negotiated', they added. Bracelets went at $10, chessboards, complete, for $250. For these people ivory is no more than a mineral to be worked and sold, like wood; it is a material to be sculpted and turned into money. No thought is ever given to its origins. When we asked if they had ever seen an elephant,

The initial meeting between Stanley and Chief Ngalyema (who gave his name to Mont Galiema, the seat of government today) had all the flavour of a grand reunion.

they all answered no: none of them had ever actually seen a tusk on an elephant, or given any thought to the massacre and plight of these noble animals.

They took us into the centre of town, where the ivory carvers work on the raw tusks; it was like an elephants' graveyard. Hundreds of tusks, most of them small, were piled about like firewood waiting to be turned into works of art. One of the carvers told us that he had begun trading in ivory in 1972 after having abandoned his studies. 'I left school in order to work with my uncle; three years later I dedicated myself to the ivory trade. I have been independent for ten years and make enough to keep my wife and five children. The ivory comes from Kisangani, Bandundu and Equator, where the ivory hunters sell it to us; it travels to Kinshasa by boat, but these days there is less and less ivory. Only we artists have permits to work the ivory in our studios; it is now forbidden to own rough ivory, and many of the sculpted pieces are worked in Kisangani.'

'So it is forbidden to buy ivory tusks, but it is permitted to sell it once it's been sculpted? Rather an interesting situation, I would say,' Lorenzo remarked.

'Yes, exactly, you have understood,' the carver replied, unaware of the irony.

What seemed even more ironic in this story was our earlier encounter with Brother Bernard, an eighty-year-old, long-ginger-bearded priest at the Procure in

In the Kinshasa artists' market one of Africa's largest arrays of 'art' is displayed and hawked — manifestations of the country's artistic temperament range from the worst of naive kitsch to some, but not many, prestigious antiques.

Kisangani, who had a sizeable collection of ivory figurines, bracelets and boxes for sale in his office. When we asked him about it, he replied, quite unconcerned, that he was helping out the carvers and bringing in some money to the Procure. Neither he nor anyone else seemed in the least aware of the consequences of this gruesome trade.

Beside the ivory sculptors in the market are the wood carvers with their beautiful wooden figurines, simple, elegant bowls, ornate combs, ebony spoons and knives; and beside them the terra-cotta and stone carvings and bas reliefs, beaten copper trays, plates and hangings, and the silver swords and amulets. Thousands of pieces are displayed on individual stalls one beside the other beneath a long, open, tin-roofed shed; outside, beneath the trees, hundreds of paintings, oils and water colours and gouaches depicting Zairian life, scenery and people are on sale, propped up on stones and sticks beside the hungry-eyed artists.

The *marché des artistes* in Kinshasa is one of the highlights of the sprawling metropolis; it says a lot about the people of Zaire. Most, if not all, great African art comes from Zaire and West Africa; it was from here that Picasso drew some of his inspiration.

L'Ecole des Beaux Arts in Kinshasa caters to and encourages the artistic nature of the Zairians, but it also influences and channels it on European lines, which is a pity, for it thwarts the instinctive expression, the very fibre of their art, which is so much more interesting when allowed its own authenticity. The artists' ideas, inspirations and impulses are naturally derived from their legends, their music and their struggle, but incentives to encourage the development of a genuinely native art are unfortunately sorely missing. It is a pity that so much artistic fervour does not find a wider, and more understanding, audience.

Frère Joseph Cornet was the curator of President Mobutu's extraordinary collection of African art, which has been accumulating over the past twenty years, ever since he came to power. Catalogued, tagged and numbered, it is stowed away in row upon row of dusty shelves in two great hangars within the confines of the royal compound on Mont Galiema. A team of connoisseurs and collectors, headed by Frère Cornet, have for two decades scoured the jungles of the country and tracked down a massive and priceless collection of ancient art and artefacts.

Frère Cornet, himself an eminent connoisseur of Zairian art, has lived in Zaire for forty years; his knowledge, we found, talking to him as we walked through the lines of shelves in the hangars, was not only substantial but stretched way beyond the confines of art into the realms of history and sorcery. He told us that this important collection was the greatest in the world. It contained antique masks from Bandundu and Bayaka, one of the oldest tribes in Zaire, who produced some of the finest art in

Africa. Many of the cowrie shells embroidered on the masks came from the Indian Ocean, not the Atlantic; that is why they are so rare in the interior, and are of such value. These cowrie shells had been there for centuries; they were found during the tomb excavations in the Saba region and are about a thousand years old. The great fetish masks from the Bayaka tribe are reserved for witchdoctors who have particular powers.

Frère Cornet showed us a fetish of great value, with enormous supernatural powers that manifest themselves through a series of sharp objects inserted into the stomach or the head of the victim. The shell on the head of this fetish symbolizes the power within. When the witch-doctor is asked to make magic for purposes of revenge or in order to hurt people he uses a statue (which represents the fetish) in which pieces of iron, especially blades, and nails are inserted. One can determine the age of the fetish from the blades. If the death of a certain person is requested, the blade is bent at right angles. It is difficult to say whether the curses really have an effect, but they often appear to do so because the person who has commissioned the fetish usually gives it a helping hand; auto-suggestion reinforces the victim's vulnerability, and poison does the rest.

Negro art is functional; it often represents the tangible elements of magic. The mysterious encounter between divinity and humanity takes place within the masks, between the living and the spirits of the dead. Fetishes, statues and masks are mystical symbols of good and evil.

A final reminder of the tragic history of slavery in Zaire stood in silent dignity on the road to Matadi.

—Overleaf—
The joyousness of Africa often appears in Zairian paintings.

We left Kinshasa a week later and, thanks to the generous help of the American Ambassador, to whom we had a letter of introduction from his counterpart in Dar-es-Salaam, Lorenzo was able to obtain a helicopter from the Inga-Shaba Construction Co., the company that maintains the huge hydroelectric plant at the Inga Rapids. It was in these devilish rapids that the French team of seven men perished dramatically a few months before our arrival.

Three of the five remaining members of our team dropped out in Kinshasa. Brian took the expedition equipment overland by lorry to Boma, where we were to relaunch the boats for the last time, and Lorenzo, our cameraman Mario and I took off in the Inga Dam Company helicopter, which offered us a superb bird's-eye view of the sprawling city and the great river with its ferocious cataracts.

315

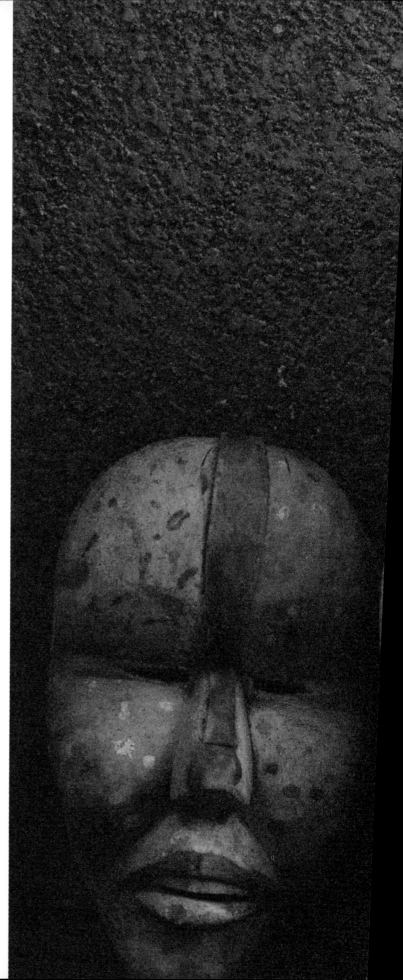

— Above and right —

Negro art is functional
and often represents the
tangible elements of
magic. Inspiration is
derived from legends,
sorcery and struggle.

— Far right —

A mysterious encounter
between humanity and
divinity, between the
living and the spirits of
the dead, takes place
within the mask.

On our way to the heliport we passed a forlorn parking lot where some derelict vehicles had been abandoned. Beside them, slightly to one side, one of Stanley's last river craft, the *Ada*, lay in regal corrosion, the year 1870 still clearly visible beneath the name. Rust had eaten filigree holes all over it, weeds and long grasses grew in the dust that had accumulated over the years in its belly, and across it from one end to the other lay, face down, the great steel statue that had once stood proudly on Mont Galiema looking out over the Livingstone Falls below. It had been severed at the shins; the missing feet gave it a strangely grotesque air of ostracism and revenge. Further on, the great statue of King Leopold of the Belgians astride his haughty steed, which had once stood in the centre of the main square, rose from a pile of discarded tyres and tubes, rusting pipes and nondescript trash. His proud, hard face with its elegant beard still retained its imperious demeanour, despite the cobwebs stretching from his ears and the fallen leaves rotting at his crutch. His time of grandeur had passed, as had Stanley's; Zaire no longer recognized them.

Approximately twenty minutes after take-off we circled over the Zongo Falls, one of the most spectacular and powerful waterfalls on the river. We could hear the giant billowing brown water pouring over the cliff edge long before we saw it hurtling downward to the valley bottom in, as Stanley wrote, 'a deafening roar like

In a forlorn parking lot on the outskirts of Kinshasa, rust had eaten filigree holes into Stanley's last rivercraft, the Ada; *across it his immense metal statue lay face down, the legs severed.*

the thunder of an express train through a rock tunnel'. We landed about a hundred yards from the falls and wandered down along the Ingisi river, which at this point is compressed into a rockbed a hundred yards wide, before it slips through a crack in the rock and plunging downwards for 300 feet into the valley below. It crashes uncontrollably over the mighty boulders, through the trees and on down the canyon to the Zaire river approximately two miles further on. We circled low over the falls several times; they disappeared and reappeared in a cloud of water mist as we were thrown about like a bird in a storm by the displacement of the air; the water leapt up at us hundreds of feet in a great transparent spray that merged with the low clouds and fell in misty rain over the great dark trees growing up from the valley sides.

From Zongo we followed the river, flying low along the steep, dark rock cliffs where giant kites rode the thermals like hang gliders and nested in caves or on the tops of trees growing on ledges. 'This stretch of the river was named the Child-Mother-Father by an old chieftain,' Stanley wrote:

...the Child is a two hundred yards stretch of broken water and the Mother consists of half a mile of dangerous rapids; but the Father is the wildest stretch of river I have ever seen. Take a strip of

King Leopold's days of grandeur had passed, as had Stanley's, and Zaire no longer recognized him; but his proud, hard face with its elegant beard still retained its imperious demeanour among the cobwebs and weeds.

sea blown over by a hurricane, four miles in length and half a mile in breadth, and a pretty accurate conception of its leaping waves may be obtained. Some of the troughs are a hundred yards in length and from one to the other the river plunges. There was a first rush down into the bottom of an immense trough and then by sheer force, the enormous volume lifts itself upward steeply until, gathering itself into a ridge, it suddenly hurls twenty or thirty feet straight upward before rolling down into another trough . . . the most powerful ocean steamer going at full speed on this portion of the river would be as helpless as a cockle-boat. I attempted three times, by watching some tree floated down from above, to ascertain the rate of the wild current, by observing the time it occupied in passing between two given points, from which I estimated it to be travelling at about thirty miles an hour.

Such was the might of this giant among rivers as it crashed towards the sea.

The Inga Falls, approximately a hundred miles beyond Matadi, the first and most important river port, lived up to Stanley's description:

As I looked up or down along this angry scene, every interval 50 or 100 yards of it was marked with wave towers, that collapse into foam and spray, the mad clash of watery hills, bounding mounds and heaving billows, while the base of either bank, consisting of a long line of piled boulders of massive size, was buried in the tempestuous surf. The roar was tremendous and deafening . . . we had scarcely ventured near the top of the rapids when the current swept the boat from our hands. Away into the centre of the angry, foaming, billowy stream the boat darted, dragging one man into the maddened flood; never did rocks assume such hardness, such solemn grimness and bigness, never were they invested with such terror and such grandeur as while we were the cruel sport and prey of the brown-black waves, which whirled us around like a spinning top, swung aside, almost engulfing us in the rapidly subsiding troughs and then hurled us upon the white, rageful crests of others . . . the flood was resolved that we should taste the bitterness of death . . . we saw the river heaved bodily upwards as though a volcano was about to belch around us . . . I was beginning to congratulate myself when to my horror I saw the huge canoe captured at the Stanley Falls, now with six men in it, in mid-river, gliding with the speed of an arrow towards the falls. Human strength availed nothing now and we watched it in agony, we saw it whirled round three or four times, then plunge down into the depths, out of which the stern presently emerged pointed upwards and we knew that the canoe mates were no more.

How well we related to those excited, evocative words, now a vivid reality beneath us, and our thoughts went out to the unfortunate French team who perished here with their rubber boats in similar circumstances a hundred years later, sucked in by the vicious whirlpools and catapulted into the waves as they hit the submerged rocks. At this point in the Zaire river the water is compressed into a narrow passage about 1,000 yards wide, causing a current that reaches a speed of thirty miles an hour in a series of whirlpools, swishbacks and waves, crashing over the rocks and sucking down anything that passes even close to them. Danger lurks everywhere.

We landed at the American hydroelectric HQ, where we were invited to lunch by James Miller, the director of the site. He told us how he had sat on the top terrace above the turbines and watched helplessly as the French team were sucked to their death.

'The boats rose like matchsticks straight into the air, hovered for a moment on the crest of the waves coming at them and then disappeared from sight. They reappeared a hundred yards downstream, upside down; there was no sign of the men. No one even ever found their bodies; they were just annihilated in front of me,' he said emotionally.

James took us for a tour of the giant turbines and complained bitterly at the lack of care and supervision, the indifference and the ignorance of the Zairians in charge of maintenance. One turbine had already ground to a halt; the other three, he told us, would follow suit if the situation didn't change soon. This mammoth investment, financed by a World Bank loan, was but one of many such projects which were suffering a similar fate in the country. As in so many new Third World countries, the heads of state had not yet understood that it wasn't enough to obtain the machinery if the maintenance infrastructure was lacking. Machinery, like people, has a life span in proportion to the care expended on it – a concept the Zairians – and other Africans – find almost impossible to comprehend.

From Inga we motored to Boma on a beautiful tarmacked road in a car James put at our disposal. Brian had arrived the night before and had set up our last camp on a small ledge beside two rusting steamboats waiting to be absorbed by the river in a hundred years' time – or more.

It was here in Boma that Stanley, with his 'wayworn, feeble and suffering column', ended his gruelling 4,000-mile trek across the African continent. Here in Boma, on 31 July 1877, he finally said goodbye to his faithful boat *The Lady Alice* and 'consigned her to her final resting place above the Isangila Cataract, to bleach and rot to dust'.

For three days we struggled forward through the cruel, punishing Crystal Mountains . . . up and down the desolate and sad land wound the poor, hungry caravan. Bleached whiteness of ripest grass, grey rock-piles here and there looming up solemn and sad in their greyness, a thin grove of trees now

—Overleaf—
The tall, elegant trunks of the giant mangroves rose skywards; from them vines fell in long tentacles to the water, where they rooted in the mud.

325

and then visible on the heights in the hollows — such were the scenes with which every uplift of a ridge or rising crest of a hill met our hungry eyes.

On the fourth day they reached a village called Nsanda and here Stanley called a halt. The party was over; the people were dying. 'To any Gentleman who speaks English at Boma,' he wrote:

Dear Sir, I have arrived at this place from Zanzibar with 115 souls, men, women and children. We are now in a state of imminent starvation. We can buy nothing from the natives for they laugh at our kinds of cloth, beads and wire . . . I do not know you; but I am told there is an Englishman at Boma and as you are a Christian and a gentleman I beg you not to disregard my request . . . we are in a state of the greatest distress; but if your supplies arrive in time, I may be able to reach Boma within five days . . . the supplies must arrive within two days or I may have a fearful time of it among the dying . . . what is wanted is immediate relief and I pray you to use your utmost energies to forward it at once . . . until that time I beg you to believe me.

He signed it 'H. M. Stanley', and then added rather pathetically, 'P.S. You may know me by name, I therefore add, I am the person that discovered Livingstone in 1871.' Two days later, six men returned at the head of a luxuriously provisioned caravan: 'The gracious God be praised for ever, the long war we had maintained against famine and the siege of woe was over and my people and I rejoiced in plenty . . . On August 9th, the 999th day from the date of our departure from Zanzibar, we prepared to greet the van of civilization.'

In Boma there is a great baobab tree known as 'Stanley's Baobab' which stretches up about two hundred feet in a great spray of gnarled branches and leaves. It is hollow inside; legend has it that Stanley spent the first night here upon arrival in Boma; his faithful blacks lay around it on the outside in order to protect him from the wild animals. A fitting end to an epic story, even if it is not true.

We camped that night on the river not far from Stanley's Baobab. Next day, according to Lorenzo's calculations, we were to arrive in Banana at the Zaire delta where the river spills into the Atlantic. The water hyacinth we had first encountered 800 miles upriver and which had travelled with us downstream towards the salt water where they would finally die bobbed on our wake. A friendly jungle dweller offered us a pineapple; he threw himself into the water to bring it to us so that we would not get wet – a touching gesture from one who lived his life in the jungle to us who had just passed through it.

At the end of a journey such as this, which had been our life for so long, a feeling of melancholy begins to creep in, giving rise to an unbearable apprehension of returning to mundane life where the unexpected does not exist.

We entered a final labyrinth of magnificent mangroves, whose giant exposed roots, bleached white by the sun, resembled carcasses of mammoth prehistoric crabs confined to an endless liquid graveyard of black mud. Their tall, elegant trunks rose skywards like thin pencils, and from them vines fell in long tentacles to the water, where the claws root them to the mud.

From Matadi and Boma to Banana, the Zaire river stretches from a width of eight hundred yards to ten miles. I sensed the Atlantic before I saw it. In the last mile the river runs between Angola on the left and Zaire on the right. We hugged the right bank, flying the Zairian and Italian flags. We came around a point, the last point, the last bend in the river, beyond which lay Banana Point and the ocean.

A slim sliver of land jutted out into the ocean in front of us; it was barely visible: a row of palm trees silhouetted against the bright light which ricocheted from the waves stood out starkly against the limpid sky. This was the Atlantic Ocean, the end of our 3,750-mile journey; we had arrived. 'I felt a sense of loss, like when a close friend goes away for a long time or when I get to the last page of a good book,' Lorenzo confided to me later that night.

It was four o'clock in the afternoon; the sunlight bouncing off the sea was blinding. We remained silent. Lorenzo had a look of mingled sadness and satisfaction on his face. The deep creases around his blue eyes, his shaggy beard and his frayed straw hat told a story of adventure, of perseverance, of courage, of vision and, like Stanley, of a touch of madness.

Before turning into Banana Bay, where we would abandon the boats, we sped, at full throttle, a mile into the ocean. 'I was glad to be with Mirella; we had seen Africa as few people have,' he scribbled in his notebook. He put his arm around my shoulders and said nothing; his silence spoke louder than words.

The inflatables pulled up alongside each other. We switched off the engines and bobbed on the long waves of the Atlantic Ocean as Lorenzo reached for his water gourd.

'Indian Ocean, Atlantic Ocean,' he spoke solemnly, with just a touch of emotion in his voice as he emptied the gourd of Indian Ocean water he had scooped up eighteen months before in the Rufiji delta where our journey began. He turned to shake each one of us by the hand. 'We made it. Thank you all,' he said, holding the Italian and Zairian flag in each hand.

Before he could say any more, Brian and Mario joyfully seized Lorenzo and tipped him overboard to resounding cheers from the rest of the crew.

—Overleaf—
At Banana Lorenzo was heaved overboard into the Atlantic, as is the custom on such occasions.

ACKNOWLEDGEMENTS

Without the generous help and support of the following persons and organizations, the African Rainbow expedition could not have taken place. We are deeply grateful to them all:

The Hon. Bettino Craxi, Prime Minister of Italy; Mr Roberto Vallarino Gancia; Mr Massimo Pini; Mr Mario Raffaelli, Italian Ministry of Foreign Affairs; On. Paolo Pillitteri, Mayor of Milan; Dr Stefano Rolando; Mr Nerio Nesi, President of BNL; Mr Gian Luigi Valenza, Italian Ambassador, Kenya; Marchese F. Rossi Longhi, Italian Ambassador, Tanzania; Mr V. Farinelli, Italian Ambassador, Zaire; Mr Beyeye Djema, Commissaire d'Etat, République du Zaire; Mr Job M. Lusinde, Tanzanian Ambassador, Kenya; Mr John William Shirley, US Ambassador, Tanzania; Mr Brandon Grove Jnr, US Ambassador, Zaire; Mr Alberto Pirelli, Pirelli SPA, Milan; Dr Carlo Rivetti, GFT (Gruppo Finanziario Tessile), Turin; Dr Cesare Romiti, Fiat, Turin; Mr Jean Henry de Saint Marc, Total, Africa; Mr Bill Garrett, Editor, *National Geographic Magazine*, USA; Mr Massimo Osti, C.P. Company, Bologna; Comm. Alberto Rusconi, Rusconi Editore, Milano; Dr Franco Castoldi, Castoldijet, Abbiategrasso; Mr Struelens, Sabena Airlines, Bruxelles; Prof. Muratori, Mariner Outboard, Rome; Mr T. Davies, Mariner Outboard, Power-Marine, Belgium–USA; Mr Gian Ludovico Pennacchio, UNDP, Kenya; Mr Richard Morgan, Mrs Mary Anne Fitzgerald and Miss Cynthia Goodman of the *International Herald Tribune*; Mr Lorenzo Berni, San Lorenzo Restaurant, London; Mr Ludovico Gnecchi; Mr and Mrs Michael Cunningham Reed; Mrs Rex Dobie; Mr Charles Dobie; Mr Julian Friedmann; Mr Marcello Lenghi; Mr Franco Rosso; Mr Guido Rosada; Mr Muni Gastel; Mr Filippo Panarello; Mr Stefano Mazzone; Mr Ari Gramatica; Mr John Powis; Mr Roberto Grazzini; Mr Thierry Marmouget; Mr Patrick Hays; Mr Viero Cognigni; Mr A. Fumagalli; Mr Lelio Picciotto; Professor Bohny; and many, many more.

SPONSORS AND SUPPLIERS

Presidenza del Consiglio dei Ministri della Repubblica Italiana; Pirelli (Moldip) Superga, Italy; C.P. Company (Gruppo Finanziario Tessile), Italy; Total, France; Fiat, Italy; Sabena Air Lines, Belgium; Castoldijet, Italy; Mariner-Power Marine, USA; Filli. Gancia, Italy; Italian Television–RAI 2, Italy; Télé-Hachette, France. *National Geographic Magazine*, USA; Banca Nationale del Lavoro, Italy; Rusconi Editore, Italy; Marconi Radio, Eddystone, UK; Pennel et Flipo, France; San Lorenzo Restaurant, London; Farmitalia, Italy; Beaulieu Cameras, France; Lake Naivasha Hotel, Kenya; Amrec–Flying Doctors, Kenya; Star, Italy; Mase Generators, Italy; Ellebi Trailers, Italy; Trapper–Pubblipull, Italy; Motomec, Italy; Tarpo, Kenya; Governor's Camp, Kenya; Gifil, Italy; Ditron Inno-Hit, Italy; SGEEM, France; DAI Frigoriferi, Italy; TNI–Tapezzeria Nautica, Italy; Aereotecnica Coltri, Italy; SMC, Italy; Dacor, Italy; Lab-Line, Italy; Air-Camping, Italy; Eurovinil, Italy; Italrope, Italy; Uno Tachting, Italy; Incar–Fiat, Tanzania; Autan Bayer, Italy; Bonemelli, Italy; Ponte, Spaghetti, Italy; Curti Riso, Italy; Pirotecnica Industriale Mugnaoni, Italy; Manfrotto, Italy; and Mr Steven Mills.

EXPEDITION MEMBERS

Richard Bonham, Lorenzo Camerana, Gianfranco Peroncini, Marco Fulvi, Shona McKinley, Elisabeth Ryeri, Byrdine Melton, Sally Dudmesh, Amina Ricciardi, Brian Larkey, Hugo Douglas-Dufresne, Charles Babault, Adam James, Juliette Westlake and Giovanni Mitcheunig. Film-makers attached to the expedition: Antonio Climati, Bruno Brunello, John Brunello and Mario Gianni.

We are greatly indebted to Stephanie Powers, Jane Goodall, Shirley Strum, Richard Leakey, Kamau Kimeu, George Adamson, Maurice Krafft, James Ash, Frère Joseph Cornet, Alfred Liyolo, Hubert Wells, Dori Sitterley, Eddie McGee, Dr Philip Reece and Citoyen Mushenzi for sharing their knowledge with us and appearing in the *African Rainbow* TV films.

INDEX